Parentless Parents

ALSO BY ALLISON GILBERT

Always Too Soon:
Voices of Support for Those Who Have Lost Both Parents

Covering Catastrophe:
Broadcast Journalists Report September 11

Parentless Parents

How the Loss of Our Mothers
and Fathers Impacts the Way We
Raise Our Children

Allison Gilbert

ⓗⓨⓟⓔⓡⓘⓞⓝ

New York

Library of Congress Cataloging-in-Publication Data has been applied for.

ISBN 978-1-4013-2351-6

Hyperion books are available for special promotions and premiums. For details contact the HarperCollins Special Markets Department in the New York office at 212-207-7528, fax 212-207-7222, or e-mail spsales@harpercollins.com.

Book design by Nicola Ferguson

FIRST EDITION

10 9 8 7 6 5 4 3 2 1

We try to produce the most beautiful books possible, and we are also extremely concerned about the impact of our manufacturing process on the forests of the world and the environment as a whole. Accordingly, we've made sure that all of the paper we use has been certified as coming from forests that are managed, to ensure the protection of the people and wildlife dependent upon them.

For my children, Jake and Lexi, and their grandparents, Sidney and Lynn

Contents

Author's Note

With few exceptions, the parentless parents I interviewed for this book allowed me to use their real names, and for that I am exceptionally grateful. In cases where details were deemed too private, I gladly agreed to change identifying facts to ensure anonymity.

"There are only two lasting bequests we can hope to give our children. One of these is roots; the other, wings."

— *Hodding Carter*

Parentless Parents

Introduction

M*y dad all but predicted* I would crumble after he died. For years after my mother passed away from ovarian cancer, he and I would meet for lunch in New York City. We both worked in midtown Manhattan and loved getting together, alone. No stepmother. No son-in-law. Just us. We called them "dates," and he was the perfect companion: great at conversation, always interested in what I had to say, and he would never let me pay. Once when I was two months pregnant and craving spicy food, he suggested we eat Mexican. After we left the restaurant, he took my hand into his thick, calloused palm and we began walking in the direction of his office. When we got to the corner and were waiting to cross the street, he mentioned something that seemed so innocuous at the time that I barely paid it any attention. In fact, I remember shrugging it off. He said, "You better be okay when I die. Because it *will* happen."

My father was trying to be helpful, I'm sure. To brace me for the inevitable: that one day I would be parentless. But hadn't I been all right since Mom passed away? I had gotten married, was expecting a baby, and had a great job. I loved my mother and missed her completely, but I assured my dad (convinced myself?) that I was fine. But my dad was prophetic. Two years after that conversation, he, too, was dead. And to be truthful, I wasn't okay. I was devastated.

My dad had an energy that filled rooms. His ego was even bigger. So when he was diagnosed with lung cancer, his rapid deterioration was all the harder to watch. His world, which had been full of business trips to Moscow and tickets to the latest museum exhibitions and cultural events, shrunk almost immediately to a footpath between his apartment and his doctor's office. The disease not only sucked the life out of him, it drained it out of me, too. I had seen this show before and knew how it ended. My sadness more than doubled. It was worse because since my mom had died, I'd become a mother myself. I not only mourned my father, but also grieved the loss of him as a grandfather. And Jake, at eighteen months, would never remember him. He never even met my mother. I had become a parentless parent.

Since then, and with the birth of my daughter, I have learned that so much of what parentless parents miss is irreplaceable. My husband, Mark, is affectionate and loving, and his parents are warm and giving—but it's not the same. No matter how supportive our spouses and in-laws, no matter how deep our bench of babysitters, no matter how many parenting books and magazines we read, nobody can fill the void our mothers and fathers left behind. Our parents can't pass on family traditions. Our parents can't share stories about living relatives or ancestors. And they can't tell us what we really need to know as parents—how we behaved at certain ages and stages. If we had even one parent, there'd at least be the possibility that some of that information could be passed along directly.

Holidays are particularly difficult. My parents divorced when I was six, and my brother, Jay, and I always had two Thanksgiving dinners. Mom and Dad would alternate who got us on Thursday night and who would host Thanksgiving—again—over the weekend. Every year I ate turkey, stuffing, and pumpkin pie in duplicate. The year my father died, my brother decided to host Thanksgiving, and as my husband and I barreled toward Pennsylvania with Jake snapped into his car seat behind us, I had trouble even faking a smile. I didn't feel old enough to be a parent without parents. For thirty-one years, I had been the one taken care of. I had been the child. I was good at being the daughter.

By the time our car rolled into my brother's pebbled driveway, I couldn't wait to get out and hug him. I hoped he would hold me, knowingly, lovingly, perhaps the way my parents would have, if they were still alive. Jay was standing in front of the house waiting to greet us. As soon as I saw him, though, I felt worse. His freckled arms were outstretched and raised high in anticipation of good times ahead. A smile ballooned across his face. I pretended not to see him and bent down underneath the glove compartment, gathering imaginary belongings that had fallen out of my bag. I stayed there so long I felt blood pooling in my forehead and cheeks.

Oblivious to my charade, Mark got out of the car, took Jake from the backseat, and started walking to the house. I hoped their arrival would keep everyone busy so I could be left alone just a little longer. But I saw my brother coming. I steeled myself, opened the door, and reached out to him. But my arms were lower than his, and our hug was mismatched and awkward. I was prepared for a comforting embrace, the kind you give someone at a memorial service, but he seemed ready to celebrate.

It has taken me years to understand and accept that my brother and I mourn differently. Sometimes in the past, it has made me feel like an only child. In January and September, on the anniversaries of our parents' deaths, I always call him seeking solace and connection. My calls are almost always met with surprise.

Everything inside the house looked and smelled fantastic. My sister-in-law, Randi, had a pot of apple cider on the stove, and her parents were sitting with Cheryl, my stepmother, and Cheryl's two sisters, in the family room. They were having fun watching Jake and his older redheaded cousin, Dexter, play with Thomas the Tank Engine on the floor. A collection of unlit candles had been arranged in the center of the dining room table and twelve places were set, ready for dinner.

Except for me, everyone seemed relaxed and normal. My dad and brother's favorite Charlie Mingus CD was playing and we were all talking and laughing. But all that normalcy made me feel unsettled, lonely, and sick. This was Randi's family. These were Cheryl's sisters. Jay was there, but our family was gone.

I went through all the motions of happy; I smiled in all the right places and laughed at all the right times and pretended to be interested in the cheddar cheese and crackers on the kitchen counter. Part of me wanted to call attention to myself and be comforted, but mainly I just wanted to show our son a good time.

When we finally sat down to dinner, I had no appetite. I had been stuffing my emotions down my throat all day and was full. Throughout the meal, I tried to participate in various conversations but found myself unable to take my eyes off my nephew Dexter and his grandmother. I stared at her as she wiped cranberry sauce off his cheek, and then I looked at Jake in his high chair, face splattered with gravy, mashing turkey with a fork. My mother would never be able to show such affection to her grandson.

Rationally, seeing that scene unfold shouldn't have mattered. But my emotions resulted from the same jealous ache I felt watching my in-laws hold Jake's hand or give him a bath. And though my stepmother, Cheryl, was loving with Jake, I had trouble allowing her to fill that role. Cheryl had been the "other woman." When I felt my eyes filling with tears, I excused myself from the table and walked toward the bathroom in my brother's bedroom, far from the main event, thinking it would be the safest, most private place to get myself together.

I never quite got there. Outside the bathroom was my brother's walk-in closet. At first, I just stopped in the doorway, glancing inside at nothing in particular. Then I was pulled in. I remember raking a group of hangers to the side and standing there, unable to move, looking at a flannel shirt that I was sure had belonged to my dad. The last time I had seen him wear it was the year before, when he and I took Jake to the Metropolitan Museum of Art for the first time. The excursion was my dad's idea. His six-month-old grandson would learn about art and he would be the teacher.

The shirt was a fabric memorial. I had to touch it. Bring it to my nose and inhale it. I began to cry and then dissolved into full-blown tears and, soon, sobs. *How could I possibly make up for all the lessons my parents would have taught?*

I hid in the closet with all of my inadequacies. The job of being a parentless parent was just too hard; I couldn't teach myself everything a mother needed to know and offer Jake the kind of special relationship his grandparents — the two from *my* side of the family — would have provided.

My arms didn't feel strong enough to bridge three generations.

It has been nearly ten years since my father died, and each day has brought new challenges and rewards. After my mother passed away, I learned that time lessens the pain. But as a mother of two growing children, I am constantly reminded that no matter how much I miss my parents, their absence doesn't just affect me. Because my children never got to know my parents, the void is also theirs. How much richer would their lives have been if my parents were alive? Would they be sprouting into different people?

Loss is always difficult, but I have found that talking with other people who share similar experiences helps. That's what I discovered when I wrote *Always Too Soon: Voices of Support for Those Who Have Lost Both Parents* — a collection of interviews with men and women who had also experienced the death of their second parent. After it was published, I was gratified when readers would tell me they felt better and less alone after finishing it. But I was surprised to learn what they felt I should have spent more time addressing.

Men and women wanted to discuss what it was like to be a parent without parents. These parentless parents told me how lonely they felt because so many of their friends still have one, if not both, parents. And they told me how few places they had to turn to for support; most of their spouses hadn't been through such a loss. It was because of this response that I helped organize the first Parentless Parents support group. There are now Parentless Parents chapters forming in California, Florida, Michigan, New Jersey, New York, Oregon, Pennsylvania, Rhode Island, and Washington, D.C. After talking with men and women in these groups, I knew this book needed to be written.

The number of parentless parents in America is increasing. According to the U.S. Census Bureau, the age at which men and women enter their first marriage is the highest it's been since the government began keeping records in 1890 — for men, the median age is twenty-eight; for women it's twenty-six. In addition, according to the National Center for Health Statistics, a division of the Centers for Disease Control and Prevention, the average age for a woman to have her first child is now twenty-five — also a historic high. These statistics by themselves point to an interesting trend, but as I dug into the numbers further I was convinced that an even bigger shift was taking place.

I took my hunch to Kenneth Land, a director at the Duke Population Research Institute at Duke University and editor of the scientific journal *Demography,* who assured me, after crunching the same figures on my behalf, that I was correct. Life expectancy, while also on the rise, isn't growing fast enough to guarantee the children born to these parents will have more time with their grandparents. "That increase is by no means dramatic enough to overshadow the importance of the increasing age at first birth. A significant population of children born to these women will have fewer years with their grandparents."

What this means is that our assumptions about grandparents being around longer than ever before—because they're living longer, after all—are simply inaccurate. For the first time in U.S. history, millions of children (and their parents) are actually vulnerable to having less time with their grandparents than more. Between 1970 and 2007, the average age for a woman to have her first child rose 3.6 years. During the same period, life expectancy for a sixty-five-year-old increased 3.4 years. While that doesn't seem earth-shattering on its own, consider another trend. According to the latest government statistics, while women overall are having fewer babies, mothers between forty and fifty-four are having more. The increasing age of motherhood underscores a dramatic shift that's been taking shape for decades. In 1972, approximately 180,000 children were born to mothers thirty-five and older. By 2008, that number had more than tripled to 603,113, a 235 percent increase, a jump so significant it can't be explained away by increasing population size. Unquestionably a revolution is happening in the way generations are connected in America.

Despite this, I wasn't able to find a single book or study that exclusively investigated how being parentless—regardless of age at time of loss and independent of gender—impacts parenting. Moreover, parentless parents have never been examined as a distinct demographic. The Roper Center for Public Opinion Research tracks virtually every public opinion survey conducted since the 1930s, and its archives contain data on how the public feels about seemingly every field of research: politics, education, health care, and various social issues, such as abortion and poverty. It also has a clearinghouse of information about our evolving views on work, family, and raising children. But when I asked about any data they've collected about being a parent without both parents, the Roper Center told me no survey had ever been done.

"The subject has not been studied fully in professional circles, and it should be," says Dr. Molly Poag, clinical associate professor of psychiatry at NYU School of Medicine and former chairman of the Department of Psychiatry at Lenox Hill Hospital in New York City. "I see more and more older patients coming in who are dealing with being parents while their own moms and dads are dying or already dead. It's clear to me that this subject deserves attention."

To counter this vacuum, I used every tool at a journalist's disposal. I conducted dozens of in-person interviews and many more on the phone. I led focus groups in Los Angeles and New York and launched the Parentless Parents Survey, the first of its kind, which received nearly thirteen hundred responses from across the United States and a dozen countries.

As I listened to these conversations and tallied the data, what surprised me most was how intensely felt certain subjects and challenges turned out to be — no matter when a parentless parent lost his or her own parents. For example, even with big families and devoted spouses, the majority of parentless parents felt isolated. Fifty-seven percent of respondents reported not having had enough support when their children were young, and approximately 69 percent said their friends, the ones with living parents, truly didn't understand what it's like to be a parent without parents. Nearly 70 percent said they felt jealous when they saw other children with their grandparents.

Also unexpected was how often this sense of isolation spilled over into marriages. Parentless parents said they received nearly double the amount of emotional support from friends who had also lost parents (82 percent) than from their own husbands and wives (42 percent). In addition, more respondents indicated their spouses *didn't* understand what they were going through (48 percent), than *did* (42 percent). Moreover, since the majority of respondents had spouses with one or two living parents, an uneven balance of power often develops within these relationships. A major cause of tension is the lopsided

presence of grandparents. Nearly 30 percent of respondents resented the disproportionate influence their in-laws had over their
children.

These findings were striking, yet oddly comforting. Through the
anonymous click of a mouse, thousands of parentless parents told me
they often grappled with the same issues I did. There's validation in
numbers.

As these and other patterns began to emerge, I sought the analysis
of experts in various fields, including parenting, psychology, marriage, and grief counseling. I also went to the library to read. My goal
was to incorporate what had already been written about double parent loss and parenthood (very little) and use that material to augment
my findings.

I set out to explore the issues and challenges facing mothers and
fathers who have lost both parents due only to death. This targeted
approach upset a number of people who tried to take the Parentless
Parents Survey, but were prohibited from doing so. "Hi Allison," a mom
named Betsy emailed me, "I feel there is a whole segment of people
you are not recognizing. My mother passed away when I was 18 from
breast cancer. My father is still alive but has not been a part of my life
for over 15 years due to his mental illness. This kind of loss can make
parenting even more difficult." And from another parent: "I don't even
know where to begin. I wound up at your Parentless Parents Survey,
eager to participate, and was basically told I'm not parentless enough.
Being dismissed by your survey felt like a punch in the gut."

There are certainly many reasons other than death to be without
parents. But every study must work within boundaries, and as I got
deeper into this subject I became more and more convinced that having both parents no longer living is a very specific experience. And
the majority of emails I received supported this focus — like this one:
"I feel like you tapped right into my life, my heart and my soul. It
is comforting to know that at least one other person in the world has

gone through similar tragedies and has some understanding of what I deal with on a daily basis."

Certainly, not all parentless parents share the same background or outlook, and undoubtedly many parents will identify with the stories presented here even if one or both of their parents are living. We are a complex and multilayered group, and our choices and parenting styles are informed by more than our losses. It is my hope that from reading these pages you will learn what links us — how being parentless not only shapes the way we raise our children, but how we relate to those around us and, ultimately, how we see ourselves.

Chapter 1

Early Parenthood

"I definitely felt like I was operating without a safety net. Without my mom and dad, I found myself awash in doubt and anxiety."

"I don't know anyone else who has given birth without parents by their side. It can make you feel alienated very quickly."

"No matter how many times I read up on parenting a newborn, I just didn't feel like I knew what was going on with my baby."

—from the Parentless Parents Survey

By the time my doctor arrived, I was already six centimeters dilated and fighting to keep the contraction monitor strapped around my enormous belly. The band wouldn't stay where the nurse wanted it, and she was annoyed that she couldn't get the proper readings off the machine behind me. I tried my best to hold the band in place, but every two minutes a wave of excruciating pain made it impossible and I'd let go of the monitor and seize the arms of the chair I was sitting in instead. My knuckles turned an elephant skin of pink and white.

There'd be no time for anesthesia. No epidural. "You're progressing too quickly," the nurse told me. "Even if we could get an anesthesiologist down here right now, it would be too late."

Jake, our first, had arrived the same way nearly two and a half years earlier. Back then, in April of 2000, my husband and I left our apartment in Hoboken, New Jersey, in a downpour of rain and sped across the George Washington Bridge to New York–Presbyterian Hospital, located on the northernmost tip of Manhattan. It was midnight when I was admitted, and at 2:29 A.M. we became parents for the first time.

The swiftness of Jake's birth shocked us. Mark had dashed out of the delivery room at about two in the morning to call my dad and let him know the baby was coming. (My father had told him to call, regardless of the hour, so he could be there as soon as his grandchild was born.) Mark left after one contraction, thinking he'd be back in time for the next, but my body was ramping up for delivery and my cervix soon stretched to nine centimeters and I started screaming. Mark heard me yelling all the way down the corridor and outside the maternity ward. "I gotta go. I hear Ali," he recalls telling my dad. But because of security, the double metal doors had closed behind him and he was locked out. Mark pounded on them and tried to make eye contact with anyone at the nurses' station, but nobody was at the desk. They were all with me, or so it seemed. I was hysterical. Fast deliveries are exceptionally painful. Your body doesn't have time to gradually expand. It simply explodes. Did it hurt my mother so much having me? I wondered.

When Mark finally got back to my side, the doctor — who in my pre-birth fog looked like Kathy Bates in the movie *Misery* — sternly warned me, "Get control of yourself, Allison. You. Are. Wasting. Energy. Stop yelling. Focus!" It was the verbal slap in the face I needed to rechannel my energy and begin pushing.

Twenty-six months later, delivery number two was happening the same way. Every twist of this new baby's head and shoulders made me shriek. I was later told a woman down the hall thought I was having an emergency C-section without anesthesia. But it wasn't just the intensity of my labor that made me cry that second time. It was self-pity and anger. Even contractions couldn't distract me from what I knew lay ahead. In the morning, Mark's parents would be coming to the hospital to coo over their newest grandchild, and they'd be helping change Lexi's diapers and play with Jake when we got home. But who'd be fawning over me? Even with all that support, even with my husband holding my hand, I felt completely alone.

That's what I was thinking about when the nurse came back into my hospital room to check on me and Lexi the night after she was born. That, and how lucky I was to have a daughter. I remember musing over her name and gazing at her tiny hand wrapped gently around my index finger. *Lexi, with an "L," because my mom's name was Lynn. Lexi, with the middle name Syd, because my dad's name was Sidney.* And then, just like that, my cheery thoughts evaporated. Yes, I had a daughter. But I didn't have a mother. Or for that matter, a father. I let the nurse take Lexi back to the nursery until she needed to be fed again. I turned on my side, pulled the hospital sheet up to my neck, and closed my eyes.

When Jake was born, he slept in the bassinet right by my hospital bed. I felt stronger and happier because both of us had a cheerleading squad. My dad snapped one of the first pictures in Jake's baby album. It's a photograph of Cheryl and Grandma Bertha, my dad's mother, peering affectionately over the bedrails at me nursing Jake. Dad took it as soon as they got to the hospital, at about three in the morning.

I missed my mom when I had Jake, but the hours after Lexi was born were different. When Mark had left for the evening to be home for Jake, my hospital room was achingly quiet. I had no middle-of-the-night visitors and I had cut myself off from my daughter on purpose. My grief eclipsed my happiness. In just a few days, Jake would need his mommy and I'd have double the amount of mothering to do. And while Mark would be right by my side, and his parents, members of my family, and our trusted babysitter would provide all kinds of support, neither of my parents would be there and that was all that seemed to matter.

The Crisis of Confidence

Many parents, even those with living mothers and fathers, find new parenthood hard. And even if they have parents to call, it doesn't necessarily mean they want to call them or that their parents would be willing or capable of providing support. "You don't want to presume that not having parents is a deficit. I think that's very important to the discussion," cautions Lois Braverman, president of the Ackerman Institute for the Family. "Yes, there are times, for some people, that not having parents to ask questions feels like a loss. On the other hand, sometimes not having a parent around means you're not grappling with what *they* think you should do and you're not meeting their disapproval."

True as that may be, I think it misses the point. Parentless parents don't have the option to ignore their parents or filter their remarks. Not having a choice is the reason why so many feel abandoned, deprived, and cheated. Hope Edelman, author of the landmark books *Motherless Daughters* and *Motherless Mothers,* sums up the difference from personal experience. Hope's mother died when she was seventeen, and her father passed away when she was forty. "I have a lot of friends whose parents don't live nearby, but they don't have the same kind of deep feelings of loss and deprivation that those of us who've had parents die do," she says. "Just the possibility that their parents could get on an airplane and be there is enough to help them feel as if they still have that kind of protection in the family."

Parentless parents face challenges other parents don't. When they have even one parent, new moms and dads can often rely on that remaining parent for help and guidance. When both parents are gone, there is a penetrating void. This could explain why 60 percent of respondents who took the Parentless Parents Survey and indicated having lost both parents before their first child was born reported being overwhelmed a lot or most of the time during the beginning years of parenthood.

Julie Hallman was fourteen months old when her mother died, and nineteen when her father had a fatal heart attack in his sleep. Her father and stepmother were on a Caribbean cruise, and he died on the ship. Julie was in college and found out when she got a phone call in her off-campus apartment.

Today Julie is the mother of twin twelve-year-old girls. I met her on a beautiful August day, at her postcard-ready South Florida home: a light beige ranch with a thick front lawn of emerald green grass and in the middle of the lawn three palm trees rising out of a manicured island of dirt, plants, and flowers. I shifted my rental car into park, gathered my notebook and digital recorder, and walked up her paved walkway to the front door. From our multiple phone conversations and emails, I imagined Julie would greet me warmly, and I was looking forward to our afternoon together.

Julie opened the front door and enthusiastically welcomed me inside. She had dirty blond hair that went past her shoulders and she was wearing a turquoise T-shirt and a pair of jeans. She looked like she was in her early thirties, but I knew from our phone conversations that she was forty-two. We exchanged small talk in the foyer and then I followed her to the kitchen to meet her daughters, Drew and Madison. A few minutes later, Julie took me to her office so we could talk in private.

The clutter of Julie's work space revealed the busy life of a working mom. Post-it notes were tacked to the computer, and papers covered nearly every inch of the L-shaped desk. Letters, packages, and envelopes leaned against the wall, and cardboard boxes were stacked under the desk. All of this made me feel comfortable. Julie would be a straight shooter.

"I was twenty-four when I got married, and I did not have my children until I was almost thirty," Julie told me almost as soon as we sat down. "I had a fear of having children."

"Why were you so concerned?"

"The truth is I didn't think I could be a good mother. I didn't feel very maternal. I was scared. I didn't know how to do anything with a baby. I needed to know how to hold a baby, how to feed a baby, how to burp a baby."

Julie's lack of confidence also affected how she viewed her capabilities once she became a mom. She remembers, for example, when the girls were two or three months old and both had reflux. "One day I was sitting on the couch and I was feeding one in my arms and feeding the other in a bouncy seat. Simultaneously one started to vomit, and then the other. I was by myself, and I just started to cry. I felt like I couldn't handle it."

The likely reason Julie didn't feel competent is because parenting may not be as innate as we think. We *need* our family. Help *is* required. According to Charles Snowdon, a professor of psychology at the University of Wisconsin-Madison, believing that parenting skills are somehow acquired automatically and that new mothers and fathers know what to do instinctively is entirely misguided.

Snowdon came to this conclusion after spending thirty years studying the child-rearing habits of monkeys. With grants from the National Institute of Mental Health, he focused his research on two specific species—marmosets and tamarins—because, unlike gorillas and chimpanzees, they raise their young in groups nearly identical to human families.

At the height of his investigation, Professor Snowdon and his small, one-pound monkeys took over approximately seventeen hundred square feet on the top floor of the University of Wisconsin Psychology Building. He began his work with eleven monkeys and observed them as they mated, gave birth, and cared for their young. When the monkeys reached the lab's full capacity — seventy-five — Snowdon would donate some of them to zoos and educational institutions around the country and then watch the same patterns emerge again when new babies were born.

What became clear to the professor over time was how critical it was for new parents to have the support of the entire family. When new mothers and fathers didn't receive such support, they weren't nearly as successful as those who did. "When these new mothers were removed from the family group, they had no idea what to do," Professor Snowdon says. "They held their babies upside down to nurse and failed to get their babies to the nipple. They also didn't tolerate carrying their young, which is the equivalent of human beings refusing to hold their newborns. Fathers would knock them off their backs, only to have the babies run back and attempt to climb on again. These mothers and fathers simply didn't learn what they needed to learn."

Not having these new parenting skills literally became a matter of life and death for the baby monkeys. Without food and other necessities normally provided by both parents, they died within two to three days.

How relevant is this extreme example to humans? Surely we can learn how to parent from reading books, observing other parents, and by talking with friends and relatives. While all valid, Professor Snowdon explains, those avenues have significant limitations. "The lessons we learn from other sources may not be specific to our own situations. Our families, especially our parents, know our individual needs and can provide reassurance that what we're doing is right. Clearly, parenting skills are not inborn. They need to be taught. Nothing can replace that intimate transfer of information."

Our parents are our primary teachers. And our confidence is

often shaken in early parenthood because it's these key teachers we no longer have.

The Difference Between Parentless Mothers and Fathers

Since women still do more at home, the earliest stage of parenthood is usually harder on parentless mothers than fathers. In the Parentless Parents Survey, women reported significantly more negative emotions surrounding their pregnancies, the births of their first children, and all births thereafter. Mothers felt angrier, sadder, and more isolated than fathers, who reported feeling more optimistic, peaceful, and confident. The only time women reported being a tick happier than men was when their children entered school.

This is not so surprising. The latest data from the Families and Work Institute show that "mothers still spend significantly more time per workday, on average, caring for their children than fathers." Women report taking on more responsibility for child care (67 percent), cooking (70 percent), and cleaning (73 percent). These findings, by the way, are for *working* women. Men who parent without their parents have an easier time during these early years because they don't face the same parenting and household responsibilities women do.

Take Richard Rivera, for example. Richard, a forty-year-old father living in the Bronx, New York, lost his father three years before he became a dad; his mother died a month after his daughter, Indi, was born. Richard didn't have his parents' support or guidance when he became a father. But he did have something that made all the difference in the world: a wife.

Richard never truly doubted his abilities as a dad, because he knew he could rely on his wife, Cyndi, and her family. "I was really scared," he said as we sat in his sixth-floor apartment. "But when I picked her up [from the hospital], Cyndi's mom was with me and came back home with us." That level of support continued months down the road. "I was just starting a new job and Cyndi wasn't going to work. She was going to be home all the time and be the primary caretaker. I kind of just went with the flow."

All of this is not to say that Richard doesn't miss his parents. He wishes they could be part of Indi's life and his life as a father. The difference, though, is that Richard doesn't need his parents the same way parentless mothers do. He simply doesn't grapple with the same day-to-day parenting challenges.

This disparity explains why I felt so alone when Jake and Lexi were little. Not even my brother could appreciate how dense I felt, how needy I was, and how much I ached for Mom and Dad. Mark was, and remains, an incredibly engaged dad — but I was the one who picked the kids' pediatrician, chose their car seats, and researched nursery schools. I could never go "with the flow" as Richard Rivera did, and my brother Jay's parenting experience was, and still is, wholly opposite of mine. While he runs his own company, my sister-in-law, Randi, stays at home and works a few hours a week teaching yoga and volunteering with children in the foster care system. Randi is the point person in my brother's family. She decided when to start feeding Dex and Ria solids, and she was the one who went to the store to buy all the paraphernalia the kids needed. And if she had any questions along the way, Randi could just call her mom and dad. I'd joke to Mark that I wanted a wife, too.

Stepping back, I realize I could have relied more heavily on my in-laws. They were always around, but I kept them at a distance. They'd babysit and let Mark and me catch a movie, but I couldn't bring myself to regularly ask their opinion or get their advice. Mark's mother in particular would have been a wonderful resource, but I found fully embracing her nearly impossible. If I depended on her, it felt like I was taking away an experience that should have been my mother's.

Immaturely, I didn't want Marilyn to be so involved. I resented how eager she was to swoop in and take over. When she visited, it was as if my mom never existed. Pushing Marilyn away preserved what little of her I had left.

When Marilyn did come over and help, which was often, she was remarkable. She'd run the dishwasher without being prompted, make dinner from whatever I had in the fridge, and enthusiastically play with Jake so I could focus on Lexi. Unquestionably, she made my life easier as a new mom. But accepting all that help was complicated. And it was never enough.

Marilyn could substitute for my mother only so far. She'd show me how to change diapers and boil bottles, but she couldn't tell me what I really wanted to know — What was *I* like as a baby? She couldn't share the story of my birth or recount how old I was when I started eating solid foods. And with all the questions I had when Jake and Lexi were small, seeing her with my children just reminded me of what I was missing even more.

Without my parents, so much that I needed as a new mother was lost forever.

Chapter 2

The "I" Factor

"I miss not being able to ask them questions about my childhood to compare them with my daughter's experiences."

"Each milestone — first smile, first giggle, walking, talking — everything has something missing because you can't share it with the two people who birthed you and raised you."

"I feel like I don't have enough support and yet I have to perform and behave just like my friends who have tons of parental support. It is overwhelming."

— from the Parentless Parents Survey

W*hen I was eighteen weeks* pregnant with Lexi, I had an abnormal ultrasound. My obstetrician told us flatly, "The lateral ventricles of the brain appear dilated. If you'd consider terminating the pregnancy, you should see a specialist." The fear was Down syndrome.

We needed to wait three weeks for that appointment — until the baby grew a little bigger and the brain could be more easily analyzed under a different, more powerful machine.

At night, Mark would update his parents and reach out to them for consolation. I'd call my brother, stepmother, my aunt Ronnie (my mother's sister) in New Mexico, and while they'd all listen attentively, I couldn't help feeling an invisible clock ticking away the minutes when we were on the phone. They weren't my parents and I wasn't their daughter.

The expert we were advised to see was a high-risk obstetrician specializing in fetal abnormalities and diagnosis. The procedure began like any other sonogram—by the doctor squeezing a mound of that cold, clear ultrasound jelly onto my belly. Mark and I gripped hands. When the exam was done a few minutes later, the doctor pronounced, "Everything looks fine. To be safe, you may want to consider having an amnio. Then you'd know for sure."

The amniocentesis was scheduled for the following week, and during those seven long days I felt completely battered. It had been five months since my dad died, and I was worn out from missing him, exhausted from worrying about the baby, and I longed even more for my mother.

The amnio was performed on schedule and without incident. Mark and I were told everything was fine. And the baby was a girl. A girl! I was overjoyed that the baby was healthy, of course, but I was also elated because I felt like I was getting part of my mother back. Since she died, I had yearned to have that special mother-daughter connection again. So when I was getting ready to go to bed that night, I took out the pregnancy book I'd been keeping on my bedside table and filled in the section, "The things I am looking forward to as a mother." I wrote, "Because I know you're a girl, I can't wait to do a ton of mommy/daughter stuff . . . and I can't wait to dress you in fun girly clothes. All I can do is think pink!"

This story, while it had a happy ending, was a sobering experience for me. Mark and I both had support from our families during those terrifying weeks, but he alone had something else. His mom offered Mark encouragement with stories from her own pregnancies. And his father provided his own brand of solace by recounting how healthy Mark was when he was born, despite the nervousness he too, had felt as an expectant parent. All of this gave Mark peace — the kind I never had.

Did *my* parents face a similar scare when they had me? Did *my* mom ever consider having an abortion? I never got the answers. My brother, only two and a half years older than me, couldn't be very helpful, and the times I asked Aunt Ronnie, she didn't know for sure. My questions echoed on and on. In many ways, I felt like an adopted child. Without that same direct tie to my past, I felt entirely unmoored and off balance.

This is the "I" Factor. "I" stands for irreplaceable, which correctly describes so many of our losses.

A Severed Link to Your Past

For a great number of parentless parents, the unease experienced during these early years stems from not having access to their own developmental histories. That living connection to their childhood — which frayed with the death of their first parent — becomes completely severed with the death of the second. Here's how one respondent summarized the experience in the Parentless Parents Survey: "After Sophie was born, not one day has gone by that I haven't wanted to talk to my parents and ask if I did that at that age. How old was I when I sat up, crawled for the first time, walked for the first time? All of these milestones are suddenly so important."

Another parent wrote that the most important issue facing her as a parentless parent was "not having any memory of my childhood."

Hilari Graff lives just outside New York City and lost both of her parents by the time she was twenty-seven—before she was married and had her two children. "To this day," she told me in her living room, as her three-year-old son, Alex, played enthusiastically with wooden blocks nearby, "there are so many questions I wish I could ask—because I read a lot of books and I do talk to people—but sometimes you want to know about your own childhood to see where there are similarities. Did I do something that my kids do now? I just want to know more about what I was like."

"Or even when you got your first tooth," I said empathetically.

"Exactly," Hilari said. "I was very close with my parents, but at sixteen or twenty I wasn't as interested in all the details of what my sleeping patterns were the first year of my life. There are so many times I wish I could ask them how I was at this age, or how did they handle me when I acted like this." And she half-joked, "They did a decent job with me. So how did they do it?!"

How *did* they do it? What stopped our tempter tantrums? How exactly did our parents parent us when we were young? We wonder because the information might help us understand our children's behavior and better gauge their physical and emotional maturity.

When Lexi turned three, she started to stutter. She was unfazed, but Mark and I were worried and heartbroken. It was painful hearing our daughter stumble over the simplest words. For me, what made it worse was that as a child I also stuttered and I had no recollection of how my parents helped me. Did they take the "wait and see" approach as Lexi's pediatrician recommended? Or did they whisk me off to a speech therapist for immediate intervention? Whatever they did, it worked. Mark and I ended up choosing the aggressive line of attack, and Lexi stopped stuttering almost instantly. Perhaps we would have reached the same conclusion if my parents had been alive, but the scare would have been easier to handle if they'd been there to help us along.

Jeff Gelman, a clean-cut writing teacher at a small private high school, says that if he knew more about his childhood it would have helped him manage his son, David's, sensory issues. As a baby, David never liked to be put down and always needed to be in motion. He couldn't tolerate loud noises or how certain textures felt on his skin. From birth to age three, David saw specialists for speech, OT, and PT. Jeff remembers having similar issues when he was small.

I first met Jeff when I interviewed him for *Always Too Soon*. He, along with his wife and two young sons, lives in a handsome old house in Pennsylvania and is the only person I chose to reinterview. Jeff wasn't a father when we first spoke, and I wanted to find out, now that he is, what affects him most about being a parentless parent. "It certainly would have been nice to have my parents there saying, 'Don't worry, Jeff. We went through this with you. You didn't like wearing certain kinds of clothes and you didn't like wearing turtlenecks because they felt funny on your skin.' It would have helped having my parents to talk to about all these problems." But those avenues for advice were permanently closed when a drunk driver killed his parents when he was fourteen.

Parentless parents could read every book and article ever written about parenting, and not one sentence would answer the question we really want to know: "Was I like that, too?"

Absent Cheerleaders

The isolation parentless parents experience sometimes feels inescapable. It is often the poisonous current that runs through our most exhilarating moments and transforms them into painful reminders of our parents' absence. That sense of loneliness that made me sulk under the covers after having Lexi also chipped away at Hilari Graff's happiness during her pregnancies. "Every step of the way was bittersweet because I couldn't share these experiences with my parents," she said that day in her bustling home. And what about the moment Tarah Epstein

Baiman, a thirty-six-year-old mom near Philadelphia, found out she was pregnant? That special time, even more meaningful after an earlier miscarriage, quickly became tarnished, too. "I remember that feeling, who am I going to tell? Who's going to be that phone call?"

Fathers also feel this pull. Psychologist Dr. Brad Sachs, author of numerous books on children and families and founder and director of the Father Center, says a man who has lost his parents faces a specific kind of loss when he has children. "What he'll miss is that sense of continuity, his desire to proudly show off this new generation to his father, and to earn his father's blessing. That's what he'll be deprived of. That's when he'll feel the emptiness."

The need to connect with our parents doesn't end when our children grow out of babyhood. Tarah Epstein Baiman says what she misses now is the validation that she's getting the toddler phase right. As illustration, she told me about an incident that happened just a few days before we met. She and a girlfriend had finished eating lunch and were saying good-bye outside the restaurant. While they talked, Tarah held her son, Jesse, on her hip. Out of nowhere, Jesse got impatient and wanted to leave. Tarah told him to hang on a few more minutes and he smacked her in the face. "At that moment," she reflected, "I thought to myself, *I don't know what to do right now*. There were people watching me. Like they were thinking, *Oh, how could he have just hit you? What a spoiled child.*" Not knowing how to react, her mind spun with options. "Should I put him in a time-out right there on the street? Do nothing and ignore it? There are moments like that when I would have liked to have picked up the phone and asked my parents, 'What should I have done?'" Tarah, it turns out, did nothing.

The fact that Tarah feels insecure, and did throughout her pregnancy and toddler phase, is striking to me. Tarah is an über-confident woman who, after losing both her parents before turning sixteen, went on to finish high school, then college, earn a master's degree from Harvard, and become the founder of the Orphan Society of

America—a nonprofit organization dedicated to helping children left parentless by violence. Creating OSA was important to Tarah because she knew from personal experience just how vital it is for these particular children not to fall through society's cracks. She was one of them.

Tarah's parents divorced when she was five, and years later her mother was murdered by the man she'd been dating. Tarah's father, whom Tarah had been living with at the time, died less than two years later from diabetes. She went on to live with her uncle and then her grandparents. None of this made Tarah play the victim. Instead, she grew into an independent and self-assured woman. The fact that she feels less than capable as a mother, and craves the kind of feedback she's been without for more than half her life, seems entirely out of character. Her explanation is simple: While every parent has to figure out how to be a parent for him- or herself, parentless parents don't ever receive that all-important parental pat on the back. That specific kind of reassurance is irreplaceable. Parentless parents suffer what I call Generational Silence.

Generational Silence is especially loud every time we want to share a milestone with our parents. We want our parents to applaud our children's first steps and cheer at their preschool graduations. A father of three says he misses that now more than anything. "These years are great. They're really cute and they're learning every day—and the things that come out of their mouths! Everything they're saying would be really fun to share with my parents." What we're missing is our parents' seemingly inexhaustible interest in our lives—and the lives of our children.

Without your parents, there are simply fewer people to unapologetically brag to about your children. In a New York City focus group one parent said, "That sounds like such a little thing, but it's such a big thing. Because you can't call your friends and say, 'My daughter just stood up,' because their kid may not have stood up. And they don't care because they're going through the same thing at the same time. 'So she stood up? Big deal.' "

Too Few Babysitters

Statistics show that adult orphans seem to have less child-care support than other parents. Indeed, nearly 60 percent of parents who took the Parentless Parents Survey said they didn't have enough support during their children's early years. Government figures help explain why they might feel this way.

Historically, according to research conducted by the U.S. Census Bureau, grandparents have always been the number one child-care providers for working moms with very young children in this country. The latest analysis conducted by the agency, so new that when I spoke with census family demographer Lynda Laughlin, her detailed report hadn't yet been released to the public, illustrates that grandparents are caregivers to more children than day-care centers and nursery schools combined. Her data also show that this reliance on grandparents is inching higher over time.

AARP has done its own investigation into how much time grandparents spend with grandchildren. According to the association's two most recent studies on grandparenting, 82 percent of respondents reported seeing a grandchild in the past month, while 68 percent indicated they saw a grandchild every one or two weeks. In another study, AARP concluded that the number of households consisting of children, parents, and grandparents is also growing. In 2000, approximately 780,000 households had these three generations under one roof. That number rose to an estimated 1.13 million households by 2009. This multigenerational arrangement doesn't just benefit children. The direct contact between grandparent and grandchild also helps parents, who gain an incalculable amount of psychic and physical support.

Lacking the same assistance, it's not surprising that in response to every question in the Parentless Parents Survey regarding pregnancy, childbirth, emotions about children entering school, and celebrating important milestones, respondents of every age reported feeling more isolated than supported. A staggering 79 percent indicated feeling alone sometimes or a lot of the time after their first child was born. Irene Rubaum-Keller, a psychotherapist in private practice for more than twenty years and leader of the Los Angeles chapter of Motherless Daughters, says even among women who've lost one parent, "the biggest theme I've seen is a supreme loneliness. Just this feeling of being completely on your own and having no help."

Fred Greene, a father of two grown boys living outside San Francisco, says not being able to get away when his sons were young is what made him most envious of other parents. "We never had anybody that we could say, 'We need a break. Can you take the kids for the weekend?'" Julie Hallman, the mom in Florida, says she got the help she needed mostly by hiring babysitters. "If I had a mother, she would have been there to help me," Julie stated that sunny afternoon in her office. She quickly acknowledged, however, "I didn't ask anybody either. It felt like an imposition."

I understood exactly what she meant. The only alternative to paying for help is asking for it, and asking for it poses its own set of complications. How often can you ask friends, siblings, or in-laws to lend a hand before you become, or feel like, a nuisance? And if assistance only arrives after you request it, can it ever be guilt-free?

For parentless men and women, what makes having less support even harder is that the deficit is largely invisible to others. When Hilari and I hit this point in our conversation, she leaned forward in her chair. "No one expects a woman in her thirties to have lost both her parents. So every step of the way, people would always make reference to my parents. Like, I'd be getting my hair cut and the hairdresser said to me, 'Are you going to continue to work when you have the baby?' And I said, 'Yes, I am.' And then she asked, 'Is your mom going to babysit?' I just said, 'No,' and that we were going to put the baby in day care several days a week.' I stayed for the haircut, but then went into my car and started to cry, because it's another reminder that my mom and dad will not be babysitting, ever."

The truth is, parentless parents could have all the help in the world and it wouldn't feel like enough. Hilari had child care. She just wanted *different* child care. Feeling alone and being alone are two different things.

I had help with Jake and Lexi, too—and not just from my mother-in-law, Marilyn. Mark has always been a nurturing father, and our babysitter was so giving and warmhearted that the kids ran to her when she arrived in the morning. Mark's father (and both of our stepmothers) bailed us out of numerous child-care emergencies. I have never parented alone, yet many of my recollections of being a new mother are as if I had been a single mother without any parenting support whatsoever. I just wanted the two babysitters I couldn't have.

Getting the Support You Want

When I was about five months pregnant with Jake, I began investigating doulas. Doulas are trained to offer mothers physical and emotional support before, during, and after birth, and without my mom (and my dad only enjoying children when they could walk and talk), I needed someone who would not only teach me the basics but take care of me as well. Instinctively I knew that if I couldn't get it from my parents, this kind of support would be easier to accept from a stranger. I went online and soon found Susan Esserman, cofounder and director of Seventh Moon Perinatal Support Services in northern New Jersey. Seventh Moon's philosophy is summed up on its website:

"We believe that the ancient tradition of women helping women through the childbearing years as mentors and assistants is essential to a positive birth experience and positive parenting." This sounded perfect to me.

I was so nervous about my abilities as a new mom that I made sure Susan and Mark were in cell phone contact when we were leaving the hospital so she'd be waiting outside our apartment building when we got home. I didn't want to be alone with Jake, not even for a few minutes. And, to be honest, Mark wasn't too comfortable either. We soon discovered that hiring Susan was the best decision we could have made.

Susan was better than Mary Poppins. She was Mary Poppins with degrees and certifications. Susan is a clinical social worker (MSW and LCSW), board certified lactation consultant, and leader of several postpartum support groups for new moms and their babies. She taught me everything I needed to know: how to change diapers and apply A&D ointment, how to breastfeed and use my breast pump, how to determine if Jake was eating, peeing, and pooping enough. And she helped me in other ways, too. She danced around our apartment unpacking all the baby gifts, and kept a running list of who gave us what. She cut the tags off Jake's new onesies and socks, washed them all in Dreft, and decided how they should be organized in his closet. She also cooked when I was hungry and encouraged me to rest when I was tired.

Susan more than earned her money. She taught me and Mark the basics, and by doing so, she boosted our confidence. Perhaps more importantly, Susan took care of me like a mother would. Even in my darkest hours, Susan Esserman assured me that I could do it.

I also made it a point during those new-mommy years to increase the amount of contact I had with women from my side of the family. Because of this, the first person I told that I was pregnant with Jake was my grandma Bertha. I knew she'd be overjoyed. Grandma had told me many times that she couldn't wait to share this moment with me, her only granddaughter.

As I dialed her number in Delray Beach, Florida, I imagined my four-foot-ten grandmother purposefully walking across her yellow shag carpeting to the phone when it rang. She'd be wearing white or navy blue slacks and open-toe pumps—always a little heel, never flats. "Oh, Allison," she nearly cried. "I am so happy for you." Then the battery of excited questions: "When did you find out?" "How far along are you?" "How are you feeling?" I basked in all the attention.

I called my dad next, and then Aunt Ronnie. Reaching out filled me up. I asked Ronnie to stay with us when our two weeks with Susan Esserman ended. And she did. Happily. She parachuted in and made my life easier—and better. She told me to loosen up and not be so uptight. She taught me how to make lasagna with no-boil pasta. (A miracle in a box!) And she even successfully—albeit temporarily—resurrected my mother. One day during her visit she wrote down a grocery list—green peppers, onions, chicken breasts, chili powder. She was going to make her famous Santa Fe fajitas for dinner, and she left the list on the kitchen counter. My heart lurched when I saw it. Her handwriting had the same loopy script as my mother's, and for a split second I thought—irrationally, of course—that my mother had written the list.

Aunt Ronnie would never have flown across the country to help me if I hadn't asked. Asking is hard, but when the love and assistance arrives, it's worth it. Ronnie knew better than anyone how much I missed my mom—she missed her sister, too.

Baby Books: The Unexpected Antidote

About a year after my mother died, my brother and I sold the house we grew up in. It was the only home we ever knew; our dad had designed it. The house was ultramodern and looked like two huge cubes stacked on top of each other. The sadness I felt packing up and discarding my mother's things made it nearly impossible to be discriminating. I became a Mommy hoarder. I kept boxes and boxes of her belongings—business suits, scarves, books, platters for entertaining, and a few pieces of American crafts she collected. But everything related directly to my childhood, I shipped to Aunt Ronnie. I purged myself of every last photograph, report card, and keepsake my mother ever saved. And I made sure to get rid of my baby book. At the time, it was just too depressing to be the keeper of all those memories. That had been Mom's job—not mine.

Ronnie surprised me by sending everything back when Lexi turned four. The cardboard boxes stayed taped up in my boiler room for months. With two small children running around, it never seemed important—or urgent—to take the time to open them. Yet when I finally did, it was as if I discovered a map to a buried treasure.

Inside one of the boxes was my puffy pink baby book, and when I opened it up I saw my birth announcement. Made out of parchment paper, the announcement is the size and shape of a place card you'd get at a wedding. On the front, in black script lettering, it says:

The partnership of

Gilbert and Gilbert

is proud to announce

the completion of project two

Allison

The tongue-in-cheek wording is a nod to my dad's work as an architect and the fact that my mother ran her own business, too. On the inside flap it reads:

Outline Specifications

Completion Date ----------------- *March 18th*

Live Load ----------------- *5 lbs., 13 ozs.*

Outside Dimension ----------------- *19½ inches*

Partner in Charge of Design ----------------- *Sidney*

Partner in Charge of Working Drawings ----------------- *Lynn*

Full scale model on view at

11 Sigma Place

Riverdale, NY

Until I read my birth announcement, I had no idea what I weighed when I was born. I also didn't know, until I examined my baby book, that I rolled over at six months, crawled at nine, and I took my first steps when I was thirteen and a half months old. My parents may have told me some of this, and I know my mother showed me my baby book when I was younger, but as happened with Hilari Graff's mother, she died before those milestones meant anything to me. These numbers, these simple statistics, broke my parents' silence. Had I looked at them sooner, maybe I wouldn't have been so worried that Jake wasn't walking when he turned one; I would have known that I didn't walk at my first birthday either.

I plowed through my baby book like a *New York Times* best seller. Every page revealed new clues to my past, and each clue helped fill in the bigger picture by which I could see parallels between me as a baby and my children. I also discovered links between me as a mom and my mother that I'd never known. The best morsel was located in the story my mother wrote about the day I was born:

"Daddy took Mommy to the hospital. Daddy was there all the time to help Mommy and watch Allison be born. Mommy's labor didn't start until 6:00 pm and Allison was born at 8:38 pm."

Two hours and thirty-eight minutes. *Two hours and thirty-eight minutes??!!* Just minutes different from my labor with Jake??!! Knowing we probably had the same kind of quick birthing experience made me feel connected to her in a way I hadn't known since she died.

When you don't have living parents, your baby book can help fill in the blanks. But even the most meticulous baby books can't answer every question. They're paper and words, and no matter how conscientious my mother was — and she wasn't; I was the second child, after all — the book can never take the place of the kind of information my parents could have passed on if they were still alive.

How could anyone (or any*thing*) fill the hole my mom and dad left behind? Just when I thought I was doing okay, Lexi or Jake would bring home some amazing art project from school and I'd want to share it with my parents. "Before the birth of my son, I was aware of my orphanhood," one mother wrote in the Parentless Parents Survey, "but it wasn't as pronounced. What was black and white before is Technicolor now."

Chapter 3

Later Parenthood

"It wasn't so much the new parenting stuff that I missed talking about. It was later, as the kids were older, that I really missed my mom's wisdom."

"I'm envious of friends who have parents at every milestone and school play. Those are my lowest times."

"Even though my parents were alive to see two of my children grow into adulthood, I miss them terribly — even now."

—from the Parentless Parents Survey

W hen *Jake and Lexi were* babies, I expected that the jealousy I felt for moms and dads who had their parents would subside as my children got older. That somehow the passage of time would fill the empty space my parents left behind. But trip wires are everywhere. They stand on the sidelines of Jake's baseball games and they sit in folding chairs at Lexi's piano recitals. My grandparent radar is always on.

Like the time I went to Jake's second-grade Valentine's Day party. The flyer that came home said, *"Valentine's Day Celebration! Join us for breakfast on February 14th at 8:00 a.m. Your children will read poems they have written for this special occasion. Please let the class mothers know what you are able to bring."* The morning of the party, I arrived at Jake's school with the red plastic cups I'd promised and was in a great mood. I couldn't wait to hear Jake read his poem. But right as I bit into my umpteenth chocolate munchkin, I noticed one of his classmates showing an older man a drawing on the wall. The man studied it and leaned over and whispered in her ear. She giggled, then smiled. I imagined what he must have said. *"Oh, darling.* What a *fantastic* drawing. You are *such* a terrific artist."

My mood instantly disintegrated. I started thinking how my parents couldn't participate in even the most routine aspects of Jake's life. Even though I tried to remain focused, I became preoccupied. Soon, Jake's teacher told us to take our seats. My eyes flitted back and forth between Jake, sitting pretzel-legged in front of the room with all the other students, and this man sitting in a small chair a few feet away from mine with a camera strapped around his neck. I hadn't expected grandparents to be there; they weren't expressly invited, and I wasn't prepared for the sadness that washed over me.

One afternoon in June I got so bitter, I went into my home office, flung open my top desk drawer, and grabbed one of my white and red Reporter's Notebooks. I flipped the rectangular pad open and began marking the lined pages with the nearest ballpoint pen I could find. For the rest of the week, I was going to keep track of how many times I came across other people's parents and how often friends, neighbors, and acquaintances mentioned their parents to me in conversation. I started the experiment the very next day.

Wednesday, June 3

- Lunch with friend. He tells me about his kids and his wife and how they live in a two-family home with his mother.
- Wait at bus stop for Jake and Lexi. Grandmother, a neighbor's mother, at bus stop, too.
- Bring Jake to guitar lessons. Grandmother sitting in waiting area to pick up grandson from music lessons.
- Receive a dozen "Reply All" emails about an upcoming end-of-school party in Lexi's class. Mothers are confirming what they'll be bringing. One mom emails, "Mary will bring cups and her grandparents."

Thursday, June 4

- Two grandmothers waiting for grandchildren at Jake and Lexi's bus stop.
- Neighbor also at bus stop waiting for daughter. Her 3-year-old daughter is with her. While we wait she says, "Oh, we're so excited today. Granny and Poppy are coming for her birthday. They should be coming around the corner any minute. We're so excited!"
- After pickup from bus stop, go to local ATM. See one of the teachers from Jake and Lexi's school. She introduces me to her mother.

Friday, June 5

- "Granny" and "Poppy" from the day before now at bus stop—drop-off and pickup.
- After school, take Lexi's friend to the movies and invite him to come over afterward. His mother says he can't because his grandparents are coming over for dinner.

Saturday, June 6
- Two sets of grandparents at Lexi's softball game. Plus one additional grandmother.
- Three sets of grandparents at Jake's baseball game.

Sunday, June 7
- Three sets of grandparents at Lexi's soccer game.

I'm ashamed I kept this scorecard. What sane person keeps tabs like this? Friends and neighbors had no idea what I was doing, because I always kept my notebook inside my bag and filled it out when I was alone. Obviously, I was in a very dark and painful place. But with the exception of crawling into a cave and abandoning my children, there was no way to avoid other people's parents. I had to go to Jake and Lexi's school. I had to pick them up at the bus stop. And I enjoyed doing those things.

But I was addicted to my parents. When I was a child, they helped me forget my problems and calm my fears. No matter the trouble I had at school or with friends, they always seemed to know what to do and what to say. Now that I'm a parent, I wish I could get their advice on getting Lexi to stop talking back to me, and I'd love to know their suggestions for motivating Jake to clean his room without his usual "Mom, I'll do it later!" histrionics. It's not that my parents didn't raise an independent child capable of thinking and acting on her own. I am a fully competent and functioning adult. But in the thirty-one years that I was their daughter, it was easy to get used to their ever-available feedback and guidance.

Intellectually, I realize my parents would never have been as involved in my children's lives as I imagine. My parents were passionate about their careers and worked all the time. When I was small, I often resented that my mother, especially, worked as much as she did. I'd accuse her (falsely) of being the only mom who didn't pick her daughter up from school. And if I really look back at my dad's involvement when Jake was born, I have to admit that though he loved showing up for the big events—Jake's birth, his bris, his first haircut—he never seemed too interested in babysitting. Maybe that would have changed when he retired, but when would that have been? Even though their presence would likely have been dictated by their schedules, not mine, the amount I missed them had nothing to do with their being perfect parents.

Cindi Hartmann, a forty-four-year-old mom who lives outside Ann Arbor, Michigan, confessed that during her daughter's recent dance team competition, envy got the best of her, too. "We were in the second row, dead center, and Cami was amazing. I made it through her finishing and then I had to get myself out of that room."

It might surprise you to hear what actually made Cindi so upset. Yes, she wished her parents could have been there to see their granddaughter perform, but that wasn't the real trigger. What set her off was the seating arrangements. That amazing spot she got for the show? "If your daughter was in that number," Cindi explained, "you got to sit in those seats, and when that number was over you went back to your regular seat. So all of a sudden, you'd see this huge number of people move over there just for a solo. They've got all their family and you could tell who the grandparents were." But when it was Cami's turn to be on stage, rushing into those prime slots were just Cindi, her husband, and her other daughter, Cara. "We just took up less space."

Reminders of your parents' absence can show up even in your child's backpack. Tom Vates told me about one such incident that happened just before I arrived for our interview in his sprawling Tudor home in New Jersey. Tom, a pediatric urologist, has three daughters: Sarah, twelve; Katie, ten; and Hannah, seven. As we sat on overstuffed leather chairs in his living room, he explained what had occurred that afternoon. "My oldest daughter has this science project, and it's on eye color. They're learning what you learn when you're a sixth grader or seventh grader in science—that brown eye is dominant and blue eye is recessive. The assignment is you have to do a family pedigree, including your grandparents. So I know what my eye color is, I know what my wife's eye color is, I know what my kid's eye color is. But then Sarah asks, 'What about your mom and dad?' And I'm like, 'I don't remember. I don't know.' We had to go look at a picture on the wall and try to see. I told her, 'It looks like it's green, maybe it's blue.'"

The incident was upsetting because it caught Tom off guard. Indeed, Jeff Gelman says, "The times where it hits hardest are the ones when I'm not prepared."

Helen Fitzgerald, an expert on grieving and former director of training for the American Hospice Association, says unanticipated events are often more challenging than expected ones for individuals coping with loss. "There are plenty of times when we might assume people would have a difficult time. These are what I call the commercial holidays, the ones that everybody acknowledges. Easter, for example, or a loved one's birthday. But a whole assortment of other events that don't have special names can make you just as acutely aware that you don't have parents. Your child's first day of school might suddenly take you back to your first day of school and reactivate your loss. It reminds you that you no longer have that connection to your childhood—because who better to review those memories with than your parents?"

There are other times on the school calendar, however, that remain difficult even when parentless parents know they're coming. Take Grandparents Day. This seemingly harmless event can make some parentless parents incredibly uneasy. Christine Haynes, a jewelry designer from Maryland whose husband has also lost his parents, told me about the celebration at their eldest daughter Jour'dan's school when she was five years old.

"What do they do on Grandparents Day?" I asked.

"All the kids can bring their grandparents to spend the day with them. They have breakfast, they have special events, they put on a little show, they give them gifts."

"What did you do on that day?" I asked.

"We didn't send her to school."

"You kept her home?"

"Yes," Christine replied.

"Why?"

"I didn't know what to do. I didn't know how to handle it. I was so frazzled, because, it's Grandparents Day, and who are we going to bring? I didn't want to go in place of her grandparents. What am I supposed to do?"

Even the anticipation of Grandparents Day makes some parents anxious, like Lisa Petersen, a husky-voiced ICU nurse in Michigan. "They used to call it Grandparents Day, but now it's called Family Day. At the beginning of the year they told us when the day was going to be, and I fretted the entire year about what I was going to do. Every other person is so excited — 'Oh, this is going to be the greatest thing. All the grandparents are going to be there.' And I'm smiling on the outside, but on the inside I'm thinking, what am I going to do? I was like, do I pull him out of school? But then I thought, how do I pull him out of school if the week before all they're doing [in class] is leading up to this?"

"So what did you do?" I asked.

Chuckling, she answered, "I sent my husband."

Parentless parents I've spoken with have also sent along brothers, sisters, and babysitters. But no amount of window dressing can disguise who's really supposed to attend, and there doesn't seem to be a perfect solution. Tom Vates and his wife, Molly, even urged their daughters' school to soften the blow by calling Grandparents Day a

Thankfulness Gathering or Fall Festival. Request denied. "The school feels very strongly that Grandparents Day is what they should call it," Molly said.

In the Parentless Parents Survey, nearly 60 percent of respondents said they were more aware of their parents' absence during school events and other social settings like playdates. The constant rub leaves many feeling disconnected from their peers and may help clarify why almost 70 percent admit being jealous when they see other children with their grandparents. "I don't think people get it because they've not been through it," Jeff Nudelman, a father of three children under six, says. Christine Haynes from Maryland would agree with that. This full-time working mom is usually a bubbly, glass-is-half-full personality. She's also witty and self-deprecating — describing herself on Facebook as "just a little bit crazy." But even she feels the need to remind her friends how lucky they are, especially when they complain about their parents. "I don't wish it upon them, but when it happens, that's the only time they're going to understand." She says her friends just have no idea what they're missing.

Continuing Responsibilities and Added Burdens

There's a frustrating assumption that being a parentless parent gets easier as our children get older. My research shows that in many cases the opposite is true. Bigger children, after all, bring bigger achievements and problems. For Fred Greene, the dad just outside San Francisco, being a parent without his parents only gets harder with time. "It wasn't until my kids were getting older, eight, nine, ten, and up — when they started accomplishing stuff on their own terms and I had no one to call and share it with that I started to miss my parents," he says. "That's when it became a void in my life."

My parents' silence seems to get louder the older Jake and Lexi get, too. In their absence, I've tried to reach out to my brother Jay instead. I've called him on the phone to tell him about Lexi doing flips in gymnastics, and I've beamed about Jake hitting a double in baseball. Most of the time, though, the conversations leave me wanting. What I imagine would feel like sharing with my parents feels like bragging to my brother. Our kids are so close in age it's like we're always trying to one-up each other — as if parenting is just a new phase of sibling rivalry.

Parenting has also gotten more difficult for Nancy Dickinson, a mother of two boys from Arizona. Nancy's parents only recently passed away, and when her children were small she relied on them heavily for help. "They were great grandparents. They really were. They never missed a birthday. They never missed Christmas. They just loved being around the kids."

That level of involvement was all the more welcome because Nancy lives in relative isolation — in a town so close to the Mexican border that in an unintentional imitation of Sarah Palin she told me, "We can see Mexico from our back porch." U.S. Border Patrol agents routinely conduct surveillance on or near her property, and her closest supermarket is twenty miles away. With just a phone call, her parents would break the solitude. And because Nancy is now having problems with her oldest son, Billy, she misses that lifeline even more.

A few years ago, Billy dropped out of college and announced he was going to move back home. "He wanted to live with us, but he didn't want to follow our rules," Nancy says. "He didn't want to pay us rent." The mother-son relationship deteriorated even further when she caught Billy being dishonest. "I let him use my Suburban to go pick up his paycheck and cash it. Seven hours later, he came back, handed me the keys, and said, 'Here, I filled your car up.' But the next day, I went to get in the car and couldn't open the door. Billy had wrecked the whole back of the car and didn't say a word about it. I was livid! Ordinarily, that's something I would have talked over with my mom, as in

'Mother, what do I do?' I didn't have my mom to talk to. She couldn't pull me off the ceiling."

Melony Robinson lost her parents later in life, too, and found the transition from having their constant backing to having none at all soul crushing. "I guess their support made me feel better about myself," the mom from Tennessee says. "I was able to relax more and be a better parent. I mean, I have friends to bounce things off of, but there's a layer of support from a good parental relationship that nobody can replace. I'm not sure what I'm doing in some cases and I don't feel as competent. Most people think you go on with your life and keep your parents in the background and pull out a memory once in a while."

But that's not the case, according to Dr. Kenneth Doka, author of numerous books on death and grieving and past president of the Association for Death Education and Counseling. "Grief is not a time-bound process that simply ends and you're over it. You live with that loss. There are moments when the reality strikes you differently and sometimes strikes you harder. That's very normal and very natural." Family milestones can be particularly difficult. A parent lamented during one of the Parentless Parents focus groups, "My daughter just got married last year and that's when it really hit me."

Children also tend to ask more questions as they get older, and the fact that our parents can't help us remember "what we went through when" continues to frustrate us. Within the next five years or so Lexi will no doubt ask me, "Mom, when did you get your period?" She'll wonder, just like I did, when I asked my mother. But the response I'll give will be unsatisfying. "I don't really remember, Lex. Maybe eleven. Might have been twelve. I'm not exactly sure." My mother likely would've remembered, though. She always seemed able to recall every detail of my life.

A Different Kind of Sandwich Generation

Being part of the sandwich generation means you are caught in the middle of taking care of aging parents while supporting your own children. Usually, if life goes predictably, these competing demands end when your parents die and you can once again focus exclusively on your children. However, because their grandparents outlived their mother and father, many parentless parents find themselves pulled by a different generational tug-of-war.

After my father died, I used frequent flyer miles and visited Grandma Bertha often. I took her grocery shopping and out to dinner. The kids and I threw her a party for her eighty-sixth birthday. And when she was diagnosed with macular degeneration, I Googled specialists while Jake and Lexi were in school. On the weekends, Mark would take the kids grocery shopping just to give me time to investigate special reading glasses and lamps. Doing anything that had to be done—and more—is what my father would have done. I was doing it for him.

A few years after Dad passed away, my uncle uprooted his life in New Jersey so he could be closer to their mother. Richie got an apartment just a few doors away and ferried Grandma around to all her doctors' appointments. This would have been perfect except that they didn't get along all that well. The situation was often tense, and what made it worse was that I didn't have confidence in my uncle's ability to navigate Grandma Bertha's care. He was distracted by a new divorce and job search. So I continued to feel that I had to micromanage her care from New York.

I loved my grandma but resented having to take on the caregiver role again. I didn't want the responsibility. But there I was, forced into family triage for the third time. Soon, my once spunky grandma could only distinguish shapes and shadows, and her days consisted mainly of catching her breath and going to the bathroom. It became clear she needed nursing care, and I took on the job of finding home-care workers, too.

Then, one evening, I called Grandma to say good night. I thought I woke her up because she seemed disoriented. "Hi, Allison," she panted into the phone. "How are you, Grandma?" I sang back, trying to perk her up. "I don't know, Allison. I don't know," she said. "Grandma," I said, pushing on, "are you having trouble going to sleep?" "I don't know" was all she said back. "Okay, Grandma. I'm sure you're just tired. Go to bed. Have a good sleep. I'll talk to you in the morning." "Okay," she replied. "I love you, Grandma," I said, ending our conversation. "Love you, too," she responded.

As soon as we got off the phone, I called Uncle Richie and asked him to walk over and check on her, which he did. He called me back from her apartment and said she was fine and not to worry. He tucked her in and went home.

The next morning, I fired up my computer as soon as Jake and Lexi got off to school. I started frantically looking up hospices in and around Delray Beach, trying to line up care for her immediately. Which was the best hospice? Was there one near her apartment that took Medicare? End-of-life decision-making was familiar terrain. About a dozen calls and emails later, my phone rang. I assumed it was one of the hospices calling me back.

"Hello?" Pause.

"She's gone, Allison." I barely heard Richie. He was crying and I couldn't respond.

"I went in this morning, and she died in her sleep."

And, just like that, Grandma Bertha was gone, too.

Absence of Unconditional Love

Our parents would surely be more than just grandparents to our children. If they were still alive, we imagine in some ways they'd still be taking care of us, too. Whether you have parents or not, it's hard to take care of yourself when you're busy raising a family. Your children's needs nearly always interfere with your own. The difference for parentless parents, though, is that we no longer have anyone to parent us.

Colleen Orme, forty-five years old and mother of three sports-obsessed boys ages nine to fourteen, says that while day-to-day parenting has gotten easier over time, "it doesn't mean there weren't moments when I was so tired that I would sit and cry. And not because I needed advice, because I needed a shoulder." Colleen's parents never met her children. They died, one after the other, from prolonged illnesses, six months apart.

"I didn't complain for sixteen years," the mom from Virginia continued. "I made the best of it. But now I want to be rescued. I think that's human nature. I think it's easy to be happy and it's difficult to have challenges. And that's the sad thing about missing your parents, because nobody else in your life really rescues you. I want that luxury. You don't call your girlfriend and say, 'Oh, I'm so tired,' because your girlfriend's like, 'I'm tired, too.'"

Hilari Graff says her parents would have supported her in ways no one else can possibly duplicate. But they also died before her children, Rachel and Alex, were born. "I think I have felt most alone or most sad when I wanted them to make me feel better. When I've had a bad Mommy day, I feel it so much because that's when I want to call my parents and I want them to make me feel better in the way a parent makes a kid feel better. I have a wonderful spouse and I have friends, [but] it's just different. I still want to be the kid."

The weight we carry around also comes from knowing that our parents are missing out. "There are three different losses," Joanne Greene, Fred's wife and also a parentless parent, explains. "You're constantly thinking what it would be like if they were here—for them, for you, and for your children. You're missing out on it, your kids are missing out on it, and they're missing out on it, too." Fifty-six-year-old Anne Condon Habig, a paralegal in a law firm, says her dad would have relished being a grandfather, especially to her teenage son. "My father had always wanted a son, but had four girls. He loved us, of course, but we were raised to change the oil on the car and get up on the roof and help him put in the gutters. The year my son was born, two of my other sisters also had boys. I think we all felt my father would have just loved this."

Former bodybuilder Judy Kalvin-Stiefel says her mom's entire life was centered on being a mother, so it was certainly going to revolve around becoming a grandmother. Judy, fifty years old and still remarkably fit, talked affectionately about her mother with me, calling her the "consummate housewife." "She wanted to be a grandparent in the worst way," Judy said. Then, barely audibly, she looked down at her hands and went on. "She would have been a wonderful grandmother." That, of course, never happened. Judy's mom was hit by a car and killed before Judy got married and had her daughter.

My mother never got the chance to be a grandmother either, and my father was a grandfather for a nanosecond—a tease, really—that lasted eighteen months for Jake and a little longer for his older cousin, Dexter. The cumulative impact of parenting without my parents is that I live in something of an altered state. I savor motherhood—taking in its greatest joys—but often, just below the surface, I feel something is missing. Mark's parents love me, but I'm not their daughter. I am their daughter-in-law, and that's entirely different. The distinction means that I am no longer anyone's number one priority or concern. Mark loves me, too, but he doesn't *unconditionally* love me.

He could walk away at any time. That kind of parent love is irreplaceable.

Constantly being the parent (and the spouse, and the home owner, and the office worker, and every other imaginable role) and never again being the child leaves many parentless parents feeling emotionally depleted. The ugly truth is that I've sometimes taken my exhaustion out on Jake and Lexi. I've been surly when I should've been calm. "Sometimes you snap and you feel bad," Christine Haynes admitted during our interview. Hilari Graff has suffered the same internal battle. "You think you've damaged your kids and you're not happy with yourself. [That] you're not the best parent you can be."

It wasn't until I was putting Jake and Lexi to bed one night that I was struck by how badly I needed to get my anger and grief under control. I was in a particularly foul mood, and Jake and Lexi were pushing all my buttons. They weren't doing anything bad, just arguing about whose book I should read to them first, hers or his. As their debate dragged on and grew louder, my mouth and cheeks grew tighter, as if I'd left a face mask on too long. I finally reached my breaking point and yelled at them to be quiet and get into bed. I opened an adaptation of C. S. Lewis's *The Lion, the Witch and the Wardrobe.* We got to the part where Edmund sneaks into the wardrobe after his sister, Lucy. As I turned the page to read what happens next, I nearly choked on my words. It was as if I was looking into a mirror and saw my reflection.

The White Witch was me.

For the longest time, I thought I knew why I'd often gotten so mad. The ripple effects from my parents' deaths had been so obvious. But something else was eating away at me that I didn't even recognize until many years later.

Without my parents, I felt as if Jake and Lexi didn't really know me, as if part of me was completely invisible to them. My children get to see me as a mother and sister, but they can't observe me being a daughter. It's impossible for them to hear my parents poking fun at me or telling even the silliest stories about me when I was young. And they certainly can't listen to my parents wax on about all the ways they look and act like me when I was their age.

I worked feverishly to restore what was missing: I kept in touch with my parents' closest friends; arranged brunch with a teacher from my elementary school; invited one of my mother's longtime boyfriends (a man she nearly married before meeting my stepfather) over for dinner.

Coordinating these encounters took an inordinate amount of effort. I pursued them, however, not because these individuals could remember when I reached certain milestones — those facts they mostly couldn't recall — but because they were capable of telling other real and colorful tidbits. When one of them saw Lexi's purple flip-flops in the hallway, and her yellow ones in her bedroom, she chuckled knowingly. It was February and snow was on the ground. Grinning at Lexi, she said, "Your mom used to wear clogs and shorts to school every day during the winter. It could have been ten degrees outside, but she refused to put on anything else. Your mom was so stubborn!" Instead of embarrassing me, the story made me feel great. For that moment and others just like it, I didn't feel as if I was the only one holding the key to my past. Jake and Lexi could see me through a different prism, which also helped reestablish the parts of me that seemed to have vanished.

Once I was able to identify what had been causing me so much stress, I was able to back off. Today I am able to seek the same experiences with a lot less urgency and far greater pleasure.

I have also put enormous pressure on myself to offer Jake and Lexi the kind of experiences my parents would have provided if they were still alive. I always try to make up for the deficit by pointing out the architectural significance of buildings and by exposing them to the kind of classical music my dad loved and the type of American crafts my mom collected. If my parents were alive, all of their interests and expertise would be transmitted naturally, as if by osmosis. But now the only way to convey that knowledge is by my own sheer will and determination. It's clear that parentless parents have yet another job other parents don't. Not only do I have to be Jake and Lexi's mother—in many ways, I have to be their grandparent, too.

Chapter 4

The Grandparent Gap

"The link to family history was gone. I lost all that history with my mom and dad."

"I feel bad for my children. They are missing out on so much."

"I am solely responsible for the direction in which my children are led. They have no grandparents to look to for support, comfort, praise, or guidance. They have no escape from my husband and I. No weekends at Grandma and Grandpa's. It makes me feel like I have several familial roles to fill. This adds a lot of pressure."

—from the Parentless Parents Survey

M*ore than twenty years ago,* doctors, professors, and researchers gathered in Budapest, Hungary, for the Third European Conference on Developmental Psychology. It was June 1988, and participants came to the meeting from countries like the Netherlands, Finland, Britain, Canada, and the United States. Scientists presented papers there on the role grandparents play in the lives of grandchildren.

Peter Smith, who currently heads the Unit for School and Family Studies at Goldsmiths, University of London, was one of the experts in attendance. He also traveled to a similar conference held the following year in Jyväskylä, Finland. From analyzing the research presented at these meetings, Smith published a book called *The Psychology of Grandparenthood*. His conclusion is unambiguous: Grandparent relationships have an enormous impact on grandchildren.

Some of the work that had most intrigued Professor Smith was conducted by Piergiorgio Battistelli and Alessandra Farneti from Italy. In their study, two hundred Italian boys and girls between the ages of four and seven were given forty pictures. Each card illustrated an everyday object, like ice cream, toys, or a garden. In a game of free association, the children were asked to take the cards from a box and put them next to one of the following figures: a mother, a father, a grandmother, or a grandfather.

The results were astounding. Preschool children linked items to their grandparents almost as often as they associated them to their parents. In addition, the vast majority of children the researchers studied connected the grandparent figures with objects representing pure joy and contentment. For example, items that had oral connotations, like bottles or sugary treats. Or were associated with play, like a picture of a park or a toy. Battistelli and Farneti described their findings as the result of a "precise, constant developmental trend" and summarized their research this way: "We may thus conclude that at a younger age, the figure of grandparent is particularly rich in significance and connotation, almost reaching the parental figure."

Another researcher who captured Smith's attention was Maria Tyszkowa of Poland. Her work focused on older children. In her study, she asked high school and college students to write essays about their grandparents. One hundred and thirty-eight essays were analyzed in total. The writings reveal the specific areas of influence grandparents have on their grandchildren. I'll summarize her findings in three categories — Cultural Influence, Skill Development, and Family History and Friendship.

Cultural Influence

Nearly all the subjects remembered a grandmother or grandfather reading books, singing lullabies, or telling them stories when they were young. As they grew, the connection included the discussion of books, film, and music. These grandparent-led experiences directly influence the development of imagination and a sense of aesthetics. Grandparents also teach grandchildren about national traditions and history, and because these lessons are taught from personal experience, they're deemed more credible.

Skill Development

Grandparents teach practical skills related to their own profession and interests. A grandfather who likes to fish teaches a grandchild how to bait a hook. A grandmother who likes to garden teaches a grandchild how to plant seeds. This knowledge is more easily digested than lessons taught in school, in a book, or sometimes even by a parent.

Family History and Friendship

Grandparents were also viewed as storytellers. Students wrote about grandparents handing down information about their past and sharing details about the lives of other relatives and ancestors. Researchers view this intergenerational communication as critical.

Students also discussed the importance of grandparents as trusted allies. Having this extra support, the Polish scientist wrote, has a measured "social and psychological dimension" and "ensures grandchildren a feeling of security and belonging." This becomes even more important as children age. In the essays, students listed a number of activities they did with their grandparents. Shopping, cooking, and playing games were all mentioned. Can you guess what the number one activity was? More than half of the students said it was simply having a conversation. Take a look at the below graph and see the findings for yourself:

ACTIVITIES CHILDREN DO WITH THEIR GRANDPARENTS	
	Percentage
Conversations	52.2
Walks	23.9
Playing and games	17.4
Cooking	9.4
Cleaning, housework	9.4
Gardening, work in the field	8.0
Shopping	7.2
Looking at family pictures and souvenirs	7.1
Fine crafts	7.0
Excursions, traveling	7.0
Preparing for and participating in parties	6.5
Playing music, singing	6.0
Reading	5.1
Visiting relatives and friends	4.4
Fishing	3.6
Discussions and making more important decisions	3.2
Taking care of pets	3.0
Common prayers	1.5

Source: *The Psychology of Grandparenthood*, Peter K. Smith; *The Role of Grandparents in the Development of Grandchildren as Perceived by Adolescents and Young Adults in Poland*, Maria Tyszkowa.

Dr. Tyszkowa sums up the importance of grandchild-grandparent conversations this way:

> Not infrequently adolescents and young adults report that they slip away from home to grandparents, especially when they go through some periods of trouble. Their love and wisdom of life is a source of psychic and moral support in moments of stress and frustration quite common in adolescence and young adulthood. The possibility of a gentle conversation or simple immersion in a loving atmosphere and being personally important allows them to regain positive self-evaluation and strengthens resistance to stress. . . . Conversations carried on by adolescent and adult grandchildren with grandparents seem to be of particular significance to them because hard-working parents do not have enough time or patience for conversation with their children, and because the existence of a mutual bond with and, at the same time, a distance from their grandparents allows them to talk about matters which they would not like to reveal to their parents. Many subjects stressed that conversations with grandparents are carried out in an atmosphere of peace, understanding and tolerance.

Since these European conferences, other research has been conducted that demonstrates the profound impact grandparents have on grandchildren. The relationship is deemed so consequential it was the topic of a symposium at the 2009 biennial meeting of the Society for Research in Child Development (SRCD). In addition, the same year, a study published by the American Psychological Association in the *Journal of Family Psychology* found that children have better social skills and fewer behavior problems if they spend time with their grandparents—particularly if their parents are divorced, separated, or remarried. That's because, as we've already learned, grandchildren turn to their grandparents as confidants and sources of comfort, and do so even more during times of stress and family turmoil. The lead researcher, Shalhevet Attar-Schwartz, of the Hebrew University of Jerusalem, writes, "They can reduce the negative influence of parents separating and be a resource for children who are going through these family changes."

If grandparents have so much influence on the lives of grandchildren, where does that leave the children of parentless parents? The SRCD says it's not aware of any studies that specifically measure how the absence of grandparents, or having fewer grandparents, affects a child's personal growth and development. I contacted other organizations, including the National Institute of Child Health and Human Development, the American Academy of Pediatrics, and the American Psychological Association, and they couldn't point to a single study either.

If you examine the power of a particular kind of relationship, should you not also investigate the lack of it?

Tom Vates, the doctor in New Jersey, took an educated guess on how the void affects the children of parentless parents. "Imagine your child is a sculpture and your entire family — including your parents — is the shaper of that sculpture. You and your wife can provide 120,000 little pushes of the fingers to mold it and shape it, but your children are always going to miss some of the pushes that would have made the sculpture complete. You can still see the face, you can still see what it is, but some of those influences won't ever impact the final product."

If celebrated children's book author Patricia Polacco never knew her grandparents, "I would not have written the entire body of work," she told me from her Union City, Michigan, home. "I am sure of it." Polacco is a sought-after speaker on the elementary school circuit, and the majority of her seventy books were inspired by the close relationship she had with her grandparents.

Frank Luntz, the eminent Republican spin doctor and pollster, may never have gotten into politics — and worked for Newt Gingrich, Rudolph Giuliani, or shaped the recent health-care language for the GOP — if it weren't for his grandfather. This is what Luntz wrote about his grandfather in the first few pages of his 2009 book, *What Americans Really Want . . . Really:* "It was his influence that turned me into a political junkie and history freak, and for that I dedicate this book to him."

Writer Jacquelyn Mitchard knows what her children missed growing up. In the anthology *Blindsided by a Diaper* (edited by Dana Bedford Hilmer), she rails against having had only one grandparent to offer them. She screams from the page, "Why did we get so ripped off?"

Even though Jake and Lexi have grandparents, I can't help feeling they were also ripped off, because they never got to know my mother and father or experience their unique blend of influences. Charles de Gaulle's sweeping statement about no individual being irreplaceable is wrong. Cemeteries of the world *are* full of indispensible people. Children only get one set of maternal grandparents, and the one that belonged to Jake and Lexi is gone.

My childhood was richer because, for a while at least, I had all my grandparents. Most years we'd fly to Florida to visit them, and vacations were full of firsts — playing shuffleboard under palm trees and collecting strawberries in "Pick-Your-Own" patches. Three of my grandparents died by the time I was ten, before they could teach me anything truly transformative. Grandma Bertha, however, changed my life.

A month or so after my dad had died, when my pregnancy scare with Lexi had ended, I took Jake down to Florida for a mini-vacation. I needed the sun and rest, but mostly we went because I wanted to see how Grandma was doing. While I was feeding Jake breakfast one morning, Grandma opened her china cabinet and took out a shoe box from the lower shelf. Her sling-backs made a snapping noise as she walked back to the dining room table, where Jake and I were sitting. Inside the box were hundreds of well-organized index cards. Her feminine script marked the categories, "Electric," "Maintenance," "Groceries," and "Incidentals." She leafed through them with her fingernails until she found the one she wanted. On the left-hand side, under a list of many others, she wrote down the date and then drew a dark line with her pen to the right side of the card, where she added a dollar amount beneath an equally long column of numbers. "Grandma," I said in disbelief, "how long have you been keeping track of your bills this way?" Proudly, she answered, "I have cards here from 1938, the year your father was born."

An entire conversation then unfolded about money. I should always know how I'm spending it. I should always save it. I should never pay a bill without studying exactly what I'm being charged. Her lessons were the hard-earned ones of a woman who grew up poor on New York's Lower East Side, whose father forced her to quit high school so she could take care of her little sister after their mother died, and of a woman who kept the books for her husband's butter and eggs business. And the lessons were important to share because they were ignored by my father.

Maybe in reaction to Grandma's extreme sensitivity to money, my father spent his lavishly. He went to fancy restaurants, traveled every chance he could, and collected pre-Columbian art. If my grandmother hadn't taught me those lessons, perhaps I would have panicked during the recent economic collapse. But I didn't. Mark and I had long before set aside a protective cushion.

Grandma Bertha's lessons had skipped a generation.

Chapter 5

Keeping Your Parents' Memory Alive

> "She'll never know how green my mother's eyes were or how my dad roared when he laughed. How do I help her love them?"
>
> "I tell them stories about my parents so they become more than a name, but a real person. I hope my children share these stories with their kids so my parents are not completely forgotten."
>
> "I make a point to have photos of them accessible and simply work them into conversations with my son."
>
> *— from the Parentless Parents Survey*

M ike's the kind of guy you'd want at your wedding — outgoing, fun, and the first to pump his fists on the dance floor. Just looking at his smile, which is open and full of perfectly white teeth, makes you want to have a good time, too. People follow Mike around just because it's cool to be near him.

At least that's the way he seems to me in the black-and-white photograph Fred Greene, his father, showed me during my visit to his home in San Rafael, California — about twenty-five minutes outside San Francisco, across the Golden Gate Bridge. In the photograph, Mike, then twenty-one years old and holding an icy drink with a plastic stirrer and slice of lime, is standing slightly behind his grandfather and younger cousin. He has a Tigger-like quality to him — as if he just bounced in and crashed what was supposed to have been a more formal photo and the only thing freezing him in place is the camera.

All three are dressed elegantly — the young men both in dark suits — while their grandfather, standing proudly between them, is wearing a white tuxedo. You can tell they are related. Each has Obama-sized ears, dark eyes, and an upper lip that disappears when he smiles. They also all have short brown hair and big foreheads. The picture, you assume, must have been taken at a festive event — a fiftieth birthday? an anniversary? And each looks like he'd rather be nowhere else in the world.

The reality is that the picture never happened. At no time did Mike and his cousin ever meet their grandfather, because Fred's parents were killed in a horrific car accident when Fred was just seven years old. So how could it be that they were all looking at me — together — in this photo? "I did a little Photoshop magic," Fred explained triumphantly.

Fred created the photo in an attempt to alleviate his son's worries about going prematurely bald. "Mike has been concerned for years that he's losing his hair. He just has a high forehead. And one day, a photo passed by on my computer screen and I realized that my father had the exact same hairline."

That photo of his father was taken on January 28, 1962, at the party following Fred's older brother's bar mitzvah. In the picture, their parents are standing together while Fred, then six years old, obediently poses in front of them — his mother's long, thin arm draped over his left shoulder. His father is wearing black horn-rim glasses, and his hairline, as Fred knew, was exactly the same as Mike's.

To prove it to his son, Fred scoured his Mac for more images until he found one of Mike at a wedding in 2007. He cropped that picture and matched it in size and color to the one of his father taken at the bar mitzvah forty-five years earlier and created a fake photograph of grandfather and grandson standing next to each other. "Once my brother saw the photo," Fred said, "he asked if I could include his son in the picture, too." Flattered, Fred found a complementary picture of his nephew, taken at yet another wedding, and with a little extra fine-tuning, he created the seamless photo I was staring at in his office.

Fred brushed off my photo envy. I guess to a man who runs a media production company out of his home — complete with recording studio, professional editing equipment, and two computers — manipulating photographs is no big deal. But I was in awe. The picture accomplished what so many parentless parents aim to do but fail. It created a tangible and accessible link between Fred's father and his son. Mike can see they have the same smile. He can see he isn't losing his hair — he just has the same hairline as his grandfather. This photograph connects him to his grandfather in a way an isolated photograph can't. Fred reluctantly accepted my compliments, and before I left his home for the evening, he handed me a DVD to watch later that night.

Fred had produced nothing less than a movie short about his parents. He digitized what seemed like hundreds of family photos and hours of home video and altered every second to look and sound like an old-fashioned newsreel. Fred also included a musical score — the theme song from the Little Rascals — and text, written like subtitles in a foreign film, to narrate the story. The first shot, for example, is of his mom leaving the hospital just days after giving birth to him. She's holding Fred swaddled in her lap and across the bottom of the screen it says, "The story begins in the Greater Los Angeles area. . . ."

But Fred's film is more than simply fun to watch. By adding words to the video, Fred accomplishes a greater feat. He identifies by name the cousins, aunts, and uncles his children might never have known and fixes the moving images to a specific place and time by putting locations, addresses, and dates at the bottom of the screen. The captions are invaluable because Fred can't rely on his parents to impart family history to his sons. The storytelling chain broke when his parents died. Without them, it's his job.

Ensuring children have a connection to their grandparents requires time, patience, and creativity. Most often, according to the Parentless Parents Survey, we show our children pictures and tell our children stories. We also cook our parents' favorite recipes and display their prized possessions. Some parentless parents take their children to cemeteries and plan special trips to childhood homes and towns. Keeping the memory of our parents alive is just one more parenting responsibility we have that other parents don't.

When children are young, the best tools are often the simplest and most accessible. A mother of three children — all under seven — writes in the Parentless Parents Survey, "I like to tell them true things that they can really relate to. If my daughter is eating American cheese, I tell her how much my father liked it. Also, my mother was a reading teacher, and because she tutored at home, she had a ton of children's books. We have written 'Grandma Sheila' in each book, and we refer to them as 'Grandma Sheila books.' My kids have learned about my mother's love of literature and now they share her passion."

Telling stories about your parents, singing their favorite songs, playing music they loved — all of it can help bridge the gap between generations. The tools at our disposal, however, become more complex and far-reaching as our children age. Photographs that once had only superficial meaning now spark detailed conversations about family genealogy. Conversations about shared personality traits and professional interests are more relevant as adult children choose spouses and careers.

It's not easy. While 61 percent of parentless parents find joy and satisfaction in sharing memories with their children, others avoid it. "It is too painful for me," one respondent wrote in the survey. Another, almost apologizing, said, "I want to, but I avoid talking about them because I don't want to get sad around [my kids]." Many say they have the desire but simply don't know where to begin.

I know it's hard — especially because we have so few tools at our disposal to help us do it effectively. During Yom Kippur one year, the holiest day on the Jewish calendar, Mark and I were sitting in synagogue with Jake and Lexi when Lexi leaned over and whispered to me: "Mom, what are those lights on the wall?"

Lexi was referring to a permanent display honoring temple members and loved ones who have passed away. As in many synagogues around the world, names are memorialized on bronze plates, and next to every one is a tiny, unadorned lightbulb that shines on the anniversary of each person's death. From far away, the memorial looks like a constellation — forming patterns like Orion's Belt or the Little Dipper. As I told Lexi what the lights symbolize, my explanation seemed insufficient. If my parents' names were on the wall, would Lexi know her grandparents any better? It would do so little to convey who her grandparents were.

I'm also not convinced that donating money to an organization my synagogue chooses, or lighting a symbolic candle, or adding my parents' names to a special memorial booklet it publishes once a year, helps my children know their grandparents any better, either. I've pointed to the column where it says "In Loving Memory Of" and shown Jake and Lexi their grandparents' names printed in bold type. I can tell you it meant absolutely nothing to them.

All of this leaves me searching for alternatives. I tell them about my father's love of classical music when we hear Mozart or Tchaikovsky on the radio and how he enjoyed cooking frittatas and Chicken Parmesan. I've talked about how my mother loved to entertain and throw parties and how freely she sent out invitations so nobody would feel excluded or alone during the holidays. But mostly everything I say seems flat.

My parents cast large shadows, and offering Jake and Lexi such dribs and drabs feels woefully insignificant. My father was a Howard Roark of the Upper East Side, and he was cocky and arrogant and owned his own practice. His firm did extensive work overseas, particularly in Moscow, so much so that he ultimately opened an office there and lived in Russia half the year. Dad was elevated to the College of Fellows by the American Institute of Architects and was elected to full membership in the Moscow Union of Architects, a prestigious and unique honor. My mother was no slouch either. By the time I could understand what she did for a living, the headhunting company she cofounded with a friend in the early 1970s had become the oldest and largest executive search firm owned and operated by women in the United States.

As a child, I only "got" who my mom and dad were by visiting their offices. I felt enormous pride seeing their names (and my last name!) emblazoned in large letters across doors and walls, and I'd follow my parents around like a puppy dog while they worked. My dad would weave his way around what seemed to me like a football field of draftsmen, and when they peered up from their stools and sloping tables, they'd ask for his feedback on whatever project they were designing. I also saw how they looked at him — with respect — and felt like a big shot being the boss's daughter. I'd listen as he discussed color choices with a team of interior designers and watch as he'd tear through binders of paint and fabric swatches so thick and heavy they made a thud when he took them off a shelf and put them on a table.

My mother's workplace was also exciting. In her corner office, located high above Third (and later, Madison) Avenue, I'd sit in a cushy white chair — my feet dangling above the carpeted floor — and listen silently as Mom talked to clients on the phone. Her secretary would put call after call through, and she'd handle each one like it was the most important of the day. Her voice was strong and certain and she never ended a sentence like she was asking a question. Just by being with my parents, I was absorbing how to be professional, assertive, and bold.

How, then, could I transfer all of this to Jake and Lexi? Trying to evoke my parents was like wearing a straitjacket and gesturing wildly with my head that I wanted a drink of water. Eventually you'd figure out what I was trying to say, but it was a rather inept way of communicating. It was clear I needed better resources.

Then I read an article in a parenting magazine that gave me an idea. The story was about the different ways children learn. The writer made the point, not particularly new, that children learn best by doing, and that students who learn through memorization don't retain information as well as those who are offered interactive experiences. I suddenly realized I could talk to Jake and Lexi about my parents until I was blue in the face, but nothing I said would mean as much as providing them with something physical and real. But how?

I decided to arrange a "Grandma and Grandpa Tour" of New York City. After all, my mom's office is still there, and my father designed more than a dozen offices in Manhattan that my children would never know about unless I showed them. Field trip!

Our adventure had to start with a letter requesting permission to see my mom's office and the offices my dad designed. My first email was to Jonathan Tisch, chairman and CEO of Loews Hotels. My dad knew Jon, but had worked most closely with his late father, Bob, on the company's corporate interiors.

After several weeks of planning, a date was set to go to Loews headquarters, and I was elated that my stepmother, Cheryl, agreed to come along, too. The kids seemed to be looking forward to it (or they were just excited about a day off from school), and on that brisk Friday morning in January, I asked Lexi to wear her favorite velvet dress and Jake to put on beige slacks and a long-sleeved collared shirt. They didn't have to be fancy, but certainly they had to look nice.

The lobby was stately yet welcoming. As we walked in, the first thing we saw was a nearly floor-to-ceiling tapestry hanging against a beige limestone wall. A security guard wearing a bow tie was greeting and checking in visitors from behind an enormous desk. He was flanked by two imposing flower arrangements. "Good morning," I said, approaching the desk. "I'm Allison Gilbert and we're here to see Jonathan Tisch." As we waited to be cleared, I saw Jake and Lexi looking agape at the towering ceiling and couldn't help but smile.

We reached our floor and were immediately greeted and escorted into a conference room. I recognized the space instantly from when my dad first sketched it. The front wall was made entirely of glass, with hundreds of Chiclet-looking squares etched in to give anyone conducting meetings inside privacy. The wood that surrounded the glass was a deep, rich cherry, and neither the glass nor the wood showed a single fingerprint. In the back of the room, a pitcher was brimming with water and ice, and an assortment of cookies sat next to nearly a dozen bottles of soda and juice. "Mom, can I have some?!!" Jake and Lexi each asked in euphoric disbelief. "Sure," I quickly agreed. They took turns using the silver tongs and then sat down in two of the plush chairs that surrounded the conference table. This was by far the fanciest place Jake and Lexi had ever been.

"I am so sorry to keep you waiting!" Jonathan Tisch said, strutting into the room like he owned the place—because he did. He kissed me hello on the cheek and then said, looking down at the occupied seats, "These must be Jake and Lexi. We look forward to showing you around today." I was beaming.

Jonathan and I talked a little, catching up, and then he turned his attention dutifully back to Jake and Lexi. "It's been a long time since your grandpa designed our offices, and maybe we've needed to switch around an office here and there, but basically it's remained the same."

I looked at Jake and Lexi to judge their interest in what he was saying. They were quiet and listening and seemed to be taking it in.

"I can't stay with you very long," Jonathan continued, "but I've arranged for you to have the very best tour guide around. He knows everything about what your grandfather did for us here and can answer any of your questions." And with that he jetted off and left us in the very capable hands of Dan Johnson, the director of facilities for the Loews Corporation.

Dan made us feel that we topped his agenda for the day. He'd patiently stop our parade whenever he saw something interesting for the kids to look at, and start it again if he noticed they were becoming disinterested and restless. And I chimed in, too—like when Dan led us down an internal staircase. The stairs were made of dark green marble, and the wooden railing was so substantial and oversized, I needed to stretch my hand out like I was grasping a football to hold it. "Grandpa could have just put an elevator here, but he thought stairs were nicer," I explained.

The most significant part of our expedition, however, came as a surprise. As Dan took us from one spot to another, he made sure to introduce Jake and Lexi to nearly everyone we passed. To a man walking down the hall: "This is Jake and Lexi. Their grandfather designed our offices." To a woman sitting at her desk: "You were here when Sidney Gilbert did our offices, right? These are his grandchildren." And he said much the same to the many other men and women sitting in cubicles, who looked up curiously from their computers as we marched down the hall.

I didn't realize until that moment how long it had been since my children had heard the words "your grandfather" spoken by someone other than me in reference to my dad. Jake and Lexi get to call Mark's father "Grandpa" all the time—but how about their other grandpa? Hearing his name, spoken out loud and by others who knew him, made my dad more real, when most of the time he's just a ghost.

Thanks to Jon and Dan, my dad came alive that day in a way he hadn't before.

The same was true when we visited Janet Tweed, my mother's business partner of more than twenty years. "Allison," Janet cooed as we entered Gilbert Tweed Associates. It had been a dozen years since I'd seen her last, at my mother's funeral, and she looked just as I remembered. Petite. Blond. Thin. She was wearing skintight black pants with a matching figure-hugging black turtleneck. She looked like Catwoman except for her tasteful gold accessories.

I introduced Janet to Jake and Lexi, and she graciously began showing them around. We saw my mom's old corner office, and they were immediately drawn to the windows, marveling at the little cars on the streets below. "Mom, Grandma worked so high up!" Lexi exclaimed.

Janet showed them a framed picture of my mom at one of their company picnics. She was in a brightly colored hot-air balloon about two hundred feet off the ground. Of the tethered balloon, Janet told them, "Your grandmother just thought it would be a great idea." And she added with a genuine laugh, "Grandma Lynn just did everything big. Big parties. Big celebrations. She was just a lot of fun."

We then headed toward the main conference room. It was decorated exactly as I remembered. Along the windowsills, in homage to the company's line of work, were sculptures of disembodied heads in various shapes and forms: a profile of a head and neck made out of uneven layers of glass; a wooden bust with movable features so that you could change, for example, how far the eyes protruded from the rest of the face; and an abstract face crafted out of metal and painted white. Jake and Lexi thought they were hilarious.

On the way home after the trips, I asked them what they thought of Grandma Lynn's office and Grandpa Sidney's designs. We talked in a kid-friendly way about the responsibilities of owning your own business and how much Grandpa Sidney and Grandma Lynn loved what they did for a living. Then, as they munched hungrily on popcorn, a favorite snack, and gulped down the contents of their juice boxes, I asked the question I'd of course been planning all along: "What did you learn about Grandma Lynn and Grandpa Sidney today?"

After our visit to Gilbert Tweed, Jake wiped his buttery hands on his shirt and boiled the entire experience down to a single thought. He chirped, "I learned the word 'headhunter.'"

I'll take it.

Sharing as Healing

I was on a high for days. The "Grandma and Grandpa Tour" had worked just as I had hoped; Jake and Lexi got to know their grandparents from a perspective I never could have provided myself. But as I continued to reflect on the excursion, I realized there were other reasons for my residual good mood.

Parentless parents don't get to go home, and this was the closest I'd gotten. For those brief moments, I was fully embraced by a familiar physical space, and each room prompted a new childhood memory. I felt whole. Helen Fitzgerald, the bereavement expert, isn't at all surprised I found the trip so healing. "The reminiscing, the sharing, the talking — it all helps break up the grief and make it more manageable," she says. "In early grief, it reminds you how much you lost. But later, it can be cathartic because it's a way for children to know their grandparents."

The "Grandma and Grandpa Tour" also accomplished something else that Jake and Lexi are too young to even realize. The trip broadened their view of what's possible. As a little girl, I took it for granted that mothers and fathers ran their own companies. It was my normal. But of course I know now it's not typical at all. My children's view of what adults do for a living is so much narrower.

Mark's father was an engineer and his stepmother owned an employment agency, but both have been largely retired, and happily so, since I've known them. Cheryl, my stepmother, and Marilyn, Mark's mother, both work in part-time jobs they don't find particularly engaging. My parents would have been examples for my children of another way of working and living. That universe, after all, is what made their mom, *me*.

Malcolm Gladwell writes convincingly in his book *Outliers* that successful people thrive in large measure because of who and what surrounds them — that achievement doesn't come, as you might expect, solely from hard work and whiz-kid smarts. If Jake and Lexi have fewer actors molding and shaping them and showing them what's achievable, how am I not to fear they will grow up to be less than what they would have otherwise been? The visits I arranged for the two of them were my attempt to make up for this shortfall.

Common Obstacles

Not every parent can bring his or her children to places their grandparents worked, or want to. Some parentless parents were so young when their parents died they feel as if they don't have enough information to pass along, while others can't fathom what to say about parents they didn't respect or with whom they had strained or nonexistent relationships.

In the case of parents who died young, there are concrete steps you can take despite not having enough of your own memories as a reference. Fred Greene made a decision to doctor that photograph and digitize that movie even though his parents died when he was seven. Some parentless parents who have audio recordings of their mothers and fathers (telephone messages; in one case, a bedtime story) have played them for their children.

To help build a complete picture, Dr. Brad Sachs, the psychologist who runs the Father Center, says you should also rely heavily on people. "The best thing, and the thing I advise men to do, is to make as much contact as possible with individuals who knew their father. The father's mother may be alive, or the father's siblings, or maybe a business partner. Doing a bit of an archaeological dig to come up with a rich and deep portrait of the missing grandfather usually enables the father to more naturally and spontaneously pass on those qualities, those dimensions, those virtues."

Your own siblings can also be valuable—especially if you're specific with them about your needs. By purposefully engaging your brother or sister, you might be able to expose a side of your parents your children have never heard. This can be done spontaneously, but in my experience, the most substantive conversations require planning. If your sibling doesn't usually enjoy talking about your parents or the past, you may want to call in advance and explain what you'd like to accomplish during his or her next visit. The conversation you'd like to have is more likely to occur if your objective isn't a surprise.

For parentless parents who had conflicted relationships with their mothers and fathers, deciding how and what to say to their children is especially daunting. Throughout the writing of this book, I met mothers and fathers who were estranged from their parents. Troubled relationships were also reported in the Parentless Parents focus groups and survey. Some parents were abusive. Others were alcoholics. No matter the cause of conflict, there was near universal concern among these parents about how and when to talk to their children about the children's grandparents. What should they share? If they don't tell their children everything, are they being honest?

Tarah Epstein Baiman, who witnessed her mother's brutal killing and characterizes her mom as having been a "very troubled person," says, "With my father, there were positive stories. I'll have a harder time when it comes to my mom because there aren't a lot of fond memories. I want Jesse to have a connection to her, but I haven't yet contemplated what I'll say." She came up with what is truly the only practical solution. Tarah conceded, "I'll just have to cherry-pick."

Donna Schuurman, executive director of the Dougy Center, the oldest grief support center for children in the United States, says that is precisely what she should do. Schuurman, who before becoming director in 1991 worked as a volunteer with families who lost loved ones to suicide, says everyone makes choices about what stories to tell, good and bad, when a family member dies. (Focusing on a father's love of boating, not how much time he spent gambling, for example.) There is only one rule, she says, for talking with children about grief, death, and those who have died. "Never lie. That doesn't mean tell your child everything, all at once, no matter what. It means tell the truth. But tell the truth at the appropriate time."

Schuurman says parents will know the right time because their child will ask for more information. "When children ask questions, often just a little information will satisfy their curiosity. It's like a big meal. They need to take one bite at a time, and as they get older, they can bite off more. When your child is small, it might be enough to say, 'Grandpa died a few years ago.' Later, your child may ask, 'How did Grandpa die?' It's at that point you can share, 'He was killed. Or, he didn't take care of himself.' No child has ever said to me they were glad they were lied to. Children always find out what you think they shouldn't know, what you assume they can't handle. It's better they learn tough information from their parents."

Additional guidelines apply to older children who were able to develop a positive relationship with their grandparents, despite these obstacles. Experts say it's important to support their connection without being dishonest about your own emotions. Schuurman advises, "You might say, 'I had a different relationship with Grandpa as his son than you did as his grandson. He was different at fifty than he was at thirty.'"

I'd add that the best approach might be just listening whenever your child wants to talk about his or her late grandparents.

Ideas and Resources

Near the end of every interview I conducted for this book, I'd ask the same question: What do you do, if anything, to keep the memory of your parents alive for your children? I also asked the same question in the Parentless Parents Survey and provided limitless space for respondents to answer. While some projects floored me (like the father who made a memory box for his children and filled it with photographs, mementoes, and handwritten stories about his parents, and the mom who took her mother's old wooden spools of thread and made them into Christmas ornaments), I was mostly disheartened by the replies. Many parents say they've struggled so much with knowing what to do, they've simply given up. "It feels complicated and too emotional," one parent wrote.

Below are some ideas all parentless parents might find inspiring for keeping the memory of their parents alive for their children. They represent some of the best tips and resources I've discovered from more than five years of conversations and research.

Paper and Pictures

Gia Russo, a design expert and coauthor of *At Home with Friends,* once gave redecorating tips in a national magazine about transforming a teenager's bedroom into a tranquil sitting room or office. She advised simply, "Surround yourself with meaningful things."

I find what she said particularly useful for parentless parents who struggle with what to do with the many papers and photographs they've inherited from their parents. In the photograph illustrating Russo's design idea, a sea of white frames (all roughly the same size) line a beige wall. Inside each frame is something evocative — a black-and-white family photograph, an article from a newspaper that had particular significance. What papers do you have hidden away in your attic or basement that could gain new life and meaning by being displayed for everyone in your home to learn from and appreciate? Your parents' birth certificates? Their marriage records? Use this idea as an excuse to open those boxes and talk with your children about where your parents were born, what town they grew up in, or when your parents got married.

If you don't have the time or inclination to do this yourself, you may want to mail your family photographs and other flat memorabilia to someone like Kim Screen. Kim owns Good Stock, a business tailor-made for parentless parents. "I help people tell their family story," she told me over the phone from her Seattle home. In Kim's hands the stuff of junk drawers becomes a photo book unlike any you can make on Snapfish or iPhoto. Kim is part archivist and part therapist — gently coaxing customers into telling her exactly what they want to create and why. "We always start by clients telling me stories about their loved ones." She then prompts clients to send her letters, emails, maps from favorite vacation spots, postcards — anything that can be scanned — in order to better tell their story. "I particularly love using signatures from old correspondence because it really conveys who that person was."

The difference between uploading your own pictures and working with a professional like Kim is that this soft-spoken mom, who lost her own dad when she was five, works with you every step of the way so you never face the project alone.

Another approach is to create a one-of-a-kind scrapbook. Jessica Helfand became enamored with scrapbooks after leafing through one started in 1918 by her grandmother. Minnie Reed put anything and everything into her book — dance cards, calling cards, poems and letters, and of course, photographs. To look at it is to vicariously relive parts of her life: a class trip to Washington, her high school graduation, the young and tender courtship between her and Jessica's grandfather.

Jessica is now a senior critic in graphic design at the Yale University School of Art and the author of the exquisite coffee-table book *Scrapbooks: An American History*. Scrapbooks are "visual biographies," Jessica writes. "They seem at once an evocative and a largely overlooked class of artifact." Even though Jessica knew her grandmother, loved her dearly, and saw her with great frequency, her scrapbook (discovered in a closet only after she passed away) brought them closer together. Seeing what was important to her—the dances she went to, the young boys she had crushes on—made her grandmother even more real.

My parents never kept a scrapbook, but Jessica says that shouldn't deter me from making one out of their old photographs and memorabilia. It won't have the same aesthetics, she warns, but I can do something with it I could never accomplish with an autobiographical scrapbook—involve my children in its creation. "Photographs are so much more meaningful if they're put into historical context. You could have your children go on Google and find images of the Vietnam War, the landing on the moon, even a picture of the kind of telephone your parents used to use. You aren't your parents, but you can be the filter through which your children know them." And as with my "Grandma and Grandpa Tour," because it's a project to be done *with* your children, and not *for* them, Jessica thinks they'll be more likely to retain what they learn about their grandparents.

Important tip: If you can't identify the people in the pictures, ask for help. Siblings, especially older ones, can be a great resource. If you are an only child, you'll probably get the information you need from aunts, uncles, and cousins. When you've exhausted those options, widen your circle by reaching out to distant relatives and your parents' old friends and neighbors. You might be surprised how much information is out there if you take the time to look.

Another memory-making idea is to give new life to old family slides. In the corner of our house where Mark keeps his Shop-Vac and power tools sits a slide projector—a neglected leftover from my childhood. After my parents divorced, my mom would take adventurous trips as a newly single woman—Papua New Guinea was a favorite—and invite friends over to see her slides when she returned. My brother Jay and I would sit in the living room as Mom held court—listening to her stories and the familiar whirring and clicking noises the projector made when it popped the slides in and out like an old-fashioned toaster.

Next to that slide projector, in boxes, are hundreds of those slides. I can't bring myself to get rid of them, and really all they're doing now is taking up space. I've shown them to Jake and Lexi once or twice, but the pictures, I have to be honest, weren't that interesting even to me.

Marita Gootee found her dad's old slides one day back in the late 1990s, but because she's an artist and sees treasure where others might just see clutter, she got an idea. Marita scanned the slides into her computer and then both enhanced and altered the images into a series of photos she calls, *Recreations of Family History.* The results are powerful and have been featured in exhibitions all over the country, including in Mississippi, where she lives.

In one piece, Marita took an unremarkable slide of her grandparents' neighbor and duplicated the image three times to give the illusion, as in time-lapse photography, of her walking. She titled the piece, *Departure.* In the piece *Going Home,* Marita used an ordinary slide of her father and grandparents chatting and gave the photograph added dimension by scratching the surface with a pin before she scanned it. She made improvements to all of the original slides by adding color, etching in meaningful words or phrases, and superimposing images from other sources. "All of my work deals with the idea of memory," Marita says. "The series is about me looking back at my family growing up, and telling a larger story."

There are still other ways to recycle slides. Scanning them and making prints has become increasingly straightforward and affordable. Or you can get really creative. If you have fifty or more, you can actually create a lampshade. Thin metal rings link the transparencies together and the images become illuminated when the light goes on. Directions can be found easily online.

Slides can also be put to use during your next family reunion. To make name tags, place a white sticker behind the photograph to ensure the image is visible and then attach a safety pin to the back with a little sticky putty. They can also be used to identify wineglasses. Just make a tiny hole in the cardboard surrounding the picture and attach it to the stem with a short strand of colorful yarn or ribbon.

Clothing and Jewelry

Dawn Gerber was once featured in a *Real Simple* magazine article about unique ways to document family history. Sixty-one years old at the time, she explained the meaning behind a prize-winning quilt she had sewn. At first, Dawn said, she was going to sew a generic image of a house, but then "it struck me to weave my family's entire history into the quilt to remember those who had come before. . . . Each block holds meaning. On one I embroidered my parents' favorite song, 'Don't Sit Under the Apple Tree,' and wrote our family names on the leaves of a blossoming apple tree. . . . The quilt's scalloped border lists ten generations of relatives, ending with my own. I titled my quilt *Remembrance.*"

If you're not as crafty as Dawn, but like the idea, you can pay to have someone make a quilt for you. I handed the Gazebo, a quaint shop in Manhattan that now only exists online, a Hefty bag filled with my father's best neckties, and within a few months their magicians created a three-foot-by-three-foot quilt using every last one of them.

Every time Jake and Lexi point to a strip of silk, I can tell them a story about the time I remember their grandfather wearing it—the night we tried a new restaurant in SoHo, the afternoon I met him at a construction site on Long Island, the time he took me shopping for a new sweater when I was in college.

You can use practically anything your parents wore to make a quilt—including T-shirts, jeans, and other types of old clothing. Finding help is as easy as speaking to your local tailor.

And, if you're like me, you probably have a number of your mother's necklaces sitting in your jewelry box and perhaps several pairs of your father's cuff links. Possibly at some point, in a stroke of inspiration, you might have even brought one of your mom's stray earrings to a jeweler and had it reconfigured into a necklace. According to Robert Dancik, an artist who specializes in creating "meaningful jewelry," resetting jewelry is the minimum one can do.

Dancik says nearly any keepsake—a coin, a book of matches from a favorite restaurant, a torn piece of paper from an old map—can be repurposed into jewelry. In his book *Amulets and Talismans,* Dancik describes the power of recontextualizing such mementos. "Objects such as these serve as symbols for people, places, and events in our lives and are a gateway to emotions that cannot be tapped with words or images alone. . . . It is when we take one of these personal mementos and deliberately place it in a context to amplify its power as a symbol, that we call it an amulet or a talisman."

When his own father passed away, Dancik took a button from his sport coat and used it to make a pin. He placed the brown leather button into a delicate sterling silver setting and then for additional texture and interest, added an aquamarine to the center, representing his father's love of the sea. Hanging down from the middle of the pin is a pearl cradled in place by a twisted silver vine.

Dancik's other work is equally magnificent. He's taken the traditional charm bracelet and turned it on its head by fashioning what he calls a story bracelet. The charms on a story bracelet can be made of anything meaningful to you—buttons, photographs, bits and pieces of broken jewelry—and the bracelet is then etched with a personal story or message. I got goose bumps imagining what I could make for Lexi when she graduates from high school. There are so many objects I've saved from my parents that I could use.

Amulets and Talismans is a beautiful how-to book. It provides detailed instructions and plentiful color photographs so readers can create Dancik's work at home. But, at least for me, the best news I can pass along is that you don't have to buy any drills, files, or torches and do any of this yourself. Dancik and many other jewelers are willing to work with customers directly.

Food and Cooking

We all know that food is one of the easiest and most popular ways to connect our children to their grandparents. But how can we make what we prepare even more meaningful to our children? The answer lies, at least partly, in what you create outside the kitchen.

Fred Greene's sister, Sandy Taradash, wrote a cookbook for her family. In it, she not only provides ingredients of favorite dishes, but also the cherished family stories and sayings that go along with them. From reading the book cover to cover, I learned new recipes for roast beef and whipped potatoes and that Sandy's mother had made those dishes every Sunday night when Sandy was growing up. I also came away with information that had nothing to do with cooking at all. Several pages feature poems her father wrote while stationed in France and Germany during World War II. The book took her ten years to complete, and when she was finished Sandy published it herself and gave copies to her children, brothers, and cousins. Sandy is quick to point out that she didn't compile the book alone. From the beginning, she solicited contributions from everyone in her immediate and extended family.

There are a number of books you can purchase or borrow from the library that will give you a good feel for what Sandy created. The one I recommend most highly is really a memoir in cookbook clothes. It's called *Falling Cloudberries: A World of Family Recipes* by Tessa Kiros. Kiros's book retraces her life across the globe — from England, to South Africa, to the hills of Tuscany, Italy, where she and her family now live — and highlights in rich text and color photography the meals that have meant the most to her along the way. There's the vegetable soup recipe — "This is a soup that my mother made often" — and the recipe for her father's favorite dessert, a trifle made with rose water and cognac, which "reminds him of his childhood." Sprinkled throughout are her finest ingredients — full-page photographs of the individuals who shaped her love of food — her mother, father, grandfather, and on page 56, a black-and-white picture of her great-great-grandmother from Russia. At the very beginning of the book is Kiros's family tree, dotted with delicate and exquisite drawings of her ancestors.

If you're comfortable with a paintbrush, you may enjoy the following idea that comes from a woman concerned with preserving her grandma's cookie recipes. First, she and her family baked the cookies from scratch — peanut butter drops, pecan shortbread, and gingerbread — and then she took pictures of them. From those images, the Los Angeles mom made watercolor paintings and used those paintings to illustrate a cookbook. Her sister wrote a touching foreword and she put it all together on a computer. The next Christmas, the books were wrapped for family and given out as gifts.

Real-Life Experiences

Ever since Julie Hallman's twin daughters, Drew and Madison, were in fifth grade, they've helped raise money for skin-cancer awareness. To support their efforts, they teamed up with a jewelry designer who created a special necklace for them to assemble at home and sell. So most weeks, besides doing their homework, the twins sit together at their kitchen table in Florida stringing silver pendants on black, red, or brown cords, and then sell the pieces to anyone who'll buy them. Drew and Madison are incredibly motivated. It was skin cancer, after all, that killed their grandmother before they were born.

Julie has always felt that doing charity work in their grandmother's name gives the girls a special opportunity to know her and honor her memory. "My children have raised over five thousand dollars for a melanoma foundation, which has been a huge part of their lives," Julie says. A framed article in Julie's office, from the *Miami Herald,* is proof of their commitment. The headline blares, "11-Year-Old Twins Take on Skin Cancer." The girls have also been interviewed by a local television station. "They put a picture of my mom in the final piece, and I was so happy," Julie recalls. "She deserved to be on TV. I felt like it was a dedication to her. And the fact that my girls worked so hard to make it happen, it just felt even better."

Jackie Logan participated in a Parentless Parents focus group and thinks one of the best ideas she's come up with to honor her parents' memory is taking her two teenage children to France, where her father went to school. "It was great for the kids to feel connected to Paris in a way that they wouldn't have otherwise. I could talk about his life and bring those experiences alive. It made the whole trip more meaningful." But the trip wasn't only good for Jackie's kids. Jackie says, "It also brought his memory alive again for me."

Do you know where your parents grew up? If you do, why not take your kids to see their old neighborhoods? To make it even more interesting for older kids, you can create an audio walking tour for their iPods, the same kind you listen to at museums. As they walk from landmark to landmark—your parents' childhood home, their school, the pond where they used to swim—you can describe what they're seeing by telling the stories you remember your parents telling you.

If you don't know where your parents were raised, you can approach this idea from a broader perspective. You can introduce your children to experiences your parents enjoyed. If your father loved sailing, why not take your children sailing? If your mother loved painting, why not paint together?

Even if you can't go back to where they worked like I did for the "Grandma and Grandpa Tour," you can still expose your children to what your parents did for a living. For example, if your father was an electrician, ask your local electrician if your children can shadow him for an afternoon. If your mom was a lawyer, why not ask a nearby law firm for a quick visit. Think of it as the parentless parents' version of "Take Our Daughters and Sons to Work Day."

One of the most fun and exciting experiences I've been able to give Jake and Lexi happened by accident. As part of the "Grandma and Grandpa Tour," I had reached out to John Mara, president of the New York Giants. My dad had designed the Giants' headquarters, and I couldn't imagine how much cooler my dad would be to Jake and Lexi than if they saw the work he did for their favorite football team. But my timing was off, and I couldn't make it happen. Giants Stadium, along with the business offices my dad designed, was in flux because the Giants were about to move to their new stadium. All my dad's work was about to be demolished, and even if we did come, we wouldn't see anything, because every office was packed floor to ceiling with moving boxes. Instead, John Mara's assistant graciously offered, "Would your kids like to be our guests at a game and come a little early and watch the pregame warm-up from the sidelines?"

Are you kidding?!

On Sunday, December 27, 2009, all four of us went to see the Giants take on the Carolina Panthers for what would be the last Giants game ever played at Giants Stadium. For Jake, especially, watching the pregame warm-up from the field was like being on the rope at the Academy Awards. He was ecstatic. Eli Manning throwing practice passes. Brandon Jacobs running the ball. Hakeem Nicks catching. Jake and Lexi also took high fives from Domenik Hixon and met Super Bowl MVP O.J. Anderson, who happened to be standing right beside us.

If it weren't for my dad, Jake and Lexi would never have had that access. "Jake," I said on the way home after the game, "that was pretty incredible, huh?"

"Yeah!" he exclaimed. "That was awesome!"

And just to make sure he really got how special the day was, I said: "You know, that was something we only got to do because of Grandpa Sidney. Not everyone gets to see the Giants warm up like that before the game." And without a moment's hesitation he casually replied from the backseat, "Not every kid gets to be Grandpa Sidney's grandson."

The Power of Words

Letter Writing

In the *New York Times* best seller *Big Russ & Me,* Tim Russert, the late NBC News Washington bureau chief and host of *Meet the Press,* writes fondly about growing up in Buffalo, New York, in the 1950s. The tale brings to life the outsized devotion and admiration Russert had for his father, Big Russ, a World War II veteran who worked two jobs most of his life to support his family. It's the Epilogue, though, that I find particularly poignant and worth mentioning.

The Epilogue is a letter Russert wrote to his son, Luke. We learn by reading it that Luke is about to begin college and Russert embraces the milestone as an opportunity to link three generations of Russert men:

"Whenever you think your studies are tough, think about Grandpa. The example he set and the lessons he taught — work, respect, discipline — are as important for you as they have been for me. . . . Lukeman, along the way you'll hit some hurdles and experience some setbacks. I will always be there for you, as Grandpa was for me. But remember, while you are always, always loved, you are never, never entitled. As Grandpa likes to say, 'The world doesn't owe you a favor.' You do, however, owe this world something. To live a good and decent and meaningful life would be the ultimate affirmation of Grandpa's lessons and values."

Russert would have had no way of knowing how important it would be that he recorded those feelings on paper. In 2008 he was in his office at NBC when he had a fatal heart attack. He was just fifty-eight years old. Big Russ passed away the following year at the age of eighty-five. Russert, by writing that letter to Luke, left him a priceless gift. It will forever connect Luke to his grandfather and all that Big Russ stood for and believed.

Sheila Bender, founder of the online magazine *Writing It Real,* says letter writing has been used for centuries to evoke deep feeling and intimacy and is actually a recognized form of literature. She says the genre is a perfect tool for parentless parents who want a fresh way to keep the memory of their parents alive for their children. Sheila suggests that parentless parents may choose to write letters to their children as if they were written by the children's grandparents. "That's a terrific way to pass on family stories and information. The more of their voice you can translate to paper, the more you honor their place in your life and build a place for them in your children's lives."

To write a powerful letter, Sheila offers a few suggestions. First, she emphasizes paying special attention to what you want your children to know from reading the letter. "What are you trying to convey? What lessons are you trying to teach? If you keep thinking about the goal, you're less likely to have your letter go off track," Sheila says. Once you decide what you want to communicate and why, the next step, Sheila says, is choosing the right words. "Avoid words that are too general. For example, 'I love everything you do' is general. A better way of writing might be, 'I love watching you on the swing and seeing your legs pump the air.' Choosing precise words and phrases creates a fuller experience for the reader."

I followed many of Sheila's tips when I wrote my own letters to Jake and Lexi from their grandparents.

Dear Lexi,

I am so glad your mom asked me to write you a letter. What a great idea! There are so many things I'd like to say and never had the chance.

Let me start by letting you know that I heard you went to my office and met my business partner, Janet. That makes me very happy. I used to take your mom to the office when she was your age. Sometimes when school was on vacation, your mom would come to my office and "work," filing papers, making calls and earning a little money for things she wanted to buy—like cool new shoes or a new record album, which is what we called CDs back then!

Janet and I started our company, Gilbert Tweed, when your mom was just two years old. Your mom grew up with a working mom too! Back then, it was unusual for a mommy to go to work every day and even rarer for a woman to run her own business. That's part of what made it so much fun!

I know it's sometimes frustrating for you when Mommy needs to work. When your mom was little, she didn't like that I worked either. It wasn't until she got older that she understood just how much I liked running my own business. I got tremendous joy from mentoring the women who worked for me. They'd start out "green," learn the ropes, and then many of them would spread their wings and fly away to start their own businesses. It felt good to watch them become more independent, doing things they weren't sure they could do at first. Helping others become the best they could be was one of the best parts of my job.

My favorite things were crafts and travel. I loved going to craft fairs and would drag your mom around those shows for *hours*! You might have some of the things I bought around your house. Ask Mom about them.

I traveled a lot, sometimes with your mom, sometimes on my own. I flew in hot air balloons, rode on motorcycles, paddled canoes, and visited many far away countries filled with very different people. I would have loved to travel with you.

But no matter how important these passions and my work were to me, they are NOT what life's about. Life is about who you are, how you treat others, and the relationships you nurture along the way. We all want the same things in life—to be loved and heard. You don't always have to agree with those around you, but you have to communicate understanding and respect.

Your mom and I used to butt heads all the time. If she thought I did something wrong, she used to snap at me and slam doors. I spent a lot of time teaching her that even when she disagreed with my decisions, she needed to respect them. Lexi, save this letter and reread it when you're a teenager. Try to always remember that your mom has your best interests at heart.

Know that I love you and that you make me very proud. And, one last thing. You are a very talented artist. But please know you didn't inherit those capabilities just from your grandfather. My mother, your great-grandma Henny, and Aunt Ronnie were artists too!

Love,

Grandma Lynn

P.S. Give your mom a hug from me. I miss her so much.

———

Dear Jake,

First, let me say how absurd I think this is. You don't need a letter from me to let you know what was important to me or what lessons I would have taught you. If you want to know who your grandfather was, just look at your mother. Your mom is me.

Your mom is everything I was . . . for good and bad. When your mom explodes in anger, it comes from me. When she gushes with pride, I was never able to hide my emotions either. Everyone in my life — family, friends, clients — knew where I stood and exactly what I thought. I was never a diplomat, I admit. There's an old saying, "Let the chips fall where they may," and I think that's as close to a motto as I had. But the people in my life were glad for it because they didn't have to wonder if I was telling the truth. If they were weak or unsure they usually didn't like me much. And that was fine with me. I preferred to be around people I respected.

Don't worry about being liked, Jake. You can't control that. Worry about being true to yourself. That's hard enough. That, and maybe, try not to be a schmuck.

I would really have enjoyed getting to know you. I always dreamed of playing catch with you and taking you to some of my favorite places like Yankee Stadium. Like you, I loved the Yankees. Your uncle Richie and I went to a lot of games growing up. I loved Joe DiMaggio and Yogi Berra — but my favorite player was somebody you've probably never heard of. His name was Tommy "Old Reliable" Henrich. He wasn't a great player, and he didn't hit a lot of home runs, but he was a "clutch" hitter who always seemed to get the hit the Yankees needed to either start a rally or to win the game. The Brooklyn Dodgers were the enemy and your great-grandpa Willie used to joke that you needed a passport to get to Brooklyn. I would have also loved going to a Giants football game with you. Just being together would have been fun.

I always liked kids (not babies so much) as soon as they were old enough to have a conversation. I liked playing games — like chess and backgammon — but I should warn you, once you got the hang of a game, I would not have held back to give you a better chance of winning. I'd respect you enough to know that you'd probably try harder to beat me if you knew it was for real. You might be a little upset with me at first, but you'd learn, and you'd get better. And you know what? No one would have been prouder when you finally beat me, than me!

One of the scariest, and ultimately most rewarding, moments in my life came when I decided that I had the power to make a difference in the world. When your mom was 11 years old, I wrote a letter to fellow architects inviting them to join me in doing something to decrease the chances of nuclear war, which seemed like a very real possibility at the time. It was really hard for me to send that letter. Back then, businesses weren't really involved in things like that and I didn't know how my clients would react. Maybe I'd lose them all. Instead, I only lost a few, and the ones who stood by me became even better friends and respected colleagues. It was because of that letter that we formed the organization Architects Designers and Planners for Social Responsibility.

Because of the risk I took, I was invited to become a Giraffe. The Giraffe Project, as it was known back then, honors people who "stick their neck out" for the common good. Nothing is more thrilling than to exceed your own expectations. I felt I really made a difference to the planet.

There's one more lesson I want to make sure you learn. It's something I told your mom when I got sick. I believe I created my own cancer. I spent too much of my life being angry. Slow waiters. Long lines. Incompetence. Neediness. All of it. It all made me angry. It wasn't until your cousin Dexter was born that I began to calm down. Becoming a grandfather allowed me to appreciate my family more and I began to find peace. I was inching toward becoming a little gentler, a little kinder, a bit more flexible. I think I'd still be alive if I achieved this kind of balance earlier.

I love you, Jake, and don't ever be afraid to stick your neck out like a giraffe. I hope you make choices in your life that will lead you to contributing to this world.

Love,
Grandpa Sidney

Purposeful Conversation

I am conscious of how I refer to my parents around Jake and Lexi. Every time, I say "Grandma" or "Grandpa" or "your grandparents." If I happen to call my parents "my dad" or "my mom" in front of them, I feel as if I've misspoken and quickly edit my sentence mid-thought. This may seem excessive and maybe even unnecessary, but I believe how I talk about my parents shapes how my children will think about my parents and ultimately how they will remember them. Language is one of the keys to keeping the memory of my parents alive.

That's why I was shocked to hear the conversation I heard the morning Sandy Taradash invited me to join her entire family for brunch. Sandy lives with her grown daughter, Marni, and Marni's husband and two young children, in the steep hills of Walnut Creek,

California. Driving up to their home, my car was nearly vertical and I was forced back into my seat like I was flying in the space shuttle. Sandy had prepared an elaborate feast, and from the second I walked through the door, I didn't feel like a stranger. We ate and talked and laughed as if we had known each other for years.

After we pushed back our chairs, Sandy showed me around her brightly colored house and directed my attention to her father's artwork on the walls. He loved to paint and draw and had done so with great proficiency since high school. "My dad was very talented," Sandy said as we came full circle back to the dining room table. Overhearing the tail end of our conversation, Joree, Sandy's other daughter asked, "Mom, who are you talking about, your dad?"

Sandy nodded. "Yes, I'm telling Allison about my dad."

"Yeah," Joree agreed, looking at me. "Her dad was a terrific artist."

My heart jerked. "You don't call your grandfather, your grandfather?" I asked the question with a little more astonishment in my voice than I intended.

"No. I never knew him," Joree replied. "I think of him more as my mother's father, not my grandfather."

This back-and-forth struck me as odd. Sandy had spent a considerable amount of time making sure her parents were commemorated around the house. In addition to her father's artwork, pieces of her mother's jewelry were displayed in shadow boxes in her bathroom, and she had transformed a lamp her parents loved into a sculpture for her bedroom. She had also spent that decade writing the cookbook. So why not refer to them as grandparents? To me, it created even more distance between generations. I didn't press the issue that afternoon, but I asked Sandy about it in an email when I got back to New York. This was her reply:

"How can you call someone a name/label that they NEVER were??? They were NEVER grandparents! If I referred to my dad as 'your grandfather' my children would have NO frame of reference. Neither would I! To my kids, all my dad is, is MY DAD."

Does language make a difference in how our children perceive their grandparents who are no longer living? Dr. Kathy Hirsh-Pasek thinks so. Hirsh-Pasek is the director of the Infant Language Laboratory at Temple University and is considered one of the nation's top experts in the area of early language development. I asked her if she thought it matters if parentless parents call their parents "Mom" and "Dad" or "Grandma" and "Grandpa" when talking to their own children. Her response was this: "How we frame language is important, especially at the youngest ages. Children are egocentric by nature and want to understand how things relate to them. Anytime we can make what we say more concrete and more connected to who they are, children will find it more meaningful."

Further emphasizing the point, Deborah Tannen, professor of linguistics at Georgetown University and author of nine books on how language affects relationships, believes, "Language choice is always important. Starting with the word 'Hi' the words you choose shape the impressions people get and the way they think about things." Hirsh-Pasek says word choice even matters to her college students. "If I teach and only talk about myself, it will be a very boring lecture. But if I make my lesson about my students and their way of life, whatever I'm teaching will be something they'll want to learn about."

Likewise, by referring to my parents as "Grandma Lynn" and "Grandpa Sidney," I am giving Jake and Lexi the opportunity to own the relationship for themselves.

Knowing When to Stop and "Just Be"

I feel an awesome responsibility to keep the memory of my parents alive. Sometimes, though, all the talking about my mom and dad, all the picture showing, is more job than joy. Mark knew both my parents very well, and he'll often bring them up in conversation because he knows it usually makes me happy, but clearly we don't share the responsibility equally. And while my brother, uncle, and stepmother are terrific at sharing memories, too — their contributions don't seem to come often enough to give me permission to step back.

When I bring this up to other parentless parents, the usual re-action is a conspiring sigh — the type that comes when you admit a shared, invisible truth. It's yet another reason why being a parent with-out parents is sometimes harder than being a parent with parents. Because with all the jobs we share — parentless parents are the only ones who have to play this memory game. In fact, according to the Parentless Parents Survey, close to 10 percent of us consider it a bur-den. A mom from Illinois complains: "I feel like I'm too young to be introducing my toddler to her grandparents with nothing more than stories and pictures."

I often feel like my very identity has been compromised. I tell Jake and Lexi stories about my parents, but forget to tell them stories about myself. I noticed this one afternoon when I was recalling how my father played stickball in the Bronx when he was a kid. As I was talking, I realized I had never told them how much I used to love ice-skating, how competitive I was at gymnastics, or how I was the only girl in my neighborhood to choose Little League baseball over soft-ball. I had been inadvertently marginalizing my own life.

Lois Braverman, who besides being president of the Ackerman Institute for the Family is also past president of the board of directors of the American Family Therapy Academy, says all of this angst is completely self-made and unnecessary. Without a hint of sentimen-tality she says children are shaped by their grandparents whether they are alive or not. "Grandparents can be present, or not present, but that doesn't change your genetic makeup. Your grandparents are al-ways with you because of DNA."

But I find this only superficially helpful. Relying on genetics isn't enough. The reality is that I feel the need to keep my parents' memory alive as much as I need to make sure Jake and Lexi have all their pencils, notebooks, and folders before their first day of school.

Psychoanalyst Linda Fleischman's perspective is more nuanced and satisfying: "If you do something with your children that your parents once enjoyed, they will know who their grandparents were. If you behave in certain ways, your children will learn where that comes from too. Just by being who you are, your children will automatically know who their grandparents were. Even if you don't do it with words, it's conveyed. Even though it's not perfect and complete, something's getting through. You don't have to work so hard. You can take the pressure off."

Her words were like putting salve on a burn. But I wasn't fully convinced. Would it be possible for me to let go and not be so obsessive? I was lukewarm on the idea, but willing to give it a try. But in truth, I really didn't know what Fleischman was talking about until many months later when Jake and I went horseback riding more than halfway across the country.

High above Vail, Colorado, is the Piney River Ranch. Piney, as it's affectionately known, is a spectacular campground at the base of the Gore Mountain Range, 9,350 feet above sea level. It overlooks a lake so massive it seems to reflect every bit of the mountains above it. To get there, you take Red Sandstone Road and pray you'll arrive at the top alive. The one and only time Mark drove our family up there was for my cousin's wedding, and I was in utter disbelief that any road could be so dangerous. In most places there aren't any guardrails, which is mind-boggling considering cliffs seemed to be on either side of us at all times. One little distraction and we'd have plummeted to our deaths. Years earlier, we were told, one family did.

When we finally wound our way to the top, we instantly knew why my cousin, Yelena, had chosen the remote spot for her wedding. Mount

Powell, the area's highest peak, had veins of snow running down it even though it was the end of June. The air was clear and fresh, and I couldn't imagine a more awe-inspiring setting. As soon as we parked our car, I saw Aunt Ronnie and jumped out of the car to hug her.

"How'd you like that trip?" she said jokingly.

"Awful. But this is amazing!" I exclaimed, pointing to the spectacular view.

The ceremony got under way a few hours later. Guests were invited to sleep in tents, yurts, and cabins for the weekend, and while Ronnie headed down the mountain after the reception because the elevation was making it hard for her to breathe, we stayed and took advantage of everything Piney had to offer: We canoed, hiked, roasted marshmallows, and made s'mores. On our last full day at the ranch, I asked Jake if he wanted to go horseback riding. I had noticed they offered rides and was thrilled when he agreed.

The trail was breathtaking. As our horses clomped their way up the gently rising slope, there were clusters of harebells, blue flax, and Alpine buttercups rising from the grass. As I marveled at the flowers, Jake noticed the trees. "Mom! Look!" he yelled from his horse without turning around. "The trunks look like they're wrapped in Ace bandages!" He was right. Aspen trees surrounded us on all sides. The tall, delicate trees were covered in overlapping layers of white bark, making their slim trunks look like wounded legs on a stick figure drawing.

My mother used to love horses, and once took me and Jay to Arizona to ride in the Superstition Mountains. She enjoyed it so much that the last Mother's Day gift I ever gave her was a surprise ride in Central Park. I kidnapped her from her office, put her in a taxi, blindfolded her, and gave the driver the address of the Claremont Riding Academy on a piece of paper.

As Jake and I made our descent, the hooves of our horses scraping the rocks, I noticed a patch of flowers on the side of the trail. The stems were so frail that the mild breeze was whipping the flowers into a frenzy. The cluster reminded me of the Chuckle Patch from the TV show *The Magic Garden,* one of my favorite programs when I was young. I took it as a sign. My mom was somehow with us saying "Hi."

I took a yoga breath. And another one. At that very moment I decided to focus on what was right in front of me — my son, on the side of a mountain, his little strawberry blond head bobbing up and down, his untied shoelaces dangling at his horse's side. Jake was horseback riding because my mom introduced me to riding when I was his age. Yes, just by being, I was keeping my mother's memory alive.

That evening, in the communal bathroom near our cabin, I studied a framed poster on the wall while I waited for Lexi to brush her teeth. It had pictures and descriptions of all the flowers in the area. As my eyes jumped from one photograph to the next, I recognized the flowers from the Chuckle Patch. They were Alpine forget-me-nots.

Jake had only one person to thank that day for his adventure. Sure, I physically took him up that mountain, but it was his grandma who led the way. And when I tucked him in that night, you better believe I told him.

Chapter 6

Fear of Dying Young

> "I am terrified of dying while my daughters are young, as happened to me with my parents. It is often very hard to envision seeing them graduate high school, get married, have children of their own."
>
> "I want my children to be more independent. I think others, including my husband, see it as coldness. I see it as love. I don't want them to be devastated when we are gone."
>
> "I worry about how much time I will have with my kids. Because of these worries, I tend to spoil my kids more than my parents spoiled me."
>
> —*from the Parentless Parents Survey*

S*even years after my mother* died of ovarian cancer, I went to see a genetic counselor at the Mount Sinai School of Medicine in New York City to learn my odds of getting the disease, too. My gynecologist had urged me to make the appointment when my mom was diagnosed, but I didn't want to take the required blood test or hear the results. Why ask a question when you already know the answer? I also wasn't ready to deal with the consequences.

If I indeed had BRCA1 or BRCA2—the genetic mutations linked to an increased risk of developing ovarian and breast cancer—I would have a lifetime risk as high as 60 percent of getting ovarian cancer, and the recommended course of action would be surgery. Most women have a lifetime risk of 1.5 percent. By removing my ovaries, my doctor told me, I'd reduce my risk to nearly zero.

Having the operation made sense to me. Any downside of living without my ovaries—going into instant menopause, hot flashes, mood swings—would surely be outweighed by staying alive. So when my doctor mentioned the procedure, my initial thoughts weren't to question the recommendation, but to ask about timing. "How soon should I do it? Now?"

"No," he replied without feeling. "When you're done using them."

At the time of that conversation I was a newlywed and not even close to having children. Mark and I were living on the Upper East Side of Manhattan, working in our first jobs out of college, eating dinner out almost every night with friends. Until I was ready, my doctor suggested I be under high-risk surveillance. Fine with me. I was living in constant fear anyway. I'd get dressed in front of our full-length mirror every morning and study my naked profile. My fingers would splay across my abdomen and I'd press them into my belly one at a time. Was it plump because I needed to drop a few pounds or hard and distended because I had cancer? I'd inch closer and closer to the mirror—as if by getting right up against it I'd be able to see what was growing underneath my skin. At just two and a half centimeters each, my ovaries were the enemy. They were time bombs threatening to kill me at any moment.

My mom always looked like she was three or four months pregnant. She didn't know until her cancer had spread that having an enlarged stomach is one of the only warning signs of ovarian cancer. But maybe knowing wouldn't have mattered anyway. Mom dismissed every malady as a nuisance, and her answer to everything was Sudafed. To her, it was a magic red pill. She'd pop one for headaches, sore throats, irritated eyes—anything that hurt and would keep her from going to work. If she felt gassy or bloated, she'd brush that off, too, thinking she just needed to lose weight.

I followed through on my doctor's advice and started booking so many screenings and tests my calendar looked like I actually *did* have cancer. Every few months I had some kind of exam—transvaginal ultrasounds to detect ovarian cancer; mammograms, breast MRIs, and sonograms to spot breast cancer; and every six months I'd bring myself to a lab for the cancer-marker CA-125 blood test. I may not have had anything wrong with me, but I had a complete team of oncologists, radiologists, and phlebotomists. Every day I lived knowing that death could begin anytime, anyplace. My mom only found out she had cancer when it had spread so far it interfered with her going to the bathroom and she went to the doctor complaining of constipation.

Fear of death made me paranoid. If I woke up with a numb arm: Did I sleep funny, or am I having a stroke? If I had a shooting headache: Am I stressed, or having a brain aneurysm? On a near daily basis I'd have to talk myself down from brief and hysterical leaps of logic that only grew worse after my father died. I lived in this silent prison for years—until Mark and I decided not to have any more children, and I was ready to take the blood test that would tell me based on science, not terror, my chances of living past the age of my mother.

There was nothing special about the blood test, but the dramatics surrounding the results put the whole procedure in another category altogether. I had to learn the findings in person. At first I didn't understand why I was being so inconvenienced. Couldn't the genetic counselor just call me? Then my imagination ran wild. I anticipated that the conversation would be similar to how patients are shuffled off when they are told behind closed doors that they are HIV-positive. Did I have this mutation or not? Would I live or die? As I sat in an unremarkable office waiting for her to come in, I started thinking how I'd tell Mark the bad news.

The room was cold and sterile, and stood in sharp contrast to the counselor herself. She wore a baby blue sweater set and pearl necklace. The combination gave her a sweet air of purpose and authority. Her voice was silky and warm and she seemed to purr through her prepared remarks. On and on she went about statistics, numbers, and math. Her words lacked emotion, and while I know she meant to be soothing and reassuring, her matter-of-factness made me even more uneasy. I began to dig my nails into my palms. *Just tell me already.* Do I have it?

"Yes," she told me. "You have BRCA1."

Even though I'd expected it, hearing the news was like being given a death sentence. She could have told me I had cancer, it would have felt the same. My fate seemed sealed. I would die the way my mother had. Young. Jake and Lexi would lose their mom. I started to sob in the chair. The counselor handed me the box of tissues placed strategically on her desk and we discussed my options.

There was no doubt in my mind when I left the office that I was going to have the surgery, but it took me another four years to go through with it. I was scared. Being a parent raises the stakes when you're put under. What if there were complications? What if I died in surgery?

I talked about the surgery all the time with my aunt Ronnie, my mother's sister. From her artist's studio in Santa Fe, she'd sprinkle words of encouragement into our weekly conversations like fairy dust. "It's really no big deal," she'd sing into the phone, surrounded by stacks of stretched canvases and paintbrushes. "You'll be in and out of the hospital before you know it."

She knew what she was talking about. After Mom died, Ronnie's doctor also encouraged her to remove her ovaries, and she never regretted doing it. She'd say, "What do I need them for anyway? I already have my daughter." And she'd add in jest, "Heck, it's a twofer!" Ronnie meant that by removing her ovaries she'd also be reducing her chances of getting breast cancer. That's because the surgery would limit the number of years her body could produce potentially cancer-causing estrogen, which was important to her because her mom, my grandma Henny, had passed away from an aggressive form of breast cancer that metastasized to her brain. The statistics were also overwhelmingly convincing. Women who carry a BRCA1 or BRCA2 mutation have up to an 85 percent risk of developing breast cancer in their lifetime (women in the general population have a 13 percent chance), which decreases up to 50 percent depending on age at the time of the operation.

Despite Aunt Ronnie's support, and even though I knew I'd go through with it, I remained fearful. She was older when she had the surgery; I was thirty-seven and not anywhere near menopause. How different would I feel? Would it affect my mood? My sex life? Ultimately, I determined, the decision wasn't about me. It became a Mommy decision. I wasn't having the surgery to save my life; I was having it to save Jake and Lexi's mother's life. In the days and weeks leading up to the operation, I explained what I was doing in the simplest language I could manage: "Mommy's having an operation so she won't get sick like Grandma Lynn."

In November 2007, just days after Thanksgiving, I was wheeled into the operating room. It was a life-affirming decision. By removing my ovaries, fallopian tubes, cervix, and uterus, I was taking control, and for the first time since my mother died life seemed more possible than death. But I was nervous. Yes, I was concerned about not waking up, but I was also worried about the very real possibility that my surgeon would find microscopic cancer cells lurking somewhere inside. As the anesthesiologist snapped a rubber tourniquet around my arm and started to drug me into a state of oblivion, I closed my eyes and forced images into my mind of Lexi doing forward rolls and Jake running bases.

I would have done anything to avoid what my mother endured — three surgeries, thirteen cycles of vomit-inducing chemotherapy, and so many trips to the lab that her veins went into hiding every time a technician approached. "Wow," they'd say, jabbing a needle in and out of my mom's arm. "Anyone ever tell you you're a hard stick?"

I also wanted to protect my children from seeing, for as long as possible, what death really looks like. Death isn't some gentle, Hollywood fade to black. It is often an eruption of putrid colors — the purplish red of crusted blood, the yellow and white mix of coughed-up phlegm, and the muddy brown of accumulating fluids under gauze bandages and surgical tape. And, as much as humanly possible, I wanted to ensure that one day I'd be able to meet my grandchildren. In the end, it really wasn't a choice at all.

As I slowly woke up in Recovery, I could hear before I could see. The room was loud — machines whirring, beeping — and nurses were talking in regular, unhushed tones. My eyes soon opened and focused on the bright ceiling lights above my head. I turned my head slowly to the left, then right, and saw patients hooked up to monitors, and nurses walking from bed to bed. Barely awake and still on morphine, I realized I had made it through the operation, and even though I had needles stuck in my arm and a catheter between my legs, a feeling of freedom washed over me. *I did it.* But I still harbored a very real fear that my doctor might have found something wrong with my ovaries. I imagined him standing over me and saying in that patronizing, mock-concern doctor voice, "We were lucky. It's stage one. We caught the cancer early." So when he came to check on me, you can imagine the first question I asked him.

"Yes, Allison," he said and smiled. "The surgery went perfectly. Everything was normal. You are completely fine."

And with that, it was over. Tears welled up in my eyes and dripped down my cheeks. The cancer cloud that had been following me around since my mother died was gone, and all that was left was me.

My father, unlike my mom, died a quick lung-cancer death. He was diagnosed with the disease in July and died in September. Death started with a cough (a cough!) and ended with him being slowly asphyxiated by his own lungs. The illness came on so fast, and Dad deteriorated so rapidly, we never caught our breath while he lost the ability to take even one. None of us saw it coming, because he hadn't smoked in twenty years.

As the weeks unfolded, his apartment gradually turned into a fully stocked medical ward. Cheryl filled it with every supply he needed — a wheelchair to get him to and from doctors' appointments, ointments for dry lips, creams for bedsores, pills for pain, and all the paraphernalia he needed just to breathe — multiple feet of plastic tubing, a face mask, and oxygen canisters the size of fire extinguishers.

Nights were the biggest ordeal. Dad had a hard time falling asleep because he thought he'd die if he did. Sleep deprivation became such a huge problem it was like he was a victim of some sort of torture. During the day it was impossible to tell if he was fatigued because he didn't get enough rest or if the cancer was spreading. When they were in bed together, Cheryl would tell me, he'd twist himself into such a panic that she'd cradle him in her arms, like a baby, until he fell asleep.

I tried to help in the way a daughter with a toddler could. When I wasn't at Gymboree, I investigated acupuncturists and found one who made house calls. In between playdates, I'd call my father's psy-chologist (probably overstepping my bounds) to check his progress. After work and before I went home to put Jake to sleep, I'd go to the grocery store and scan the shelves for anything Dad would want to eat — thinking if he ate better, maybe he'd sleep better — and buy his favorite comfort food (rice pudding) and serve it to him in a pretty bowl, never the plastic container. He'd poke it with a spoon, but never bring it to his mouth. It wasn't lost on me that feeding my dad was like feeding Jake. "Come on, Dad. Just have one bite."

Toward the end, his appetite was nonexistent and he kept losing weight. We'd measure good days by his ability to get out of bed and walk down the hallway to the dining room table. He'd shuffle there in his slippers and velvet robe, and when he sat down we'd show our disproportionate pleasure. "That's great, Dad! Good job!" But soon we'd want him to perform other pre-cancer tricks, like joining us in conversation. But he couldn't. He'd say a few words, we'd answer, but he'd be too winded to add much more. Sometimes he'd thrill us by wheezing out a complete sentence, only to be overtaken by a coughing jag so horrible it only ended when he coughed up something and spit it into a napkin.

My dad died in the same hospital where Mom was treated and I would later have my genetic counseling and surgery. I was there when he passed away — and so were Jay, Cheryl, Uncle Richie, and Grandma Bertha. But if Dad had been one of us that morning — rubbing his cold feet, massaging his swollen hands — he wouldn't have recognized who was lying there, dying in that bed. His cheeks were hollowed by malnutrition, his eyes closed in exhaustion, and his skin had lost all the redheaded peaches and cream pigmentation that made me look like I could be nobody else's daughter but his.

Forcing Independence

How do I cast away these images? I find it impossible sometimes to remove the last days of my parents' lives from my mind. They're stuck to my brain like leeches.

No matter how hard I try to replace these memories with joyful pictures of Mark and my children, cancer and death continue to live with us, stuffed into the closet sometimes, but never too far away. Robin Romm speaks about this sense of communing with loss in her breathtaking book *The Mercy Papers,* which traces the final days of her mother's life. "Death is as available as tuna fish, as milk," she writes. "It hovers next to me all the time but I can't see it. I feel it, though, its cold fingers tapping on my neck." Given that this is how I feel, too, how can death—and my fear of it—not influence the way I parent my children?

Mark often accuses me of pushing Jake and Lexi to be too independent, too early. Part of the reason they're not shy is because as soon as they were old enough I forced them to confront uncomfortable and sometimes intimidating situations.

If we're at a restaurant:

"Mom, can you ask the waiter for some crayons?"

"Nope. If you want them, you ask for them."

If we're at a friend's house:

"Mom, where's the bathroom?"

"I don't know. Why don't you ask?"

My actions aren't the result of some hard-and-fast rule, and there are times when my resolve weakens. More often than not, though, this is my parenting approach—no apologies. I once caught a friend looking at me in mock alarm when I refused to tie Jake's shoelaces. But my biggest fear is that I'll die young and my children won't learn to fend for themselves. I don't want them ever to be afraid to talk with adults or interact with authority figures. As long as I'm alive, my job is to make sure that Lexi and Jake have the tools in place to know they can handle anything.

Julie Hallman says it's critical that her twin daughters be self-sufficient, too. In her close-knit community in Florida, it's unusual for children to attend summer camp far from home. But for Julie, it was never a question. She went so far as convincing her husband that the best camp for Drew and Madison was in Georgia—a plane ride, albeit chaperoned, away. The girls started going when they were nine. "A lot of my friends are very surprised I do that," Julie admits, before adding as explanation, "I don't do it to get rid of my children. I miss them terribly when they're gone. But I know it's good for them. They're building confidence and I think that's important. I definitely fall into the category of wanting my kids to be independent, because at nineteen I was thrown to the wolves. My father had taken care of everything, and my stepmother cut me off."

"Are you scared of dying young?" I asked.

"I don't know whether it's more fear that I will die young or that I am sure I'll die young," she says, tucking a few strands of hair behind each ear. "I just don't see living a long life. I want them to be independent just in case I'm not around."

Julie is hardly alone. Of all respondents to the Parentless Parents Survey, almost 58 percent fear they'll die young and leave their children without a mother or father. Death is an undercurrent that steers our parenting behavior. It's not the way we'd prefer it, but it's woven permanently into our parenting fabric all the same. Sometimes having an increased awareness of our own mortality makes the way we parent seem overly harsh. "I think I've been tough on her because I wanted her to be prepared for life," Richard Rivera, the dad from the Bronx, says about how he interacts with his daughter, Indi. "I feel like my job is not to protect her, but to teach her how to protect herself."

When does this push for self-reliance go too far? Christine Haynes found out when one of her daughters said, "Mommy, you're being too hard on me." Christine apologized to Jour'dan, who was seven years old at the time, but told me she finds it impossible to let up. "If she's crying about something and it's not a big deal, I'm not patient with her. I'm not indulgent with those kind of weak emotions. I'm more like, 'You can't fall apart. You have to function.' I'm really, really afraid about my daughters going through what I went through. I try not to be, but I'm obsessed with it. I don't want them to be dependent on me."

Holding On Too Tight

For every parentless parent who pushes independence, there's another who struggles with loosening the tether. Instead of forcing self-reliance, these parents transfer their anxiety onto their children and hold on too tight.

Lynn Burkholder says the fear of something happening to her son, Michael, is in her blood. "I don't think you ever get over that," the mom from Canada told me. "You got that phone call and somebody was dead. It sits with you and your mind goes to that — that people around you can die."

When I asked her how this manifests itself in her day-to-day parenting, she was quick with an answer. "Well, even with him walking to school. We live two blocks from the school, but I don't like him walking to school by himself. Walking home is okay because there are a lot of other kids around, but I have this fear that he's going to get abducted. It's so ridiculous. If you knew where I live, people don't lock their doors here. I can walk home from downtown at one in the morning and not feel fear for myself, yet I have this irrational fear for him. It's really silly. I mean, he's ten! It's just that I have a bit more irrational fear than other people do."

When nurse Lisa Petersen's son turned fifteen, he mounted a campaign for more independence. He was embarrassed that she still insisted on walking him to the door when he visited friends. The Michigan mom admits her son is on a "very tight leash" but says she just wants to make sure the homes of his friends are safe. Besides losing both her parents by the time she was twenty-eight, Lisa has seen the very worst that can happen to teenage boys from her work in the ICU. "I fear things with greater intensity," she explains. This has caused no small amount of friction. "He says I won't let him do anything and that I'm overprotective. But I'm always thinking what could happen."

Sandy Taradash admits she's a worrier, too. Even though her children now have children of their own, she still gets stressed about their safety and feels the need to monitor their whereabouts. When her daughter, Joree, took her kids on a road trip, Sandy warned her not to be distracted by their repeated backseat requests for snacks and juice and to keep her eyes on the road. When she noticed books piled on a shelf a few feet from her grandson's crib, Sandy felt compelled to let her son-in-law know her concerns. What if an earthquake struck and it all fell on top of him? Sandy says the anxiety she carries around is "24/7." "My fear is that something will happen to somebody," Sandy explained without a hint of apology. And just to make sure I understood exactly what she meant, she clarified her statement. "My fear is that the *outside* world will hurt somebody."

And how can you blame her? Her brothers weren't in the car that killed their parents. She was.

Sandy was nestled between her parents in the front seat when the crash happened. It was nearly eleven o'clock the night of November 4, 1962, and Sandy, who was sixteen years old, was getting sleepy. It had been a long day. That afternoon, one of her out-of-town friends had shown up unexpectedly with two buddies. Her parents invited them to stay for dinner, and afterward Sandy's mom and dad allowed her to invite even more friends over. About two hours after they ate, the neighborhood kids started to leave and the original pack of friends had to catch a bus back to San Diego. Sandy's parents offered to drive them to the bus depot. The boys piled into the back of the car and Sandy climbed into the front with her parents.

The drop-off happened without incident, and Sandy's dad slowly turned out of the depot to head home. Sandy rested her head on her mother's left shoulder and drifted off to sleep. Nobody can say for sure how long she slept, because the next thing anyone knows is that a drunk driver on the opposite side of the road lost control of his car and plowed into their lane. She and her mother were thrown from the car and slammed into the pavement. They landed shoulder to shoulder, her mother's glasses somehow settling on her chest. Sandy remained that way, barely mobile, as the sound of sirens got closer and closer. When emergency crews arrived, they moved her onto a gurney and took her away in a screaming ambulance. Sandy never did see her father. He'd been out of her line of sight, crushed behind the wheel. Sandy spent the next seventeen days in the hospital and couldn't attend her parents' funeral.

After she told me the story, she took a deep breath and added, "We were supposed to be gone less than an hour."

Fear is often illogical, especially when it comes to our children. We want to protect them, but so many events are out of our control. Letting go is hard when your knee-jerk reaction is almost always to fear the worst.

For me, this internal battle has taken many shapes and began when I was pregnant with Jake. Before I could bring myself to choose an obstetrician, I had to examine the doctors' medical records, on file with the State of New York, to see if any complaints had been lodged against them. After that, I checked the hospital each doctor was affiliated with and evaluated the institution's C-section-to-vaginal birth ratio. Only if the doctors passed these two tests, did I set up face-to-face appointments to see which one I liked better in person. Being an investigative producer at the time, I am sure, didn't help; I had done too many stories for television about bad doctors and bad hospitals. And not having my mother to talk sense into me just fanned the fire.

There were many decisions I made overly difficult. For weeks, I looked up the safety report for every car seat on the market and cross-referenced those results with what the magazines described as "The Best" or "Easiest to Use." When I narrowed it down to two or three, I called the National Highway Traffic Safety Administration, the federal agency that oversees car seat safety. "Off the record," I remember asking, "which car seat should I buy?" Even years later, when Jake and Lexi were well into elementary school, I struggled with my fears. When our district initiated an emergency cell-phone alert system, I quickly signed up. But soon I became so enraged by how it was being used, that I complained (unsuccessfully) to the head of their school. I'd be at lunch, and my cell phone would ring, and I'd immediately recognize the number and assume the worst: Was one of them sick? Did Jake break his arm? Had a bomb gone off? I'd open my phone in panic, praying my children were okay, only to hear a recorded message about an upcoming budget vote.

Even the supremely logical founder of the Orphan Society of America, Tarah Epstein Baiman, says there are times when her fears about her son's well-being aren't rational. "I feel like nothing will happen to Jesse when I am with him. When I am not with him, I think of all the things that could happen under somebody else's watch. I become more fearful." Tarah says she can't imagine a time when

she'll ever feel totally comfortable leaving Jesse in the care of somebody else—including her own husband.

All of these fears may come across as the hysterical worrying of he-
licopter parents. But it's far more complicated than that. We've lost our
parents, and we know from personal experience that bad things really
do happen to good people. Death is not an abstract concept. Sandy
was "supposed to be gone less than an hour."

It was just a cough.
She was bloated.

Parentless parents don't have a lock on worry. In his book *The Anxious
Parent,* psychologist Michael Schwartzman discusses the fears many
parents have raising their children. He addresses anxieties about food
and feeding, health and illness, safety and injury. There's even a chapter called "Anxieties about Elimination and Toilet Training." Throughout the book, no matter the issue, Schwartzman always comes back to
the same cure: the absolute necessity of taking control.

To Schwartzman, taking control means acknowledging your fears,
understanding what happened in your past that may have allowed
them to appear, and then reframing uncomfortable or scary situations
to envision positive, not negative, outcomes. Ultimately, Schwartzman
argues, anxiety can be managed by thinking positive thoughts: Instead of assuming your child will be hit by a car walking to school,
imagine him heeding your warnings to look both ways before crossing
the street and arriving safely; rather than predicting you're going to die
young, force images into your mind of being alive past the age of your
parents and playing with your grandchildren.

This is a head game. It challenges you to parent completely in the
moment. And it sounds very similar to the advice Jake gets from his
coaches in Little League.

Jake became a starting pitcher in fourth grade. He played AAA ball, and until that spring, I never knew that being a pitcher was so mentally demanding. Jake, tall for his age and athletic, would begin each game confident and poised. He'd be so calm on the mound I almost couldn't see him breathing. He was consistent, too, throwing strike after strike. Until he wasn't. When his game started to fall apart, Mark and I knew more balls were coming. He'd think about every pitch, except the one he had to throw. *I can't believe I walked that guy. The next batter's getting a hit; I know it.* It was an unforgiving cycle that made my heart ache from the bleachers. One of his coaches would invariably call a time-out and walk to the mound. "Jake," he'd remind him, "just throw one pitch at a time." That's all he needed. With that little verbal nudge, my ten-year-old son would pull himself together. By putting both the past and future out of his mind, Jake was once again 100 percent in the moment and firing rockets across the plate.

Dave Eiland has taught the same lesson to some of the best pitchers in major-league baseball. His squad recently included CC Sabathia, A. J. Burnett, Andy Pettitte, and arguably the most successful closer in history, Mariano Rivera. Eiland is the former pitching coach for the New York Yankees. "I always tell them to just think about locking that pitch into the glove," he told me one afternoon when I asked him about his approach. "They can't worry about the batters they've walked or the ones coming up."

It seems hard to believe that major-league pitchers need the same reminder. They've probably heard the same philosophy since *they* were ten years old. But Eiland told me maintaining that kind of focus is one of the hardest jobs in baseball. "Pitchers need to throw every pitch with conviction. They can never get lazy."

Nor can parentless parents. If we do a better job keeping our losses in the past—and pay greater attention to quieting our fears of the future—we have the potential to become better, more focused parents right now.

And that could give us back some of the control we've been missing.

"Out of Body" Parenting

A friend once showed me the journal she keeps for her son. Every day she meticulously records what he does — "Today you tried grapes for the first time" — or what they do together — "We went to the park and saw your friend Ben." Each page is crisp and neat, and she always uses the same color ink. The outside is equally handsome — made of supple leather dyed a midnight blue. Every night when she completes her latest entry, she fastens the journal together with a matching leather lace. "That's gorgeous," I said, thinking what a bad mother I was because I don't keep a similar diary for my kids.

Not to be outdone, the next day I went to a stationery store and found two nearly identical leather journals. I purchased a pink one for Lexi and a black one for Jake. I took them home like trophies, and that night, I started Jake's first entry.

SEPTEMBER 2006

Dear Jake,

Mom and Dad bought this journal so we could write down all the fun and important things that make you . . . you. We got this for you out of love; love for who you are already and who you will become.

So, who is Jake at six years old? You are full of love, enthusiasm, spirit, laughter, energy and exuberance. You are all boy. You actually love everything involving sports. There is nothing you won't try. Actually, now that I think of it, that's not true. You have been reluctant to try riding your bike without training wheels! Maybe in the spring you'll get your nerve up. . . .

I kept journaling like this for a grand total of four entries. Lexi's even fewer. I stopped because all I could think about was how Jake and Lexi would be looking at those very same pages when I'm dead. It was like I was being watched. Every word I wrote seemed profoundly important, and I felt self-conscious making any mistakes. If I had too many cross-outs, Jake and Lexi would think I was sloppy or careless. If I didn't pick the right noun or adjective, they might misconstrue what I meant to say. Or worse, they might think their mom didn't care enough.

And because of how much importance I've attached to anything with my parents' handwriting on it, even the physical act of writing was paralyzing. My writing went so slowly that every line, swoop, and dot appeared laboriously on the page as if I were working with an Etch A Sketch.

I've also noticed that I try to move out of frame when Mark turns on our video camera. If I can't escape, I smile and wave, but what I'm really focusing on is how that exact moment of video will look to Jake and Lexi when I'm gone. "Oh," they'll say, "look at Mom. I remember that day." I know it would seem more likely that I'd run in front of the camera to ensure they'll remember me — that I was there! that I loved them! — but the reality is part of me feels like I'm already gone.

This "out of body" awareness is common among parentless parents. Jeff Nudelman says he often evaluates his parenting skills in real time, as if he's on the outside, looking in. "If I happen to lose my cool, I don't want them to look at me like, 'My dad, he used to get angry at us.' It's why I try to make them aware that I'm there and love them. It's why I'm more engaged. I gotta make sure they remember me. I don't think that's easy for someone who has their parents to understand."

For Christine Haynes, the Maryland mom who spends her days crafting necklaces, rings, and bracelets out of precious metals and gemstones, it's become something of an obsession to record everything. "I come from a long line of women dying young from cancer, so I'm just terrified. I think, as a result, I desperately try to capture memories. Pictures. Mementoes. I'm constantly videotaping. I don't wait for the perfect opportunity to make a memory. There's always an opportunity. Ramsey ate her first hard-boiled egg?! That's exciting. Let's videotape it!"

Christine also puts pen to paper with the expectation that when she dies, her writing will speak for her. "When I was pregnant with my first daughter, I started writing her letters just about what type of person I hope she'll be, what type of person I was, the things I was thinking. Now that there are two of them, I will write a note, put it in a little envelope, seal it, and stick it in a Tupperware container. They each have their own." Another mom told me that she's saved so much of her son's schoolwork and so many of his art projects the collection no longer fits in her attic. With dozens of boxes already upstairs, the overflow has spilled into a closet in the hallway. "I want him to be able to go back and know how I really felt," she told me. For her, all that saving will be proof that she loved him.

I've responded in much the opposite way. I am a hard-core editor of everything my children touch. It's hard to save all of their paintings, drawings, and spelling tests when I know they'll be looking at them one day without me. Mark has been a terrific ally on this front—especially because (like me) he doesn't like clutter. Every year we pick two pieces of artwork—one from Jake and one from Lexi—and frame them for the "permanent collection" in our home office. Everything else (pretty much) gets tossed.

Children's urologist Tom Vates developed a similar approach after his dad died. While he and his brother were cleaning out their father's house, they found a box of mementos their parents had saved from when they were kids. Tom says it was like being brought face-to-face with his own mortality. "I'm looking at what they kept. A piece of my hair. A piece of my brother's hair. From that moment on, I was more conscious of what I was saving and how it would reflect on me when I'm gone. It was like skipping to the last chapter of a book."

I don't think Jake and Lexi will remember me less because I didn't keep journals for them. After years of beating myself up and feeling like I was never doing enough, I've learned to take the pressure off and do what I can. What matters most, Tom Vates believes, is how you spend time with your children now, not how well you document it.

When each of Tom's daughters turned five, he took her on a special daddy-daughter trip to Disney World. Tom would take time off from his busy medical practice and spend four days with each of his girls one-on-one. He'd do whatever she wanted. For Hannah it was Splash Mountain. For Katie it was spinning around in those extra-large teacups. For Sarah, the best part was the Dumbo the Flying Elephant ride. Each time the trip ended, Tom would sit on the plane heading back to New Jersey with a self-satisfied smile. He knew his daughter would always remember the trip. And she'd always remember it was her dad who took her.

Experiences are perhaps the most powerful memory-building tools we have. Fred Greene says going on vacation with his parents is the only activity he actually remembers doing with them. When I look back on my childhood, it's the little outings and big trips I took with my parents that I remember most, too. Playing pool with my dad. Taking the ferry to Fire Island with my mom. It's the reason I've taken each of my children away on special Mommy-only weekends and why we spent our last vacation in Rome.

And yet. I remain afraid every day of what could happen. Seeing Jake and Lexi graduate from high school and college remains more a hope than an expectation, and the idea of being at their weddings and holding their children is more fantastic still.

I try to channel my inner baseball pitcher—and doing so has improved my outlook significantly, even ousting some of my most intractable demons—but no matter how much love I have in my life, no matter how much good there is, in the back of my mind, I often worry when it will all be taken away.

Chapter 7

When Only One Spouse Is Parentless

"The feelings of jealousy I have towards my in-laws surprise me with their intensity. It makes me sick that they are here and my parents aren't."

"My marriage would be more successful if I had family backing me up."

"I know I idealize my parents and their involvement in my daughter's life and my in-laws could never compete with that image of perfection."

—from the Parentless Parents Survey

Tracy and I were hiding under a maple tree when I saw my husband, Mark, for the first time. We were eighteen years old and counselors at Camp Lakota, a sleepaway camp in the Catskill Mountains. Our mission was scoping out boys, and if either of us spotted a cute one, we'd nudge the other and giggle. The tree's massive trunk provided the perfect cover, and because there was little threat of being discovered, we lingered. We were best friends and had nowhere else to go and nothing else to do. It was June of 1988, and the entire summer lay ahead of us. College was nine weeks away, but it might as well have been years.

For an extra $50 each, the two of us came to camp a week before the other counselors to paint, sweep, mop, and pick up garbage—anything to get the camp ready for summer. So it's not surprising that the morning the rest of the staff arrived (the ones who didn't want to paint, sweep, mop, and pick up garbage for an extra $50) I was splattered head to toe in white house paint. There were flakes in my hair and crusted smudges on my cheeks. I was actually picking dried globs off my black cutoff shorts when I looked up and saw him.

Mark stuck out from the crowd of new counselors. He was by far the tallest, six-three, and he was probably the skinniest. My husband-to-be had short, curly brown hair and was wearing a navy blue shirt, plaid pants, and a pair of white canvas Sperry Top-Siders. I thought he was hot. I elbowed Tracy in her side and told her, "That's him."

For the next few days, every counselor participated in a loose orientation, and I'd see Mark at every meeting. I'd be half-listening and half-swooning as the camp's director taught us what to do in emergencies and how to help kids if they were homesick. Every night, a gang of us would head to the Counselor's Lounge to hang out. The Counselor's Lounge was really just an unused bunk across the street from the camp, and we'd go there so often to relax we quickly began referring to it as a one-word slur, thecounselorslounge. Soon it was only necessary to say, "Wanna go to the Slounge?"

The Slounge consisted of a couple of mismatching chairs, a couch, and a pay phone, and because so many of the counselors smoked, the air was always musty and thick. Ashtrays overflowed, and butts were flicked across the wooden floor. Mark and I would grab a can of soda and a bag of chips from the outside vending machine, and we'd drink, eat, and talk with our new friends for hours. Every time someone came in, his or her arrival was announced by the slam of the front screen door. Thwack! "Hey, Jason!" Thwack! "Hi, Lisa!" Sometimes I wouldn't say anything; I'd just sit back, drink my Diet Coke, and stare at my new boyfriend like a cat in heat.

Night after night, when all the other counselors went back to their bunks to go to bed, Mark and I would stay behind and splay across the one piece of furniture big enough for the two of us. The sofa had so many cigarette burns it looked like it was covered in polka dots, and there was so much ash embedded in its fibers the scratchy wool had a greasy sheen. But who cared? We'd just listen to a Tracy Chapman tape over and over and debate if this new singer was really a man or woman. And we'd talk.

We exchanged every detail about our lives up to that summer: I told Mark that I grew up in New York; he told me about his childhood in New Jersey. I told Mark about my mom and dad; he told me about his. We learned that our parents were both divorced, that our fathers had both remarried, and that we were each the youngest sibling. Oh, and we were both Jewish! Our backgrounds were so alike! I couldn't help feeling that our meeting was *besherte,* a Yiddish saying Grandma Bertha used to describe her relationship with my grandfather—*it was meant to be.*

Within days, Mark and I had become inseparable. We coordinated our days off and synched our schedules to sit "On Duty" the same nights, which meant having to stay outside your assigned bunk during evening activity. We'd write each other love notes from our separate sides of camp—Boys' Side and Girls' Side—and our campers would eagerly ferry them back and forth like messenger pigeons. My girls insisted I use their stationery—pink paper, lavender paper, and my favorite, blue paper with teddy bears sitting on clouds—and I'd write Mark things like, "I haven't spoken to you in sooooooo long. I miss you!!!" I signed one of them, "Happy 1 Month Anniversary!" in bubble letters. Mark was just as gushy. In one of his letters he said "I love you very much" and wrote the word "very" twenty-three times. I still have every origami-looking folded-up piece of paper we sent each other that summer.

When we got to college, we kept on writing and also stayed in touch (before email and cell phones) by speaking on the phone every night from our dorm rooms. I'd be on my bed twirling the plastic cord around my index finger and he'd be sitting at his desk in a different time zone while we swapped stories about our day. We may have been teenagers, but we felt as connected as a married couple with children. Our favorite TV show was *thirtysomething,* and Mark was my Michael Steadman.

Mark is still very much my soul mate, but because my parents are now gone — and his are alive — the road that brought us together has forked. Looking at a picture of us taken that summer, I see that I look so happy and peaceful. My head is slightly cocked toward Mark's and my left arm rests unintentionally across his jeaned lap. Was I really ever that carefree? Was there really a time when I posed for a picture and didn't wonder what it would look like when I'm dead? That kind of lightness, that feeling of being completely in the moment: What did that feel like, again?

I may appear largely the same on the outside (same red hair, identical blue eyes and freckles), but with each of my parents' deaths that weightlessness I had once taken for granted was swept away. This shift has had a significant effect on how I relate to Mark and how I parent our children. And it's also affected how I feel about his mom and dad and the relationship they have with Jake and Lexi. I have now spent more than half of my life with Mark, and I can tell you that nothing has challenged our relationship more than raising our kids without my parents — and the close involvement of his.

Relationships with Our In-Laws

The worst fight Mark and I ever had ended in a volcanic explosion of Doritos. When the neon dust finally settled, it seemed not an inch of our kitchen floor was clean. Days later, I was still sponging orange powder from the cereal cabinet and silverware tray. Our argument began because I didn't want Mark's mother coming over to our house — again. Marilyn is a wonderful mother-in-law. Warm. Loving. A fantastic grandma. But on that day, at that minute, I had reached my in-law limit.

It was July 4 weekend, and we'd just spent nearly the entire holiday with Mark's family. We had gotten up early Saturday morning and gone to New Jersey to spend the day with his mother and our two nieces at his sister's house. That night, after Mark's mom headed back to her home a few miles away, we went with all the cousins to see fireworks with Mark's dad and stepmother.

Sunday morning, we were at home finishing a late breakfast when the phone rang. Mark went into our bedroom to find the receiver (it's cordless and we constantly lose it), and within minutes he returned to the kitchen and gleefully announced, "Grandma's coming over in an hour, guys!"

"Today?!" I asked, clearly not thrilled with the idea.

"She just has a little laundry to do," Mark explained. At the time, Marilyn lived in an apartment building about twenty-five minutes away and came over about twice a month to do a load or two and see her grandchildren.

"Can't she come over next weekend?"

"All-i-son," he said in exasperation. Mark pronouncing every syllable of my name is the verbal equivalent of putting his foot down — which only angered me more. I shot him a look that I hoped Jake and Lexi didn't see. My voice began to rise.

"Can't we just have a day to ourselves?"

"No, Allison. She has laundry to do *to-day*."

"But I want to spend the day with just you and the kids. Just us!" Jake and Lexi were at this point looking up from their plates, and I was uncomfortably aware that they were hearing me say that I didn't want their grandmother to come over. But I couldn't help myself. To the core of my being, I didn't want her to come over. Marilyn's the one woman who reminds me most of my mother's absence, and on that day I just needed a break.

"She'll only be here for a few hours!" Mark yelled, clenching his fists into tight, violent balls. Mark is generally easygoing and hard to upset, and for the first time since I'd known him, I was scared he was going to punch his hand through the kitchen window. But I didn't relent. I couldn't. "We spent all day with her yesterday! Please," I pleaded.

Mark was furious, and I knew it was all because of me. And while he didn't strike the glass as I had feared, he started pummeling the unopened bag of Doritos on the kitchen island. He punched it again and again until pulverized chips spewed everywhere. Instantly I was sorry for what I had done — mostly because Jake and Lexi saw and heard everything.

Mark thought I was being unreasonable and unloving; I thought I was justified and wished he could have anticipated my need for space. In the end, I relented and the afternoon we spent together was more than fine. It was fun. My intention had never been to drive a wedge between Marilyn and her grandchildren, and I realized that's what I would have been doing if I had held firm.

The Dorito Fight, of course, was about more than just that day and that one visit. And it wasn't just about Marilyn. In April, Mark's parents get to come to Jake's birthday party and shower him with gifts. In May, we celebrate Mother's Day and I'm the one who buys presents for Marilyn and Mark's stepmother, Sandy. In June, we celebrate Father's Day with his dad, Jimmy, and both of his parents attend Lexi's birthday party. By the time July 4 rolls around, I have gone through six months of every special occasion (and every ordinary day) reminding me that Marilyn, Jimmy, and Sandy get to be grandparents and my parents do not. And bookending every year are the anniversaries of my parents' deaths (which my in-laws never acknowledge) and the holidays.

Unfair as it is to Mark's parents, I'm able to cut my stepmother, Cheryl, some of the slack I should be able to give them but can't. After all, she represents my side of the family. And because it was her husband who died, Cheryl always makes it a point to connect with me on the anniversary of my father's death. She even called me one year from Hawaii, where she was on vacation, to let me know she was thinking about me. It was the anniversary of my *mother's* death.

My frustration isn't just about what I'm missing. Because Jimmy, Sandy, and Marilyn come to nearly every birthday party and we're together for most holiday dinners, my children's sense of family is completely lopsided. I can tell stories about my parents and show pictures, but there's very little I can do to counter the tidal wave of influence coming from the other side. Out of sadness and jealousy, I sometimes push Mark's parents away—like I did to Marilyn that morning in July.

Unlike my parents, when Jake and Lexi are with Mark's parents, they can see them, hear them, and hug them. They can taste and smell what's cooking in their ovens and on their stoves. Every once in a while I'll be surprised (and delighted!) when Jake and Lexi parrot the little nuggets I've taught them about my mom and dad, but when it comes down to it, they're always going to remember Mark's parents more than mine. The reality is my parents can't compete with Mark's. I can't level the playing field.

Hilari Graff says she fights the same winless battle. "There's only so much I can do, especially when they're younger," she told me that morning we met at her house over a plate of muffins. "A physical presence — it just has more impact than anything I can say about a memory or by showing a picture. Like on my daughter's birthday, she got a whole bunch of board games and I tried to tell her that I remember it was one of the things I loved doing with my mom. That we would play Scrabble. But that influence can't compare to when Grandma comes over and is playing or buying her something. It's completely disproportionate."

For Colleen Orme, making her parents as relevant as her in-laws also seems unattainable. "I love talking about them. It's pleasurable to me, but I have to say, sadly, it's also a little empty. I'm looking at three little guys and they're like, 'Okay, Mom. So your mom liked chocolate-covered grahams? Good for you!!' So there's an emptiness for me. A desperateness that I feel. That I'm trying to say, 'But you don't know. She *was* special. He *was* special. They loved each other. They had real problems, but they never loved anybody but each other. These were really good people.'"

Even in the best of circumstances, when a parentless parent loves his or her in-laws, their unrivaled presence is hard to stomach day after day. In the Parentless Parents Survey, nearly 50 percent of all respondents said they were jealous of the time their in-laws got to spend with their children and 29 percent railed against their outsized influence. This tension is only exacerbated when a parentless parent finds fault — or failure — in what his or her in-laws bring to the grandparenting table. Small differences become big when they exist in isolation. You can be kept awake by a dripping faucet in the middle of the night but not even notice the *plip, plip, plip* during the day. In my house, Mark's parents are louder simply because mine are silent.

Anne Condon Habig, the legal assistant, has been married to her husband for twenty-five years and accuses her in-laws of not being as thoughtful as her parents. When her son was young and obsessed with toy cars, for example, her mother found him an antique Tonka truck collection. To this day her son still has the set. He's seventeen years old. The present didn't cost much, but it was the effort involved in getting it that made it so special. Her in-laws, by comparison, usually give her children money. "My mother would always ask what he really wanted. The money," she said, "it's just distant."

It may seem unfair to constantly compare our in-laws to our own parents, but it's an inescapable reality. Their presence makes us feel our parents' absence with greater intensity. On the condition of anonymity, a mother in Idaho told me she blames her in-laws for the lack of connection they have with her children. "My kids, especially my daughter, love to play board games, and they'd say to my husband's parents, 'Hey, do you want to play a game?' And more often than not, my husband's mom would be distracted. She'd rather invest herself in the conversation going on than just tuning everything out and focusing on the kids. I feel they should step up. You know, 'You're all they have, so when you're here with us, instead of watching golf, or sitting and talking, go to the playroom where the kids are, and say, "Can we play a game?" I really have a hard time because [they are their] only set of grandparents." Her rant ended with a reminder: "You can't print my name next to this."

No grandparent wants to be called out on not doing enough for his or her grandchildren. And no grandparent wants to be accused of not being thoughtful or involved. But statistics support what this Idaho mom told me in confidence: Grandparents prefer to spend time with the grandchildren their daughters gave birth to.

Hope Edelman writes about this in her expertly researched book *Motherless Mothers*. "Women are almost always closer to their daughters' children than they are to their sons'," she concludes. Further, researchers have determined this preference extends to grandfathers as well.

A team of psychologists came to this understanding after going to several retirement communities in Florida and recruiting more than two hundred grandparents to participate in a study. Men and women between the ages of forty-seven and eighty-six were asked numerous questions about how they were related to their grandchildren, to what degree they spent time and money among them, and how "emotionally close" they felt to each one. Only by offering participants complete anonymity (it was a written survey and each participant was given a "security envelope" to place the survey when complete) did they learn the unvarnished truth: "Among grandparents with grandchildren through both sons and daughters, grandparents invest more in grandchildren through daughters." One of the reasons for that closeness, they discovered, is that grandparents choose to live "significantly" closer to their daughter's family than their son's. The results couldn't have surprised the scientists. They wrote that their findings echoed scientific literature already published showing the exact disparity.

This reality was also corroborated in my interviews. From a mom in Washington State: "I think my husband's parents are not very interested in our children, and I feel my parents would have been. They would have been active and involved. I have been bitter about that, and that's hard not to bring into your marriage," she said. "Especially because they are much more attentive to their daughter's children." And remember Julie Hallman, the mom in Florida who cried on the couch in exhaustion when her twin daughters were babies? At the time, her in-laws could have come over to help, but didn't. They chose to be with their expectant daughter instead. "I was angry that I had these two infants and they were a half mile away with my sister-in-law, nesting. They felt the need to mother her. To parent her. That took precedence," she said. "They love my children very much, but there's a different relationship between a daughter having children and a son having children. It's something I've had to accept, and it hurt." I asked Julie why she couldn't have asked her in-laws to come over and help. She answered plainly, "I wanted it to come naturally and not have to ask."

Marilyn, Jimmy, and Sandy have never done anything to intentionally push me away, and they've expressed their love to me over the years in innumerable ways. When my mom and dad were living, all the little things that made them different from mine didn't matter. They are different people, after all. They're not my parents. The hard-to-admit truth is this: I've locked my in-laws into a no-win Goldilocks fairy tale. They can offer me, Jake, and Lexi all the affection in the world, but it will always be too much or too little, and it will never be just right.

Your Relationship with Your Spouse

There was a time when I felt Mark understood everything about me. But now that my parents are gone, I realize being completely connected to him is impossible. So much separates us.

Mark will try hard to support me, but sometimes even his best efforts backfire. Like the time we were all playing Monopoly and he got up to get the kids some chocolate pudding. As he opened the kitchen cabinet to get the bowls, Mark announced, "Jake and Lex. See these bowls?!!" He held up two canary yellow glass bowls my mom had bought at a craft show when I was ten.

"Yeah," they said, barely looking up from the board.

"Lexi, it's your turn!" Jake blurted out, ignoring Mark.

"Aren't they cool?!!" Mark continued, this time with more enthusiasm, trying to get their attention.

"Yeah," they said in unison, clearly unimpressed.

Mark pressed on and I started to wince, hoping he'd stop turning their request for dessert into a teaching moment about my parents.

"These bowls were your grandma Lynn's. Mom used to have pudding out of these bowls when she was a kid. Isn't that great?!"

My ears stung. Mark was clearly doing this for my benefit, and I loved him for it, but the gesture just felt forced.

Regrettably, that wasn't the first time I bristled at his overtures. Sometimes I just can't let Mark in because for so many years I've felt so alone — even though he's been there, all along, right by my side. Over time, I'm the only one who had to learn the lexicon of cancer patients: Cisplatin, Tamoxifen, Carboplatin, Taxol, Augmentin, Adriamycin, Cisplatinum, Neupogen, Procrit, Diflucan, Amifostine, Zyprexa, Compazine, Ativan, Lomotil, Provigil, Triazolam, high-dose chemotherapy, autologous bone marrow transplant, platelet counts, soft-tissue masses, large-mass lesions, adenoma, ascites, Port-a-Cath, Hickman catheter, Foley catheter, peripheral line, peripheral stem cells, resected, debulking, adhesions, omentum, peritoneal cavity, abdominal cavity, transverse colon, bowel wall, small cell lung cancer, non–small cell lung cancer, widespread disease, invasive carcinoma, and finally, home nursing care and hospice.

The cancer-immersion class didn't end when my parents died. As I confronted my own risk, I graduated into Honors Cancer and my vocabulary expanded to include: genetic testing, pre-cancer, previvor, preventative surgery, prophylactic oophorectomy, surgical menopause, estrogen replacement therapy, cenestin, estrogen derivatives, plant-based estrogen, and my favorite, premature aging.

These words are now so much a part of who I am they are netted to my brain like a tumor. Unlike learning a foreign language, learning cancer hasn't made my life richer — it's poisoned it by filling my head with words, phrases, and expressions I'd rather purge from my consciousness altogether. But I can't remove them. They are inoperable.

I could be lying in bed at the end of the day giving myself a breast exam and Mark will come out of the shower and see my T-shirt hiked up around my neck, baring both my naked breasts. He'll dive into bed, come toward me, pull me close, and slowly kiss my nose, my cheek, my neck, my collarbone, working his way down, until my skin begins to crawl and I gently push him away. Somehow I'm not in the mood for sex after I've just spent the last ten minutes feeling for lumps. That wasn't foreplay. My breasts lost their innocence years ago. Now they are assassins in disguise.

Masha Gessen wrote the book *Blood Matters* about her decision to have a double mastectomy to prevent getting breast cancer. She, too, had tested positive for the BRCA gene, and was determined to beat the odds. But Gessen couldn't bring herself to remove her ovaries like I did. The writer, who lives in Moscow, was nervous about what the lack of estrogen would do to her sense of femininity and libido. She writes, "Without her ovaries, a woman will often gain weight, especially around the midsection . . . her skin will lose elasticity, her lips will lose their fullness and color, and her hair will thin." Gessen thought it was better to cut off her breasts than to cut out the hormone-producing essence of what makes a woman a woman.

I have experienced only some of the symptoms Gessen discusses. My belly is a bit bigger and I am fighting off added weight, but my lips and hair look just about the same. And while my interest in sex peaks and dips, I am still wildly attracted to Mark and completely satisfied with our life between the sheets. What has changed for me — and what affects Mark and my children — is my mood. Since my surgery, my patience is shorter, I am quicker to anger, and explosions happen faster than anyone might expect.

Gessen writes about this as well:

"Women who undergo surgical menopause can have far more extreme symptoms than women who go through 'the change' naturally, sometime in their fifties. This is probably because the levels of hormones, estrogen and progesterone, drop suddenly rather than diminishing over time, and also because the hormones disappear completely — while the ovaries of postmenopausal women continue to produce a little bit of estrogen for years."

Which is why when I look at that photograph of me and Mark at Camp Lakota—and compare it to what I see now in my bathroom mirror—the images only vaguely resemble each other. Today, my face looks more tired than I think it should and the V-shaped lines between my eyebrows look too deep. Mark hasn't aged with the same speed or violence. Mark is thirty-nine and says he feels twenty-nine. "I feel better than I did ten years ago," he said over dinner one night. That must be nice. I'm forty and often feel like I'm fifty-seven, the same age my mother was when she died. Even though the same amount of time has passed since we met, I feel like I've aged more.

Death doesn't leave me alone. Three weeks after my cousin's wedding in Colorado, it even tiptoed into Lexi's bedroom as I was getting her ready for soccer practice.

"Hey, Ronnie," I said, answering the phone. I saw the 503 area code and knew it was her calling from Portland, Oregon, where she and my uncle had recently moved. I cradled the phone to my ear while I tied one of Lexi's cleats.

"Hi," she said, her voice a little higher than usual. "Allison, remember when we were at Piney River Ranch and I was having trouble breathing?" I stopped tying Lexi's cleat. "Well, it wasn't just the elevation, honey. I have breast cancer."

"Oh, Ronnie," I responded softly, so Lexi wouldn't get concerned. "When did you find out? What stage?"

Lexi looked at me. "What, Mommy? What's wrong?" I put my index finger to my lips, and mercifully, she didn't keep pressing for an answer.

It turned out that Ronnie knew about her diagnosis at the wedding but didn't want to ruin the celebration by telling anyone. She told me that since she'd been back from the wedding she'd already been through a round of chemo and found a terrific surgeon. At first I was angry she didn't tell me the moment she was diagnosed, but she said she didn't want to worry me, and what could I do from New

York, anyway? I told her I'd be on the next plane, but she insisted I stay home with the kids and that everything was under control. She even sounded upbeat.

From that phone call on, I'd call Ronnie once a week or she'd call me just to check in. In September, right around the beginning of school, I called her several times and left messages. I also sent some emails. No reply. At first I didn't think anything of it — I figured she was just busy working or painting — but after several more un-returned calls and emails, I called my uncle.

"Is everything okay? I haven't heard from Ronnie in a few weeks."

"She's in the hospital, Ali," he explained. "She has an infection."

"What kind of infection? Is it bad?"

"That's what they're trying to find out. They have her on medica-tion and we'll just have to wait and see how she responds."

"Responds?! Is she unconscious?"

"She's touch and go, Ali. But they're thinking she'll be all right."

The next morning I got on a plane, rented a car at the airport, and drove straight to the hospital. My brother had gotten there first and was waiting for me outside the main entrance.

"It's really bad," Jay said. "Just know that when you get upstairs she's not going to look like she did at Yelena's wedding."

I knew that. Even though the wedding had been only a few months earlier, this was my third time dealing with cancer; I knew what to expect.

Jay took me to the elevator and we went up to the intensive care unit. He lifted a beige plastic phone off the wall that automatically dialed the nurses' station inside. "We're here for Ronnie Brachman," he said. The doors opened and we walked inside.

Ronnie was in the room right in front of the nurses' station, and despite my brother's description I nearly gagged when I saw her. Bald from chemo and strapped to multiple machines, Aunt Ronnie was the barely living image of my mother. And Yelena was by her bedside. Seeing her was like watching my own life in a flashback: Young girl. In her twenties. Mom dying of cancer. Was this not exactly what our moms experienced when their mother, our Grandma Henny, was dying of breast cancer, too?

A ventilator heaved Ronnie's chest up and down, and every few breaths her neck would twitch like a person with Tourette's. Doctors told us she had gotten this sick so quickly because she picked up a strep infection during chemo. Ronnie had sepsis. She was in toxic shock. Doctors were pumping so much fluid into her veins that blisters formed on her hands and arms and still more bubbled up through tiny, invisible nicks on her skin. Her fingers, the ones that had substituted for my mother's — changing Jake's diaper, feeding Lexi homemade soup, teaching them how to use acrylic paints — were now so deprived of oxygen they were blue-ish purple and mottled with port-wine marks.

The last day I was there I spent a considerable amount of time with her alone. When I told Ronnie, just as we did with Mom, that it was okay to let go, that our family would take care of one another, I saw her eyes open for the first time since I'd arrived. The whites were bloody, and while one eye seemed to focus, the other one, her right, drifted upward. A tear formed and escaped down the side of her nose. Was she crying because she heard me and felt reassured? I like to think so, but I'll never know.

A week after I left Portland, Aunt Ronnie was dead.

When Aunt Ronnie was diagnosed, the stopwatch that had been reset to 00:00:00 after my surgery started to tick again. This time, though, the threat was breast cancer. Part of the reason Aunt Ronnie removed her ovaries was to reduce her chances of getting breast cancer, but she got it anyway. In the months following her death, Mark's life went on as usual, while I started interviewing surgeons to perform a preventative double mastectomy. With yet another gun to my head, I decided that sometime within the next few years I'll remove both my healthy breasts to increase the chances of living longer than my mom, aunt, and grandmother. I will try anything to stop the cycle. How can I look at Jake and Lexi and come to a different conclusion?

Mark tries to empathize, but he can never truly understand. The below list represents only our immediate family when we met. I've left out, for example, cousins.

Mark's Family — Summer of 1988
Marilyn (Mother)
James (Father)
Sandy (Stepmother)
Debra (Sister)
Barry (Brother)
Lani (Stepsister)
Steven (Stepbrother)
Janet (Aunt)
Shirley (Aunt)
Bill (Uncle)
Arthur (Uncle)
Jacob (Grandfather)
Irma (Grandmother)

Allison's Family — Summer of 1988
Lynn (Mother)
Sidney (Father)
Cheryl (Stepmother)
Guy (Stepfather)
Jay (Brother)
Ronnie (Aunt)
Richard (Uncle)
Bertha (Grandmother)

Now, let's take a look at our families today.

Mark's Family — Today
Marilyn (Mother)
James (Father)
Sandy (Stepmother)
Debra (Sister)
Barry (Brother)
Lani (Stepsister)
Steven (Stepbrother)
Janet (Aunt)
Shirley (Aunt)
Bill (Uncle)
Arthur (Uncle)
~~Jacob (Grandfather)~~
~~Irma (Grandmother)~~

Allison's Family — Today
~~Lynn (Mother)~~
~~Sidney (Father)~~
Cheryl (Stepmother)
Guy (Stepfather)
Jay (Brother)
~~Ronnie (Aunt)~~
Richard (Uncle)
~~Bertha (Grandmother)~~

If you look closely, you'll see that Mark's day-to-day family life is largely as it was when we were at Camp Lakota. And more to the point, it looks just as it did when he was a boy. Mark is still the baby of the family. When his family gets together, the beehive is still noisy and swarms with the same love it did the day he was born. That's not to say Mark didn't love his grandparents dearly. He was close to them and adored them, and in many ways, as we've seen earlier in this book, his grandparents touched his life in a manner his parents never could. I loved them, too. But Mark has never felt the yank between his sick and dying parents and his own life. He's never had to wet a cotton ball with water and dab it on his mother's or father's cracked and bleeding lips. Mark's never had to write a eulogy for his parents or make their funeral arrangements. And when his paternal grandparents passed away, his father handled all the logistics. Mark grieved, but at a distance. It's like he's been in the audience of death, while I've been on stage.

Our children are the focus of our days, but we often circle them in opposing orbits. Birthday parties are the worst. Mark leaps between his parents, the cake, the streamers, the kids. He will hug me and love me and offer as much compassion as he can, but it's impossible for him to really "get" how I'm feeling. When we belt out "Happy Birthday," there is no way he can appreciate just how bittersweet those moments are for me, because his parents are right there singing along.

Different Approaches to Parenting

When one spouse is parentless and the other is not, couples often approach parenting from completely different camps. Parentless parents' heightened sense of mortality permeates everything we do: how we interact with our children, our expectations regarding their behavior, and our decisions concerning their health and welfare. This influence is powerful and can be a source of conflict in otherwise healthy marriages. And how could it not?

This became clear to Tarah Epstein Baiman when her son, Jesse, was just a baby. Tarah, as you may remember, lost both of her parents before she turned sixteen.

"When Jesse was six months old, my husband and I had just come home. It was Sunday night and we had just picked up Chinese food. It was a chaotic situation because we had two dogs, and they hadn't been fed. So I told Jim, 'You take Jesse upstairs; I'm going to feed the dogs.' Jim undid the buckles on the car seat, and when I came upstairs I saw that he'd put Jesse, still in the car seat, on the kitchen island.

"We had been through this so many times. I had specifically said to him, 'I don't like him up there.' And he just blew up at me. We were having a lot of clashes on control issues at the time. He was more laissez-faire when it came to parenting, saying things like 'We don't have to be so uptight,' 'Don't be so paranoid,' 'Don't be so neurotic.' And, if we were in the car and Jesse was crying, he would say, 'Oh, just take him out.' And I'd be like, 'What are you crazy?!' He *has* to go in the car seat. In my mind, there are certain rules you have to follow. You can't control the uncontrollable, but if you don't try to control the controllable, you're really in trouble. But Jim's not trained to think of the worst-case scenario. When I see a situation, my mind goes immediately to what could happen. His doesn't.

"So Jesse was on the counter, and because it was winter and he had a blanket over him, I didn't realize Jim had already unbuckled him. He had expected to take Jesse out, but something distracted him. Jesse wiggled his way out and fell off the island. There was this moment when we heard nothing and then Jesse started to just wail. He was hysterical and Jim just froze. I screamed to him, 'Call 911! You have to call 911!'

"The ambulance came and only one of us was allowed to go inside. There was no question. 'Jim, get out!' Same thing at the hospital. Jesse had to go through an MRI machine because they were worried about brain damage and somebody had to hold his head. So I pushed Jim away. I kept yelling, 'My baby! My baby!'

"It turned out that Jesse only had broken his arm, but I held Jim accountable even though I tried not to."

Jesse's fall was Jim's first brush with a potentially life-ending event. His parents were both living and the near catastrophe made him understand—the way nothing else had previously—Tarah's need for control. Now, Tarah says, "Jim is more scared about the realities of what could happen." Their son's accident ended, at least for a time, her husband's laissez-faire attitude.

If your wife "doesn't have that idea of mortality at all," or if your husband "has never lost anybody in his family," how can he or she be expected to understand how these experiences inform your parenting decisions? It is because we have experienced such loss that we parent the way we do. The deaths of our parents and the way we parent our own children are inextricably linked. And in the very real world of two-parent parenting, this can create conflict in marriages, as it did for Tarah and Jim. Andrea Karl, a parentless parent who lives about an hour outside New York City, says it "definitely caused problems" between her and her husband. It also caused trouble for Jeff Gelman and his wife, Lisa.

The morning I came to their house, Lisa made Jeff pancakes and then surprised me by sitting next to him during large portions of our interview. And when I asked Jeff, "Do you think the deaths of your parents have shaped, at all, the way you parent?" it was Lisa who chimed in with an answer first.

"Jeff is just really hesitant to take a strong discipline role. When it comes to the kids, he really was more comfortable being their friend. And it worked out really well when they were infants, and it worked out great when he could just give David all the attention in the whole wide world and just play, play, play. But you know, toddlers need a little more strict hand at times."

"Do you agree with that?" I asked, looking at Jeff.

"Yeah, it took me a while. I struggle with it," he said.

"What do you mean?" I asked, hoping he'd give me an example.

"The other night I knew I was going to be gone the next day because I was going to be at work and then an office party. I was trying to put them to bed, and the kids were being difficult and I was going to have to discipline them. And I'm thinking: *I'm going to be gone all day and what if something happens to me and I never come home and the last memory of me they have is me yelling at them?* That is not what I want. So it's on my mind, for sure."

This echoed what Jeff Nudelman told me. "I think there are times when I can be a little less strict with the kids than Cindy. I am not consistent, which is tough as a parent," he acknowledges. "But it's because of the mortality issues. I mean, I want to support my wife, but I don't want them to think that I'm angry at them for doing things that kids do. What if something happens and I'm not around? I don't want them to remember me being a mean guy."

The death of South Carolina writer Jayne Jaudon Ferrer's parents "has had a huge impact" on her marriage, but in a different way. "My perspective on life is you better enjoy today because you don't know that you have tomorrow. Everything has to be a big occasion and a big deal and special. It's like I would spend my last nickel to make a celebration." Jayne's zeal for making elaborate and frequent celebrations would be fine except that her husband, Jose, approaches parenting from an entirely different point of view. "His perspective on life is that you'd better work hard and save every nickel. 'I've got to work eighteen hours a day because I've got to provide for my family.'"

It would be too simple to dismiss the tension between Jayne and Jose as a money issue. This is not about Jayne, a blond with a penchant for bold and animal-print blouses, being a spender and Jose being a saver. During our interview, the real root of her need to create big celebrations became clear: Jayne does all the work out of fear. She wants to make sure her children never forget her. "We have to make these memories," she explained in her friendly Southern twang. Jayne says that need, her sense of urgency, is something Jose, who still has his mother, doesn't understand.

Mark says I've always been the more nervous parent. He thinks I might have been this way even if I hadn't gone through the deaths of my parents, but because my parents died before Lexi was born and when Jake was so young, we'll never know the kind of mother I would have been otherwise. Would I have trusted my instincts more? Would I assume the best, not the worst?

In the back of my mind, no news doesn't mean good news. I know the phone can always ring.

Who's in My Corner?

Jake and Lexi's birthdays aren't the only reminders of how different our lives have become. There's Mark's birthday in November, when his parents call and give him presents, and every conversation he has with his mom and dad about work, our house, the kids—life! His parents try to be there for me, too, but they can't replace my mom and dad. On rare occasions, they'll say things to me that are just puzzling, the kind of things I imagine my own parents would never say. Once, Mark's father returned from Texas after visiting his newest grandchildren, and overcome with joy he urged, "Al, you still have time to make more grandchildren!" I skipped a breath. "Jimmy, that's impossible," I said, reminding him of my surgery. Or the time I was upset that so few people called me on the anniversary of my father's death, and Marilyn consoled me by saying, "Allison, Aunt Ronnie would've called you if it was your mother's anniversary. She probably doesn't remember your dad's." Except that Aunt Ronnie had already died by then.

Am I even being fair? There were plenty of times my parents misspoke, and unintentionally hurtful things would slip from their mouths, too. With my father's immense knowledge of current events and art, he'd make me feel stupid if I couldn't keep up with dinnertime conversations. He was often unapologetically pompous. Yet I'm able to overlook my parents' mistakes while expecting my in-laws to always know and say just the right things. Mark's parents are generous and thoughtful. They always remember my birthday and ask to speak with me specifically when they call our house. Truly, I couldn't ask for better in-laws. But I miss my parents, especially when Mark and I disagree about big issues facing the kids. Mark can get his parents' perspective and use their input to support his argument. His family has always been bigger than mine, but now it overpowers. It's never a fair fight.

Five hundred miles away in Guelph, Ontario, less than a two-hour drive from Buffalo, Lynn Burkholder faced similar challenges. When her son was a baby, it was very important to her that she breastfeed him exclusively and soothe him whenever he cried. Her husband wasn't too enthusiastic with either of those ideas, and neither was her mother-in-law. "My husband wanted to start letting him cry himself to sleep. He believed in 'Ferberizing' the baby. And he wanted to introduce solids well before I was ready. I wasn't comfortable with any of it," she said. "And his mother was concerned that I was over-attending the baby, that I was spoiling him, because I'd nurse him whenever he cried."

With neither of them supporting her, Lynn felt like she was constantly being judged. When Michael was about nine months old, her mother-in-law even asked her point-blank when she was going to stop nursing. Lynn, who had no intention of quitting until he was one year old, felt blindsided. She thinks her mom would've understood and approved of her more natural approach. "That support from my side of the family wasn't there. It highlighted the fact that my parents weren't around. It's like you're not backed up by anybody."

Without our parents, we often feel alone carrying our family's flag. You might feel self-conscious hanging Christmas stockings if your spouse (and his or her entire family) celebrates Chanukah. If your parents believed kids shouldn't be planted in front of the TV and your in-laws have the television on every time your children visit, you may feel like you're swimming upstream, especially if your spouse follows his or her parents' example at home.

Catharine Hays says she felt suffocated by her husband and his family. When her parents were alive, it didn't matter as much that he preferred going to the movies and not museums. It didn't bother her to the same degree that he and his parents preferred taking big family vacations to all-inclusive resorts, while she favored places that offered culture and history. For most of their marriage, Catharine says, she tried to make her husband happy and conform to his (and his family's) needs, interests, and values. But it grated on her. The tension, she says, grew over time and became unbearable when her parents died—a choking feeling she described as "Asphyxiation. It was this feeling of not being able to breathe. How do you explain it? You were raised with a certain passion in life. A certain set of core values. It can be any kind of difference, but it's fundamental. My soul. What's important to me."

The fifty-one-year-old mom said that without her parents' support, she was the only person who could provide the kind of experiences she wanted her daughters to have. Her husband would come along on any outings she planned, but he was seldom going to take that kind of initiative. And her daughters were never going to get what she was looking for from her in-laws. Without her parents, Catharine felt deserted. She and her husband are now divorced.

Dr. Sue Johnson might have been able to help Catharine feel less alone in her marriage. Johnson, a clinical psychologist and author of four books on love and relationships, is the creator of Emotionally Focused Therapy for couples, a highly regarded method of psychotherapy practiced across the United States and many regions of the world. Emotionally Focused Therapy, or EFT, as it's commonly referred to, is similar to the attachment theory in parenting. It stresses that couples are dependent on each other in much the same way children are dependent on their parents — that spouses, too, rely on each other for comfort, nurturing, and security.

In her book *Hold Me Tight: Seven Conversations for a Lifetime of Love,* Dr. Johnson argues that marriages, like the bond between a parent and child, suffer when partners feel their needs and fears aren't being heard or respected. She admits this can be especially complicated if what's bothering you is the influence of your spouse's parents. That's pretty personal. "That's the tricky thing about relationships. It's a dance, and one person can't change the dance. Both of them would have to sit down and have a conversation and talk specifically." In Catharine's case, "She would have to say, 'I feel ignored. I feel helpless. I feel I have no say with my kids. I feel out-influenced.' She would have to tell him exactly what she needs and what her fears are for herself and her children if those needs aren't met. And he would have to hear her and not dismiss her. He would have to reinvest in the marriage by putting her needs above his own attachment to his parents."

Dr. John Gottman, the world-renowned marriage expert and cofounder with his wife, Dr. Julie Schwartz Gottman, of the Gottman Institute, says couples often get into trouble when partners feel they've lost their voice. One of the best ways to regain that voice, Gottman says, is by approaching points of contention in a more philosophical manner when times are calm. "If you take yourself out of the immediate situation and say, 'When I dream about my kids' lives, this is what I see for their future. I want them to be independent. I want them to have access to culture. I want them to stay alive.' This approach is a very effective tool."

Maybe Catharine's marriage would have been saved if she and her husband had had the kind of conversations Drs. Gottman and Johnson suggest. Maybe not. Marriages are invariably complex, and there are always multiple factors contributing to their dissolution. Regardless of any other reasons, Catharine is certain that "losing my parents was 90 to 95 percent of the reason I ended up getting divorced. It shed a white-hot light on the differences we had. I needed to have what was important to me be a bigger part of my life. I needed to stop pretending. That's why I had to be on my own. Because if I was on my own, I could bring those things to the table 100 percent of the time."

Marriage experts agree that relationships are affected when spouses have differing views on money, religion, and how they should discipline their children. But when it comes to parentless parents—and the men and women they're married to—I think marriage experts are overlooking a critical factor: the differing experiences of parental loss. No matter what our backgrounds and experiences, losing our parents has the potential to shape us as mothers and fathers and husbands and wives as much, I think, as anything else.

Which is why, according to the Parentless Parents Survey, nearly 50 percent of all respondents feel their spouses don't appreciate what it's like for them to be a parentless parent. And, it's precisely the reason parentless parents say they're much more likely (nearly doubly so, in fact) to find the kind of support they're looking for among friends who have also lost their parents—than their own husbands and wives.

This could explain why even the ordinary task of choosing a baby's name can be so problematic. "Naming our daughter was a horrible process," Amy, a former journalist, told me in an email. She and her

husband, Bruce, struggled for years to have a child, eventually con-
ceiving with the help of a donor egg. "I wanted her middle name to
be my maiden name. My husband was furious, saying that I was
'stealing' his chance to name his child. He demanded that we have
two middle names so that he could choose a name too. Never mind
that she already had his last name, and genes, and that his parents
would play a huge role in her life. I felt two middle names detracted
from the honor to my parents. How could he not get that giving her
this middle name was an important way to honor my family?! Eventually, I guilted him into legally dropping the middle name he wanted.
The name is still a sore spot in our marriage. I am STILL stunned a
year and a half later by his lack of understanding."

In some cases, parentless parents are just less willing to compro-
mise. Amy dug in her heels. Catharine Hays wasn't prepared to nego-
tiate her "core values." And Colleen Orme, the mom from Virginia
with those three sports-crazy boys, refused to settle.

About twenty years into her marriage, Colleen's husband, Tom,
started pulling away, and nothing she could do seemed to bring him
back. The rift got so bad the two separated for four months. "I didn't
want to be roommates. I wasn't interested in staying in an unhappy
marriage. Emotional intimacy is very, very important to me because
of the loss of my parents. I don't think we have all the time in the
world like everybody else thinks they do, and I want to make the most
of it." While the couple has since reunited, and Colleen still refers to
Tom as the love of her life, she says she'll call it quits for good if their
relationship deteriorates again. "I know from personal experience
that life can be over in a flash. I'm not interested in wasting time."

No matter how much a couple tries, some marriages simply don't
make it. Julie Hallman in Florida was married when I first met her,
but told me during the writing of this book that she and her husband
were getting divorced. Both Catharine and Julie say the fact that they're

parentless parents, and their spouses are not, contributed to the termination of their marriages.

But grief can also make relationships stronger. Scott Stanley, co-author of the book *Fighting for Your Marriage* and codirector of the Center for Marital and Family Studies at the University of Denver, says spouses can adjust to differing experiences of loss in much the same way couples fine-tune their relationships after one partner develops drastically different interests. "We call these changes 'world-view differences.' When a wife decides to become vegan. When a husband abandons or changes religion. These represent major shifts, just like losing a parent, that redefine you as a person and change who you are as a spouse. Couples are rarely on the same path throughout a marriage. Those who recognize the differences and accept them, not resent them, will have more success than others."

Ultimately, I've come to terms with the fact that Mark and I have been forced down different roads. I'm even glad. I know all too well what we would have had to go through if we'd been able to walk arm-in-arm.

One day Mark will know much more fully what I've been feeling — perhaps not everything, but at least more of it — and I will be there for him, just as he's been there so willingly for me. In the meantime, and even though I love him completely, I still feel as if I'm standing alone and there's a sharpshooter trained on my side of the family. One by one the gunman lines us up, fixes us in his crosshairs, and takes us down. I parent with the expectation that I'll be next, and it's because of this that I mother the way I do. I need to create memories. I must teach lessons. I have to be both parent and grandparent to my children.

Mark doesn't bear the same fear or urgency. He can just be.

Chapter 8

A World of Support

"Opening up about my fears and insecurities, and having others tell me they experience the same things, has helped the most. It makes me feel like I'm not the only one who feels that way."

"My faith group feels like an extension of family. It encompasses people of all ages so I am able to be with people of my parents' ages. I gain from the wisdom they so generously impart."

"It's so freeing not to have to explain to someone who can't possibly understand."

—from the Parentless Parents Survey

very summer throughout Japan families celebrate the holiday Obon. Depending on the region, Obon takes place in July or August, and marks the time when the dead are believed to return home. Families prepare elaborate feasts and await their loved ones' arrival with great anticipation and joy, and of course, for many of the bereaved, a touch of sadness as well. In her book *The Mourner's Dance,* Katherine Ashenburg writes, "To welcome them, what seems like the majority of Japanese clog the nation's highways to return to their family village and cemetery. There they clean the family graves, light a fire at home so that the smoke can guide the dead back, and make offerings of food and drink to the dead at an altar set up in the home."

What's most remarkable about Obon is that loved ones are celebrated in perpetuity with the Japanese "holding memorial services on the first anniversary of death, then after three, seven, thirteen, twenty-five, thirty-three, fifty, and sometimes one hundred years," Ashenburg explains. As I read her account of Obon, my mouth fell open in astonishment. What would it feel like to be part of a community, an entire country for that matter, where I was surrounded by people who not only expected me to remember my parents, but encouraged me to?

Hundreds of people attended the memorial services for my parents, and friends of mine (and theirs) stayed for shiva, the Jewish period of mourning immediately following death. After shiva ended, though, only a handful of people who attended the funerals were still in touch. While my closest friends and family would call me to make sure I was okay, outside this tight circle my parents were hardly mentioned to me again. Year after year, it's me, by myself, deciding how to remember them: Should I go to my mother's grave, or not? Should I light a memorial candle, or not? Should I go to synagogue to recite a certain prayer, or not? Unlike the fraternity of mourners I read about in Japan, the kind of support I have isn't universal or automatic. Mostly, I remember my mom and dad alone.

In North America, this is usually how grief goes — a lonely enterprise rarely acknowledged after a loved ones dies. And because of that, when I learned about Obon, I longed to go to Japan and experience the holiday for myself. My desire, though, was more in the way I'd fantasize about going to an exotic island but never actually visit. With two young kids, I didn't think I could swing a trip to Asia. It would require me to be gone for too many days. But as I did a little more investigating, I learned about a similar holiday closer to home. The best known Western equivalent is Mexico's Dia de los Muertos, or Day of the Dead, and the more I researched it, the more I knew I wanted to make the trip.

The Day of the Dead is one of Mexico's most popular holidays—second perhaps only to Christmas. As on Obon in Japan, Mexican families celebrate the return of the deceased to spend time with the living. The celebration, which takes place on November 1 and 2, is so entrenched in the fabric of Mexican life that it's part of the curriculum in schools. During the actual holiday, in fact, schools shut their doors in observance, and because children aren't in class, they fully participate in all the activities alongside their parents. The Day of the Dead is a family event in every imaginable way.

I decided the best way to learn about the Day of the Dead would be to spend the holiday with a Mexican family. My plan wasn't easy to execute. At the time I began looking into where to go, Mexico was experiencing a wave of drug violence unseen in recent years. And the murders were especially repugnant. Decapitated heads were left in plastic buckets and people were being ripped from their cars never to be heard from again. Despite the alarming headlines, I learned the bloodshed was mostly concentrated in the border states, and if I could avoid those areas I could make the trip work.

I wanted to know what it would feel like to witness people grieving without self-consciousness or apology. I needed to see how the Day of the Dead connected children to their grandparents—the grandparents they no longer have in their lives or the grandparents they may never have known.

My Journey to Hunuku

To help me during my visit I hired Lalo Hernández. Lalo, who was born in Mexico City and now lives in Cancun, makes a living taking foreigners on private tours of the area's most popular cultural sites, like Chichen Itza and Tulum. He also leads unusual eco-expeditions on bicycle, horseback, and sailboat. For my trip, however, I asked him to do something even more atypical. I asked him to locate a family willing to host me during the Day of the Dead, and even though I can carry on a conversation in Spanish, I also requested that he stay with me as guide and interpreter. I only had two requirements: the celebration had to be authentic (meaning, not a fabrication held for my benefit) and the family had to consist of at least one parentless parent.

Lalo spent the next three months locating the right family. When he emailed me about the Tuz family, I knew he'd found the perfect fit. Jose Inocensio Tuz and his wife, Fidelia, are both parentless parents and live in a small village far outside Cancun. They have six children and twenty-six grandchildren and had never before hosted a foreigner in their home.

On October 31 I flew from New York to Cancun, and within a few hours of my arrival I was sitting in the massive open-air lobby of my hotel, waiting for Lalo.

"*Hola!* You must be Allison!" I heard from a few feet away. "Welcome to Mexico!" Lalo bounded into the reception area with his arm stretched out to shake my hand. He was about my height, five-eight, and with his knee-length shorts, sneakers, and closely shaved head, he looked like he could've worked at Camp Lakota.

Lalo had a great, big smile, and he immediately leaned over to give me a friendly kiss on both cheeks. "Let's sit," he said, gesturing to the bench I'd just been sitting on. "How was your flight?"

"Easy, thanks."

"So glad to hear it!" Lalo seemed truly relieved that my trip had been uneventful, as if a bad plane ride would have reflected poorly on him. "You will have much to do in the next few days, so you should take the afternoon and have a rest."

"That sounds perfect," I said. Then, as nonchalantly as I could, I asked, "Is everything still okay with Mr. and Mrs. Tuz?"

I didn't want to offend Lalo, but I was uneasy about the logistics surrounding my interview with the Tuz family. Usually, in my work as a television news producer and writer, I conduct what are called pre-interviews with anyone I might include in a project. Pre-interviews are invaluable because they allow reporters to screen potential interviewees before committing all the time and resources required for a full, in-depth interview. In the case of Jose and Fidelia, however, all I had to go on was trust. All the communication about my visit had been through Lalo and their adult son, Benito. The Tuzes didn't have a phone or a computer, and even if they had I couldn't have had much of a conversation with them anyway. Jose and Fidelia don't speak any English—or Spanish for that matter. They only speak Mayan.

"Of course!" Lalo said to my immediate relief. "The Tuz family is expecting us. I suggest we leave the hotel at seven-thirty in the morning. That will give us enough time to make our way to Hunuku."

Lalo had told me about Hunuku, the tiny Mayan village where the Tuz family lives, in the dozens of emails we had exchanged planning my trip. Hunuku is so small, he said, most Mexicans don't even know it exists. Before I'd left for Mexico, I tried to find it on Google Maps and couldn't. At the hotel Lalo and I spoke a little longer and then parted ways until the morning we left for our trip.

The roads getting out of Cancun looked like I could have been in Miami. Outside the passenger window of Lalo's air-conditioned pickup truck, I saw a long strip of hotels and a McDonald's. But soon we were on a major highway driving away from it all. For miles, we traveled down the same pencil-straight path, until we finally turned off and continued onto a smaller two-lane road. There were no other cars, and it seemed we could keep driving forever and never see another human again.

Lalo made an otherwise long and boring drive entertaining. Even though English isn't his first language, he talked fluently about every random topic that came up during our two-and-a-half-hour road trip. In fact, Lalo likes to talk so much that I was taken aback when he stopped. "Don't talk now," he said as nicely as he could. "I need to pay attention or I'll miss the turn." We slowed down as if we were in bumper-to-bumper traffic, and I soon saw what Lalo was looking for: a small road winding its way into a jungle of trees. The only indication a village existed beyond our view was the small handmade sign planted into the scraggly overgrowth by the side of the road. In red painted letters it read "Hunuku," with an arrow pointing to the right.

The only sound I heard for the next few minutes was the crunching of small rocks and pebbles underneath the tires. "Their house is just up there," Lalo said, pointing to nothing in particular. Around a final bend, thatched huts popped up on both sides of the road and dogs and chickens darted in and out of view. As we drove farther into the village, children stopped playing and pointed at our car. Lalo pulled up next to the Tuzes' home, and Benito was waiting for us outside. He was wearing jeans and a white, collared short-sleeved shirt. He approached Lalo first, then me, and invited us inside.

The one-room home was packed with adults and children. Taking a quick look around, I easily counted between fifteen and twenty people. Light peeked in through the stick walls, and I felt as if I were inside a wicker basket. There was no kitchen. No running water. And except for the candlelit table holding the family's Day of the Dead offerings and a few wooden chairs, I saw no other furniture.

Benito introduced me to his parents, who cautiously stepped forward to greet me. His mother was short and round, and with her brown hair pulled back, it was easy to see her kind and gentle face. She wore a typical Mayan dress that fell shapelessly to her knees. It was all white, with a square neckline embroidered with red, blue, and purple flowers. Benito's father, wearing a worn yellow T-shirt and beige pants, was slim and had silver hair. The temporary altar setup in the middle of the room sat under an arch of green vines and pink flowers, and on the table were four tan bowls, each about the size of a cantaloupe cut in half, made out of the cored, dried, and smoothed shell of a jicara fruit. The bowls were filled with liquid resembling chocolate milk. I was offered some and drank it. It was thin and watery and tasted only mildly sweet. And, as yet another gesture of welcome, we were offered whole peeled oranges.

Benito soon motioned for everyone to sit down. Some of the younger children sat on the laps of the older ones, and for the next forty-five minutes the entire extended family sang, chanted, and prayed together. Incense burned on the altar and there was so much fragrant smoke wafting in every direction that my clothes, hair, and skin smelled like a campfire for days afterward. What I noticed most during the ceremony was how willing the children were just to be there. No one was whining and no one needed to be placated with juice or snacks. They were listening. They were participating.

After the ceremony, I was invited to begin my interview with Mr. and Mrs. Tuz, which was an elaborate undertaking. The conversation unfolded like a complicated game of telephone. My interpreter needed an interpreter. Lalo would translate my question from English to Spanish, and then Benito would translate it again from Spanish into Mayan. Five minutes later, with the game of telephone reversed, I'd finally get the answer to my question. With the children surrounding us and watching every second of our interview, I discovered that Jose was sixty-eight and had lost his final parent, his father, three years ago, and that Fidelia, ten years younger, had been without her parents for sixteen years. I directed my first real question to Mr. Tuz.

"Why is this holiday so important to you and your family?" I kept my pen and paper ready for when his answer circled back to me in English.

"It is our way of honoring the dead. It is part of my responsibility. It is part of my job as a parent."

"Does it help to connect your children to your parents?"

As I waited for Jose's answer to come around in English, I took a moment to look around their home as surreptitiously as I could. The handmade roof had a single bare lightbulb dangling from it, and I couldn't see one decorative object. And when I looked down at the earthen floor, I couldn't help noticing Jose's feet. Even though he was wearing sandals, they looked like he'd walked barefoot most of his life.

"Yes," I was finally told. "And it was done this way when I was a child. I saw my father doing it for his father. It's a tradition."

I turned my attention to Mrs. Tuz and asked her if she found it difficult to include her children and grandchilden in a day that seems, on the surface, to be so morbid and sad. "When I first lost my parents, it *was* sad. Now we celebrate them," she said, her hands resting on her lap.

"What kind of support do you get from your family, from your neighbors?"

"Nobody can feel the way I feel," Fidelia admitted. "You have your own emotions. But," she continued, "you are just happy that other people are there. That they are with you."

We continued talking until it was time to leave for the public memorial. As we walked out of the Tuzes' hut and ambled down the road, I noticed Benito plucking a flower off a branch of a tree. He held it between his thumb and forefinger as we walked into the village cemetery, which was located right in the middle of the community.

The cemetery was enormous. It took up the equivalent of two city blocks, and the grounds were enclosed on all sides by tall cinder-block walls. "Grounds," actually, might be the wrong word. Not a patch of green grass was anywhere in sight, and if there hadn't been gravestones and crosses popping up out of the dirt and rocks, you might have mistaken it for an abandoned lot.

It seemed that every man, woman, and child in Hunuku was there. Standing among the graves, they formed a wide semicircle five people deep around the village priest. Each grave site was in worse condition than the next. Some tombstones were crumbling, while entire plots in some areas were sinking. In the scorching heat, with a small number of women holding umbrellas to protect themselves from the sun, the priest led the village in prayer and then offered Communion.

Nobody left when the service ended. The entire village fanned out into the cemetery to spend additional time at family graves. Women who appeared to be in their late seventies leaned over tombstones and placed candles and handpicked bouquets on top of them. Children as young as two knelt down and adjusted the wooden crosses that had the names of their ancestors painted on them. Benito placed the pink flower he'd just picked onto his grandfather's grave and stayed there, head bowed, for ten minutes in silent reflection.

When people began to leave, not a single grave appeared untouched. The same cemetery that had been dull and lifeless just an hour before was now splattered like a Jackson Pollock painting in a sea of pink, yellow, and purple flowers and green stems. Before my journey to Mexico, I had never been to a cemetery like the one I saw in Hunuku. At first glance, it was so ugly and in such bad disrepair it was shocking. But as Lalo and I drove away that afternoon, I began to think it was the most beautiful cemetery I had ever seen.

In other parts of Mexico, the Day of the Dead is celebrated in more extravagant ways. Xcaret (pronounced, Esh-kar-et), a gargantuan cultural amusement park located on Cancun's popular Riviera Maya, devotes four full days to the holiday. The rest of the year, visitors snorkel off the park's artificial reefs, visit replicas of Mayan villages (which look strikingly similar to the Tuzes' home), and see costumed actors re-creating pre-Hispanic games. On the day I went, families stood in line for tickets like they were going to Six Flags or Busch Gardens.

As I walked through the turnstile, I was immediately welcomed by Xcaret's Day of the Dead mascot—an adult-sized clown skeleton. It was a woman, I think, wearing a hot pink dress, with a yellow boa around her neck. On her head was a black sombrero with fake purple and yellow flowers clustered on top. Her face was painted to look like a skeleton's, and fake teeth were drawn across her upper and lower lips to make her mouth look even more grotesque. Children posed for pictures with her like she was Mickey Mouse.

Throughout the park various Day of the Dead souvenirs were for sale, including colorful candy skulls. The skulls were made out of sugar and were displayed in baskets like Easter eggs. Children traditionally pick one with their own name on it or the name of a deceased family member. Popular Mexican names are printed on the foreheads—Jaquelin, Cleofas, Iris—and my favorite, Gilberto. No matter which direction I explored, something magical was unfolding. I sat in an audience of hundreds as puppets chatted back and forth about life and death; I walked through a torchlit plaza to see how artists painstakingly and beautifully arranged thousands of red, beige, and black uncooked beans on the ground to look like freshly dug graves; and I saw a juried group of paintings depicting traditional Day of the Dead altars. Large groups of children were everywhere, and I saw many congregating in front of several outdoor mirrors. The park had provided the mirrors—and endless tubs of black and white face paint—so they could make themselves look like skeletons, too. The kids looked as happy and excited as if it were Halloween.

By far the biggest attraction at the park was the Bridge to Paradise, which wasn't a bridge at all, but an artist-created cemetery. The line of families waiting to see the make-believe burial ground snaked around a large courtyard, and it took me about an hour just to reach the entrance. Tombstones and graves had been elaborately fashioned out of various materials, including concrete, glass, and wood. Some looked like luxurious beds, others like miniature cathedrals. All were highly imaginative and whimsical, and while children pointed, their parents took pictures. At night the entire spectacle was lit by the flash of digital cameras, and from far away the hill looked like it was covered in fireflies.

The park's celebration is so popular that the day before I came, officials counted four hundred children participating in Day of the Dead—specific activities—a 43 percent increase from the year before. And it's not just tourists like me who flood the gates. Leticia Aguerre-bere Salido, manager of traditions for Xcaret's Festival of Life and Death, told me during my visit that 70 percent of all visitors are Mexican. I asked her why she thinks the celebration attracts so much attention. "Mexicans have no discomfort surrounding death," she said. "We believe death isn't death if people don't forget about you."

Salido's comments echoed what I'd heard earlier in the evening from a young Mexican couple who'd come to Xcaret with their five-year-old daughter, Alejandra. Alejandra was dressed head-to-toe in a Day of the Dead costume—a neon orange dress with bright satin ribbons—and her hair was pulled back into Princess Leia pigtails with matching multicolored bows. She might have looked like she was going to a fancy party except her mom, Angelica, had painted her face to look like the clown skeleton. In my best conversational Spanish, I learned that Angelica had lost her father right after her daughter was born. "Is it hard for you to talk about your father to your daughter?" I asked.

"For me," she replied, "it's not hard because since my dad die he's my angel." Angelica adjusted Alejandra on her hip and continued. "Ever since Alejandra was a little baby, always I tell her that your grandpa, my dad, is in heaven, and he take care of us."

"You talk about him openly?"

"Always. Every day."

"In America, I think parents rarely talk about the people who have died. How does Alejandra respond to talking about someone she may not remember?"

"It's natural. Because since she born I was talking with her about Dad."

"So it's just normal?"

"Yes. Normal."

It was at that moment her husband interjected with a grin that said, *Poor you. You just don't get it.* Of his late father-in-law he stated what was for him and his family so obvious: "He is part of our family."

The Power of Connecting with Other Parentless Parents

I wish I could say my parents were a part of my family. But like most Americans, I've been conditioned to live my life separate from my losses. As a country, we don't have rituals in place to keep the memory of our parents alive for our children. Experts say it's because we don't have traditions like Obon and Dia de Los Muertos (and many other celebrations like them around the world) that the United States has more bereavement support groups than any other nation on earth. We have to be proactive to find support. It's not natural. It's work.

Ed Madara, director of the American Self-Help Group Clearinghouse, has been tracking the growth of support groups in the United States and abroad for more than thirty years, and says that people seek out the support of strangers when they can't find what they need in their own communities. "Finding a support group is like finding someone who speaks English when you're in a foreign country," he says. "I use the term 'ultimate empathy.' You finally feel you are not alone. You finally can talk to someone who understands."

Madara and his team research the location and purpose of support groups across the country, and every year the Clearinghouse updates its keyword-searchable database, the Self-Help Group Sourcebook, on-line. In the latest hard copy available, hundreds of groups were listed under eight separate headings. In the "Bereavement" section I saw groups listed for seemingly every form of loss—the loss of a spouse, dealing with suicide—but not one group was devoted exclusively to parent loss. Likewise, when I looked under the header "Family/Parenting," there were plenty of groups for "Foster Families" and "Step-parenting," but not a single listing for parenting without your parents.

After *Always Too Soon* was published, men and women emailed me wanting to talk about being an adult orphan. Many of these emails specifically addressed the challenges of being a parent without parents. To manage the influx of emails, I began sorting them by state and city, and then, when I had two or three from any one area, I started playing matchmaker. It was from putting these strangers together that Parentless Parents, the organization, was formed.

Hilari Graff and Judy Kalvin-Stiefel met at a Parentless Parents meeting in Westchester, New York, and instantly hit it off. They have a lot in common, after all. They both work in public relations. They both have daughters. And they both lost their mothers first, when they were twenty-four. But the two women were most shocked to learn that they shared something else—a neighborhood. Before that March evening, Judy and Hilari had no idea they lived just three blocks apart. Of their new friendship, Judy says, "It's like, ahhhhh, there's somebody else who has a similar situation, who deals with similar kinds of things, who 'gets it.' Like when Hilari's planning her Thanksgiving dinner, she's thinking the same things I'm thinking of." Their friendship is bound to grow even more because Judy's daughter is just beginning to babysit for Hilari's children, Rachel and Alex.

Down the East Coast, in Florida, Julie Hallman says she has specifically sought friendships with women because they're parentless parents. Take her friend Sharon, for instance. Julie and Sharon met before their kids were in preschool, and even though their children no longer attend school together, they've continued to make their friendship a priority. "She understands me. I understand her. We get each other," Julie says.

"Would you not be friends if you both weren't parentless?" I ask her skeptically.

"We would not naturally be friends. We wouldn't. But we have something in common. We just relate so well. We accept each other for who we are, with all our issues, and just being there for each other if we need to talk or vent."

Cindi Hartmann, the Michigan mom who found herself overcome with jealousy at her daughter's dance performance, has found great support in a friendship she's developed with another parentless parent at work. Cindi and Lori are both secretaries in an elementary school. For open-house events, they're the ones responsible for signing in grandparents and directing them to their grandchild's classroom. When they have to call parents to pick up a sick child, they'll often hear, "Oh, let me call my mom." Cindi says their job often feels like an ambush. "I think we just look at each other and wink and know. I think we can read each other like, 'It's getting too much for me.' And she'll jump in and say, 'Let me take that for you.' Or vice versa." Cindi says she doubts they'd be so close if they weren't both parentless parents.

Indeed, more than even in their own spouses and siblings, parentless parents find comfort in one another. While close to 70 percent say friends with living parents don't truly understand what's it's like for them to be a parent without parents, a massive 82 percent say friends who have also lost their parents do understand.

If you're still skeptical about the power of community to transform an otherwise isolating experience, let me tell you about the focus groups I conducted for this book. Some participants lost their parents when they were children, others when they were grown. Some had close relationships with their mothers and fathers, others' were complicated. No matter their experiences and backgrounds, these men and women soon discovered there was more that linked them as parents than separated them. And it was from that simple realization that something magical occurred. They understood they weren't alone.

For the discussions I held in California, I attracted participants with a blurb on Jen's List — an email newsletter for parents in the Los Angeles area. Within minutes of the post going live, I received so many requests to participate I decided to conduct several focus groups in the region instead of just the one I had originally planned. For each session, when the men and women arrived at my borrowed office near Santa Monica, they sat in the reception area about as far away from one another as possible, and when I came out to greet them, they'd follow me inside silently to begin.

To help break the ice, I set up a few platters of food and bottled water. As they mulled over their choices — wraps, potato chips, fruit salad, chocolate and vanilla cookies — the room remained mostly quiet, with a smattering of small talk. After about ten minutes of eating and drinking, I'd tell them it was time to get started and encourage everyone to sit down.

I arranged it so each time we'd sit in a cozy circle. Behind me, over my left shoulder, was a video camera on a tripod. After I went through my prepared remarks, I asked the group to go around the room and introduce themselves.

"I guess I'll start," said a woman in the second group who'd been fidgeting in her seat. "My name is Rachel and I have two girls. One who'll be eleven in March, and the other one is sixteen. My mom passed away when my oldest was three, so thirteen years ago. My dad died when I was fourteen. I'm forty-eight years old."

Rachel stopped talking, and the woman sitting to her right began speaking next.

"I'm Denise and I have three kids. I have four-and-a-half-year-old twins and a two-year-old girl. The twins are a boy and a girl. My dad's been gone sixteen years. He died when I was thirty, six years after my mom died. My mom died suddenly, right before my husband and I got engaged." A gasp of empathy sounds through the group. "So she knew my husband and knew we were going to get married, but wasn't there for the . . ." Denise didn't finish her sentence, but we knew what she was going to say. After a beat of silence she ended her opening remarks on an upswing. "And I'm forty-six."

All eyes went to the next woman. She was petite and looked to be the youngest of the group.

"I'm Kim and I'm thirty-seven. My mom died when I was fourteen and she was thirty-eight, so I'm coming up on that. My dad died last year. I kinda lost my dad twice, though, because I was estranged from him for many years, and just as we started rekindling our relationship, he died." Despite what she was saying, Kim's voice had a high-pitched, happy quality. "I have a one-year-old daughter and a four-year-old son."

Next, the last woman of the group.

"I'm Tanya and I have two kids. I have a twenty-two-year-old girl who's in college and a fifteen-year-old boy. I'll be fifty-four in a couple of weeks. I lost my mother a little over twenty years ago and my dad seven years ago." I found myself taken aback a little, because Tanya went on to say that her father died of lung cancer and her mother died of ovarian cancer — just like my parents.

The final introduction was made by the only man in the group.

"My name's Steve and I'll be sixty in a couple of weeks. I have a nineteen-year-old son," he said. "For me, the dynamic is much different than anybody else here. I lost my parents in a car accident when I was thirteen years old. So I've been parentless pretty much my whole life.

The dynamic for me is different than losing them one at a time as I grew older." Steve had an edge to his voice. Was he regretting being here, or was that just the way he sounded making a point?

With introductions complete, it was time for my first question. I made it as open-ended as possible to see how the conversation flowed.

"The first thing I want to talk with you about is what is it like, emotionally, to be a parent without your parents? Do your friends 'get it'?"

Tanya was the first to jump in. "Absolutely not. There's that huge vacuum. In an emergency, they'll come forward. If I had a child in the hospital. But they are not there for the regular and happy stuff. You want to call somebody and say your kid got straight A's on his report card, and who do you call?"

"Right," agreed Denise, who was sitting on the opposite side of the couch.

"You don't call your girlfriend because they're like—" another interjected before realizing Denise wasn't done speaking.

"They think you're bragging," Denise continued.

"Yeah," Tanya said. "And even the sibling thing gets dicey." I knew personally, of course, what Tanya was talking about.

"How do you feel about being a parent without parents?" I said in Rachel's direction.

"I actually hadn't thought about it a lot until I saw your ad. But that said, it's isolating. There's no question about it." She looked around the circle, making eye contact with everyone. "A real good friend of mine, both her parents live down the street, and she made me realize how little she 'gets' my situation. She's one of those moms who complains about how hard her life is, but her mother's around the corner and she shares her house with her dad. She doesn't realize when you got your parents, your kids have that, too."

"How about you, Denise?"

"My little girl is starting to ask me questions about when I was a little girl and I don't want to make it up." Her voice was soft and barely audible. "My mother was always able to tell us about the four of us, and she loved doing it. And now my kids are asking me and I don't have the recollections. I desperately miss that. Fortunately, I can ask my older sister questions and she can fill in some memories."

"Kim," I said, directing the conversation to her, "do you feel that being a parent without parents is an isolating experience?"

Kim nodded. "Completely. There was a time when I was pregnant, I had so many complications, and doctors would ask me, 'Well, did your mom have these kind of complications?' I just had no one to ask. But it really wasn't until my son turned three—the age at which I could actually recall my own childhood—that all these memories of my mom started coming back and it made me very happy and very sad all at the same time." There was a pause or two before she added, "It was easier earlier in my life than it has been recently."

"You think it's harder now that you're a mom?"

"It is. Completely," she answered.

"When are you reminded of being a parentless parent? Are there times when you feel more reminded of your parents' absence than others?"

"It's ever-present," Denise said.

"During the course of a routine day, do you ever get jealous of other people's parents?" I asked.

All four women laughed out loud and almost in unison shouted,

"Absolutely!"

"Yeah"

"All the time!"

"Yup!"

Steve held back his comments until the women finished laughing. Then he simply stated, "No." Denise pressed on without acknowledging him. "Especially that Grandparents Day. It kills me."

"Why?" I asked.

"My kids are in preschool, and last year was their first Grandparents Day. Mine were the only children who had no grandparents there." Her voice began to wobble. "And my kids were very cognizant of the fact that there was nobody there."

Steve interrupted before Denise could say anything more. "I can't be sad for my son for people he didn't know," he stated. The comment landed like a thud, and all four women sat in silence, chewing it over.

Kim was the first to break the momentary lag in conversation with her high, upbeat voice. "The time I feel the worst about my parents not being part of my children's lives is when my in-laws are with them. I just feel my husband's mom and dad are so very different from my own parents, and they're the only grandparent influence that they have in their lives. I just feel that it's unfair, and it's probably very selfish thinking, but I just feel there's nothing from my history being contributed."

Once again there was agreement around the horn, and this time Steve was in alignment, too. "I can identify with that," he said.

"I can identify with that a lot," Rachel agreed.

"I identify very strongly with what Kim was saying," Denise added. "I'm Jewish. My husband is not. They are very supportive, but they are very different, and not just from a religious perspective but—"

"Cultural," Steve added.

"Cultural," Denise agreed.

"I have the same thing," Steve said.

"And even in education," Denise went on. "It's not a value judgment on them, but it's different. My parents were very cerebral, and that's what I try to impart to my kids."

"This whole issue of marriage seems to be a big topic for a lot of parentless parents," I added. "Are both your in-laws still living?" I said, looking in Steve's direction, trying to engage him further.

"My wife's mother and father have just passed away in the last few years. So my son had grandparents. And while they were not who I would have picked, given the dream I had for my life—I wouldn't have taken away that relationship from my son for anything."

I turned my gaze away from Steve and scanned the rest of the group. "Has there ever been envy or jealousy that's shown up because your spouse has their parents?"

All four women answered with a resounding "yes," and while Steve was the only member of the group to say he didn't feel jealous or envious of his spouse, he said there was so much about him that his wife just didn't understand. "One day she was on the phone to our son and she thought he'd gotten into an accident or somebody shot him. Someone screamed, 'Watch out!' and the phone went dead. There was about fifteen minutes when she was in like total panic mode. When we finally calmed down, she said, 'You just didn't know what I went through.' And I said, 'Honey, now you know what my life has been. Forever.' She looked at me and apologized." His story was met with multiple sighs of understanding.

"Has anyone ever pushed their in-laws away because it's a reminder of what you don't have?"

"Away from me emotionally, but never away from the kids," Denise said. "It's my issue I have to deal with. Not that I don't want them here, it's just that I'm pissed off that they're here and mine aren't." I saw heads move up and down.

"Has having been through loss impacted the way you parent your—"

Kim began nodding her head even before I finished my question.

"Kim, you're already nodding."

"Yeah, definitely," she said. "I feel that I am always cognizant of how I am speaking with my children because my mom left to go to work and died in a car accident and never came home. I never want to send them off to school or part from them in any way without us being on the best of terms. So I carefully choose my words when speaking with them. It's always on the top of my head."

"That must be really hard," I said.

Kim laughed. "Over time, it's becoming more natural."

"That's an exhausting way to parent, right?" I asked, letting her know I understood what she was getting at. "It seems to be a common theme among parentless parents. There's a lot of looking at the way you parent from the outside."

"Oh, yeah. Completely," Kim said.

"But shouldn't everybody be?" Tanya countered. "I think that would be true of any parent—but we're just more aware of it. And I think it's more adding than editing. I always say 'I love you' at the end of *every* single conversation I have with my children, which drives them crazy when they've just talked with me five minutes before. It's because I know. I absolutely know that anything can happen. It makes me feel, in a way, a little more blessed."

Steve continued the thought. "We're all just a product of our experiences, as anybody is," he said. "There's this phrase I use all the time, 'It's part of life's inevitabilities.' It's something I learned at a very young age and it's something I had to prepare my son for—and my wife would get mad at me. I remember when my son, Joey, was about five or six and the movie with the dinosaurs came out, *Land Before Time*. The mommy and daddy die because it's the circle of life. We spent a lot of time with that movie—on purpose. My wife used to get mad at me a lot, saying, 'He's a boy.'"

"What were you preparing him for?"

"Life's inevitabilities. I know a lot of parents who have raised their boys and they've grown up to be *boys*. So I need to take a little more of a mature outlook because I know what's going to happen."

"Yeah, absolutely," Tanya added. "That's the way I find myself parenting. My friends have given me a hard time about this. They say, 'I can't believe you have your children make their own dentist appointments.' When my daughter went to college, she said, 'Mom, I'm the only one who learned how to write a check because you had me doing that stuff so early.' I'm not saying, 'Prepare yourself, I might die.' It's more giving them the skills that would make me feel that they wouldn't be completely lost if I wasn't there."

"Has anyone responded differently and become more controlling because you're scared something will happen to your children?"

"Every day. Scared every day," Steve quickly announced. "When you have children, they start to crawl, and then they start to walk, and then they start to run. But nothing is scarier than when they start to drive. That's when all hell breaks loose. And having lost my parents in a car accident, when he's behind the wheel, you're scared."

"Did you ever prohibit him from driving?"

"No, but the preparation was thorough and goes on to this day. He's incensed, like 'Dad, I'm old enough. I can drive!' But it's a learning process," Steve continued, "always a learning process." Steve was really getting animated now. "He's driving back to college this Sunday because his winter break is over, and I'm going with him. Not because he wants me to. But it's an eight-to-ten-hour drive and I'm not prepared for him to do it alone."

"Is he resentful?"

"Yes."

"Do you care?"

"No." Steve laughed and everyone else laughed, too.

"How about you, Denise? How do you feel your parenting has shifted?"

There was a pause, and we all turned our eyes on Denise while we waited for her to respond. Instead of talking, though, her chin started to tremble. "Should I switch topics?" I asked. "What's making you cry?"

"I'm not separated from the loss. It's too big a void," she said. "People always say it gets easier and I always say, 'No, it just gets different.'" The two women sitting closest to Denise reached out to her. One took her hand; the other rubbed her back.

I tried to gently continue the conversation. "Rachel, do you think your parenting has been impacted by loss?"

"It's funny," she said. "I hadn't thought about that at all until now. I do want my girls to be independent, self-sufficient, and I'm not the kind of parent that tries to do everything for them. They have certain things they're responsible for. At eight or nine my youngest was doing her own laundry. Like you were saying," she gestured to Tanya, "they make their own dentist appointments. I think there's some positive to that."

With Rachel looking in her direction, Tanya started to speak again. "Sometimes I won't go to certain things," she said. The fifty-three-year-old mom recalled how she couldn't bring herself to join her family for Christmas Eve services last year because it was too painful without her mom. And in reference to Denise's earlier comments about Grandparents Day, Tanya added, "For years my kids and I just didn't go."

"You pulled them out?"

"Yeah, we just wouldn't show up at school," she said. "Because they went a couple of times and came home in tears. There was this no-show because my ex-husband's parents are gone, too." Tanya called her boycott an act of "self-care."

"There's one major thing related to parenting that was influenced by my parents' deaths," Kim said, "and that is to have two children. I felt so utterly alone with no siblings after losing my parents that I was not going to have one child."

Steve agreed and took Kim's conviction one step further. "I feel more guilty about not providing my son a sibling than a grandparent." There were nods of acknowledgment all around.

"Let's talk about keeping the memory of your parents alive for your children. Do you feel like it's a parenting responsibility like any other?"

"It's important," Steve said quickly.

"Do you ever find yourself purposefully telling stories about your parents?"

"All the time," he continued. "Because that's who I am and it's important that he knows who I am. It's about legacy." There are limitations, though, Steve said. "I can't force the memory of my mother and father upon him because that was decades ago," he said, referring to when his parents died. "That's ancient history."

"It comes naturally," Tanya offered. "I want to talk about my parents and it just comes up."

"I avoid it," Kim said sharply.

"You avoid it?" I responded, encouraging her to continue.

"I do," she went on. "Because immediately my facial expression will change and I'll get sad. I mean, my four-year-old is probably at the age where I probably could say, 'Grandpa liked to do this, or . . .' But it makes me very uneasy. I want to do it later, I just . . ."

As Kim stopped speaking, Rachel immediately tried to make her feel better. "You know what?" she said affectionately. "I felt that way when mine were younger, but now I'm finding I'm sharing more. I think part of the reason I held off for so long was because I didn't want to risk sharing something that wasn't good. My parents were both alcoholics. It was a bad marriage. So I think I waited awhile because I didn't want to slip up and start telling a story and then go, 'Ooops! Can't tell you that part.' I've gotten more at ease with it, and now that they're older I'm starting to pull out the good stuff."

"I try to talk about my parents all the time," Denise added. "Part of it is a responsibility and part of it is desire. My twins are each named for my parents, and so I talk about my parents so they understand who they're named for. My conflict is choosing what I should be sharing. What's age appropriate? Because my children will understand me better when they know where I come from. But when I do talk about them, I completely romanticize and idealize the relationship I had with my mother, and I don't think they should grow up thinking that my mother was the greatest mother, because she wasn't."

Steve offered a solution. "You tell them how you want them to remember her." He added, "It doesn't have to be the whole person."

"You can be selective," somebody else encouraged. I could see the gears working in Denise's head, and also Rachel's.

"It's almost eight o'clock," I said, looking at my watch. "I'm sensitive to everyone's schedules and wanting to get home. There's one last question. If you can summarize: What is the biggest challenge you face as a parentless parent? What is *the* issue that makes parentless parents different from parents who have their parents?"

Rachel was the first to answer. "It feels heavier. It just feels like the responsibility is bigger because I don't have extended family to help."

"I'd say keeping my family history alive," Denise added. "In religious school growing up, every year we did a family tree and my parents helped. I realize I've got to be able to sit down with my kids and it's going to be hard for me."

"Because you don't have the information?"

"Because I don't have the information. It's a burden and responsibility because I want to do it well. I don't resent it. I want to do it. I feel it to be incredibly important. [But] it's really hard. My mother kept everyone alive. She told stories about everybody."

"I think just having to be all things to them," Kim said next.

"Just keeping the strength up for the journey when there isn't the reserve behind you," Tanya offered. "I now have a fifteen-year-old and he's getting very snarky. He's right on schedule, in other words. And because I'm not married right now, there's really nobody in my corner. Just someone saying, 'Don't talk to your mother that way.' Just to have my back a little bit. I think that's the biggest challenge."

Steve got the last word. "My dad died when he was thirty-eight; I was thirteen. I didn't have him a long time. But I still feel as though we had enough time. He taught me some important things, and I've imparted them to my son because the only thing we do as parents is prepare them for when *they* are. It's the things you want to carry on."

And with that final thought, the focus group ended.

As the participants gathered their belongings, the conversation continued among them. Nobody left the room until everyone was ready. I was the last one out and followed closely behind, listening. Down the hall, past the reception area, and into the hallway, they chatted. And while they waited for the elevator, I noticed two of them exchanging phone numbers and email addresses.

I walked back to the office after the elevator doors shut. It would take me a half hour to clean the room and leave it in such a way there'd be no trace of what had just taken place. As I slid my voice recorder back into its nylon sleeve, dismantled the video equipment, and threw away all the dirty plates and cups, I replayed the last ninety minutes in my mind. And I noticed how little had been eaten.

Chapter 9

A Day to Call Your Own

"I wanted my children to see their heritage from my side of the family."

"All they talked about was how much she looked like 'so and so' on their side of the family. In my head I was screaming, 'She looks like my side of the family!! Can't you see that?!' But the hard part was they couldn't see it. There was no one to see it."

"I am sad that my daughters will never know my parents. They will always be just people in a picture to them."

—from the Parentless Parents Survey

There's a simple explanation for why this group of strangers, when put in a room together, would find comfort. I think the reason can be summed up in just one word: relief. It is a relief to know you are not the only person who still grieves the loss of his or her parents (even though it may have been years since they died), and it feels good to know there are other parents who struggle with the same challenges raising their children.

Sharing common experiences is why support groups are often so successful. And why, for much the same reason, the focus groups I conducted for this book were as constructive as I'd hoped.

Researchers have long sought to measure the effectiveness of support groups. In 2002, Dr. Keith Humphreys, a professor of psychiatry and behavioral sciences at the Stanford University School of Medicine, collaborated on a scientific review that is still regarded as the most comprehensive on the topic. Specifically, but not surprisingly, Humphreys and his colleagues found that groups led by members (like every chapter of Parentless Parents) are frequently more helpful to participants than meetings run by professionals who don't share the same problem or condition. Smokers in these peer-led groups quit the habit for greater periods of time, widows and widowers feel less depressed, and breast cancer patients live longer. When you don't have to pretend everything's okay, even to the leader of your own support group, you can simply exhale. And heal.

Deep breaths, though, are harder to come by outside these settings. If we take even a moment to remember our parents during any of the major holidays, will our children feel like we're inserting something artificial or, worse, depressing into their celebration? If we acknowledge our own sadness, might we dampen their good spirits? As a parentless parent, I think it's easy to say that most holidays in America — even religious ones — are primarily set aside for festivity, not reflection. We are a nation, as author Barbara Ehrenreich argues in her book *Bright-Sided,* that expects syrupy happiness and a positive outlook all the time.

The holidays that seem to have the greatest push-pull are Mother's Day and Father's Day. Remarkably, nearly 50 percent of all parentless parents find themselves grieving more on these special days than celebrating. It is often difficult to remember your mother and rejoice over your life as a mother at the same time. From nursery school on, we are trained to celebrate Mother's Day and Father's Day, first by making our parents cards out of construction paper and pipe cleaners, and later by buying them gifts. Our role as sons and daughters is clearly defined. And when we become parents, we also know what we're supposed to do: receive all the attention and smile, smile, smile!

But what if on Mother's Day and Father's Day you'd rather crawl under the covers? What if we don't want to buy our mother-in-law a card, make all the plans to see her, or cook dinner for her, either? Every year Americans purchase more than 200 million cards for Mother's Day and Father's Day, and I used to be one of those people. What am I supposed to do now that my parents are gone? Just move on as if nothing has changed? As if being a mom myself has somehow removed the part of me that was also a daughter?

A Day to Call Our Own

In early 2008, Hilari Graff and I were discussing this very point. Since we met, she'd become leader of the Westchester County, New York, chapter of Parentless Parents. She and I were complaining that there wasn't any time of year set aside just for us—parentless parents who want to honor the parents we no longer have in our lives. Our telephone conversation went something like this:

"Maybe we could get all the chapters of Parentless Parents together and create something?" Hilari suggested.

"Like what?" I responded eagerly. "You mean something like Motherless Daughter's Day?" I had attended several Motherless Daughters' luncheons in California, New York, and Michigan and always found them cathartic. The events are almost always held the day before Mother's Day so women who attend can honor their mothers' memory on Saturday and still be available to their own families on Sunday.

"Yes," Hilari agreed. "But we'd need to include our dads, too."

Hilari was right. I remember giving a speech about being a parentless parent at a Metro Detroit Motherless Daughter's Day luncheon and a woman came up to me afterward to thank me for coming. She was animated and excited. "I've always gotten something out of these events, but most of the people who come, their fathers are still alive. I was a young girl with a dead father before I was motherless. When I come here, I grieve for both of them. This," she said, referring to my talk, "was finally about me."

"You're right," I told Hilari. "We can't hold an event tied to just Mother's Day or Father's Day. We need to honor both." We started brainstorming. "Is there some sort of 'Parents' Day'? Or maybe just a day we could set aside to honor our parents as grandparents?" I asked.

Ironically, the idea that ultimately got us the most excited was to informally re-purpose the mission of Grandparents Day to honor, in the case of parentless parents, those grandparents who are no longer with us. We thought the holiday provided an unparalleled opportunity for celebrating the memory of our mothers and fathers.

Digging through the National Grandparents Day website, I discovered it was the brainchild of Marian McQuade, a stay-at-home mom of fifteen children living in West Virginia. Her chief motivation, according to the home page, "was to champion the cause of lonely elderly in nursing homes." She also wanted to "persuade grandchildren to tap the wisdom and heritage their grandparents could provide."

In 1973, McQuade began a grassroots campaign to create a special day honoring grandparents. After months of letter writing and telephone calls to her local and state representatives, she found sympathetic ears in state senator Shirley Love and United States senator Jennings Randolph. Her efforts were indefatigable, and culminated in the 1978 signing of the National Grandparents Day proclamation by President Jimmy Carter. President Carter said then, "Just as a nation learns and is strengthened by its history, so a family learns and is strengthened by its understanding of preceding generations." From then on, National Grandparents Day would be celebrated every year on the first Sunday after Labor Day.

Before we put our plan into motion, I felt we should let Marian McQuade know. I wanted her blessing to add this new dimension to her work. Within a few days I was in touch with Kathleen McQuade Eye, one of Marian McQuade's daughters, and we arranged a time and date for me to meet her mom in person. I'd be the first journalist to speak with her mother in more than ten years.

On April 26, 2008, I set out for the long drive to the Hill Top Center—a nursing home tucked away in Oak Hill, West Virginia. Hill Top, aptly named, sits alone at the peak of Saddle Shop Road, and when I pulled into the parking lot it reminded me of a motel. The redbrick exterior was long and slim, and its small windows were decorated with beige shutters.

Kathleen was waiting for me in the entryway, and I instantly liked her. She talked about her ninety-one-year-old mother with a great deal of love and enthusiasm, and she even brought a manila envelope full of newspaper clippings and photographs for me to see, related to her mother's life's work. Dressed in a plain shirt and without makeup, Kathleen was every bit the no-nonsense woman I imagined her mother to be.

Down the hall, inside Room 312, we found Marian McQuade. Her eyes were closed and she didn't seem to notice that Kathleen and I had entered. Marian's petite body was covered head to toe in a colorful quilt, and she had a ploof of white hair peeking out from the top of the blanket. Kathleen went over to her mother's bed and told her I was in the room. "Mother," she said in a loud, deliberate voice. "Allison Gilbert is here. Remember, you're having a visitor today." When her mother didn't respond, Kathleen, unconcerned, tried to get her mother's attention again. "Allison is the journalist I told you about from New York. She's here to meet you, Mama." I stood a few feet behind them, closer to the door, and while I could hear that Marian eventually did reply to her daughter, she spoke so softly I couldn't hear what she said.

As Kathleen continued to talk with her mother and adjust her matching quilt and pillow, I noticed that nearly every inch of the room was covered in photographs, articles, and typewritten letters — reminding Marian and anyone who entered of the crusade that had consumed her younger life. It looked like a time capsule had exploded. There was even an enormous greeting card taped to the wall that wished her a "Happy Grandparents Day." It was hand-signed by at least forty people, with the inscription "Thanks to you from all of us at Fayetteville Walmart for making this day a reality." And there were so many snapshots of her grandchildren, Kathleen told me forty at last count, that the bulletin board next to her bed couldn't hold them all and the overflow was tacked with pushpins directly into the wall. When Kathleen was done making sure her mother was comfortable, she welcomed me to sit next to her.

I drew up a chair next to Marian's bedside, and with her eyes still closed, I told her how honored I was to meet her. I also told her about my mom and dad and the plan Hilari and I had to use Grandparents Day to extend the legacy of all grandparents — even those who are no longer living. After every sentence or two, I'd pause for a few moments, purposefully leaving her an opening to talk, but she never did. I began to wonder if she understood anything I was saying. Periodically I'd look up during my monologue and ask Kathleen with my eyes if I should continue. Every time, she nodded that I should.

When my visit came to an end, I slowly stood up from my chair and thanked Kathleen for allowing me to come. She was apologetic that her mother was having an "off" day, and she even seemed a little embarrassed that I had come all that way for what she thought amounted to so little. I told Kathleen I'd never regret meeting a national hero. Before I left, I leaned over to give Marian McQuade a kiss good-bye, and when my lips briefly touched her cheek, she said in a voice so weak that I had to strain to hear it, "Thank you."

I drove away from the nursing home completely elated and got myself back on the highway. Within a few minutes, I passed one of those huge green traffic signs standing tall on the side of the road. In white letters it announced for every motorist to see, "Home of Marian McQuade: Founder of National Grandparents Day."

The First Grandparents Day Celebration— Just for Parentless Parents

On Sunday, September 7, 2008, members of Parentless Parents extended the mission of Grandparents Day. We gathered at Tibbetts Brook Park in Yonkers, New York, and celebrated the grandparents our children no longer had in their lives.

We had activities for kids of all ages. Children decorated wooden frames to hold pictures of their grandparents and they planted forget-me-not flowers. Below are some of the activities we offered and some others we added in subsequent years. (The first two were modeled after events created by an extraordinary group of women for the inaugural Motherless Daughter's Day celebration in May 1996 and continue to flourish to this day.) You may want to consider them for your own celebration.

Circle of Remembrance. Parents and children joined hands and formed a big, open circle. Beginning with one of the adults, we went around the circle and one at a time said the names of our parents or grandparents out loud for everyone to hear. For example, I said, "Allison, daughter of Lynn and Sidney." Lexi said, "Lexi, granddaughter of Lynn and Sidney." The impact was enormous. It's rare that we have the opportunity to say and hear our parents' names spoken out loud.

Balloon Launch. Each adult and child received a helium-filled balloon. With a dark-colored Sharpie the adults wrote messages to our parents, and our children wrote messages to their grandparents. After everyone was done, we walked to a clearing and released the balloons into the sky. It was heartwarming to see so many balloons representing all our parents. Since our first launch, we've found biodegradable balloons, making the exercise both touching and environmentally responsible.

Make-a-Frame. Children decorated wooden frames to hold pictures of their grandparents. For the youngest children, we provided paint, glue, gems, buttons, and glitter. Older children used permanent markers and wrote notes to their grandparents along the perimeter.

Forget-Me-Nots. Children received a packet of forget-me-not seeds and a plastic, recyclable pot. Each child filled a pot with soil, planted the seeds, and decorated the pot with paint and markers.

Recipe Exchange. Each parentless parent took an index card and wrote down a favorite recipe that belonged to his or her mother or father. After Grandparents Day concluded, the recipes were typed and distributed via email to any participant who wanted them.

Potluck Lunch. All the adults brought dishes to share that reminded us of our childhoods. I was surprised how much this activity ended up meaning to me.

While I have a number of my mother's recipes, I have a block about making them. I find myself paralyzed because I don't think I can truly replicate them. What if it doesn't come out just how I remember it? So it wasn't until the second Parentless Parents Grandparents Day celebration — more than thirteen years after my mother's death — that I dug out my mom's famous (okay, maybe just famous to me) fruit tart recipe and with Lexi's help tried to make it. It was one of my favorite desserts growing up, and I hadn't tasted it or smelled it since my mother passed away.

My mom's recipe is handwritten on an index card and reads exactly like this:

FRUIT PLATTER PIE   *(serves 12 – 14)*

1 Pkg—2 Crust Pie
1 Pt. Strawberries/Halved (Save 6 whole w/ leaves)
1 Can (20 oz) Pineapple Spears
1½ Cups Seedless Grapes
1 banana
2 TBSP. Sugar

Prepare 2 Pie Crusts. Roll Dough 1" larger than 14" Pizza Pan. Flute edges. Prick bottom + sides. Bake 8–10 min. Cool.

Arrange in concentric circles — strawberry halves around edge, pineapple, grapes, bananas, whole strawberries with leaves. Sprinkle w/ sugar + orange sauce. (over)

ORANGE SAUCE

1 Cup Sugar
¼ Tsp. Salt
2 TBSP Cornstarch
1 Cup Orange Juice
¼ cup Lemon Juice
¾ Cup H_2O
½ Tsp Grated Orange Peel
½ "   "   Lemon   "

Mix sugar, salt, cornstarch, stir in OJ, lemon juice + water. Cook Med. Heat. Stir constantly until thick + boils for one min. Remove from heat + stir in ½ Tsp grated orange peel + ½ lemon peel.

As soon as I began shopping for the ingredients, I felt an unexpected rush of happiness. In trying to read my mom's handwriting and decipher her directions, I felt like she and I were having a conversation. And not unlike some of the ones we used to have, I was confused by her very first sentence. Did she mean one of those graham cracker crusts? They couldn't be the ones she meant, because when Lexi and I saw them in the supermarket, I told her they didn't look anything like what I remembered. We went to customer service for help.

"Hi," I said, cheerfully. "My mom's [My mom's! When was the last time I said that to a stranger?!] recipe calls for pie crusts and I know she doesn't mean the graham cracker shells. Do you sell pre-made dough?"

I knew my mom would never have made crusts from scratch. She was one of those moms who bought supermarket cupcakes, unpacked them from the plastic container, and passed them off as her own at school bake sales. "No, we don't sell dough," the woman behind the counter said. Hmm. I was really confused. How did my mom make this pie? Then the woman behind the counter made a suggestion. "Maybe she means the pre-made crusts?"

I never heard of such a thing. "Oh, that must be it! Where can I find them?"

"Go to Aisle 6. They're right next to the milk."

Lexi and I dashed off to Aisle 6, and sure enough, we found boxes of ready-made pie crusts. I squeezed Lexi's hand in excitement and she jumped up and down. *Mom, we found it!* We finished the rest of the shopping and went home.

I washed the grapes and strawberries and handed them to Lexi to slice with her bright red child-safe knife. As she cut, I looked at Mom's index card for further instructions and started laughing hysterically. I may have even snorted! Who writes "concentric circles" on a recipe card?! My mother was a math major in college, and right at that moment her presence radiated through me like I had just settled into a warm, luxurious bath. Concentric circles. H_2O. That was Mom, all right. Everything done with precision. And quickly. Who had time to write down a recipe longhand when you were busy running a company and raising two kids?!

Lexi asked me what was so funny, and I showed her what Grandma had written. That launched me into telling her a story about Grandma Lynn I'd never thought to share. Throughout my childhood, Mom had told her secretary to always put my calls through. Anytime, no matter what. I told Lexi how good this made me feel. That even though Grandma Lynn worked full-time and was always dealing with important meetings, she made me feel I was the most important girl in the world. "That's how you make me feel, Mom," Lexi said, picking a stray leaf off a strawberry. My heart melted. In some very real way, my mother was with us. She was helping her daughter and granddaughter make that pie. And when the sauce began to simmer, it smelled like it, too.

I now look forward to Grandparents Day with the same kind of excitement as a child anticipating Christmas morning. It's a day when I can take care of my own needs and without any self-consciousness join other moms and dads in remembering our parents and honoring their place in our children's lives.

And by knowing that I'll have the time and space to grieve and reflect in September, I am more fully able to engage with Mark's parents in May and June. It also leaves me room on Mother's Day to celebrate my life as a mom—not just mourn my lost life as a daughter.

Fredda Wasserman, clinical director of adult programs and education at Our House, a grief-support center in Los Angeles, says setting aside time to focus on loss and remember can make even the toughest times easier. "While it's important to take time for yourself—maybe journaling, maybe spending time in the fresh air, maybe doing something in memory of your parents—it's also really helpful to be with other people, and often it's healing to include your children. You can say, 'I'm your dad, but my dad died and I really miss him.' That is part of our healing process and it's part of the legacy we provide for our children. We can show them that people have strong reactions to death and that grieving goes on for a long time and it's not a bad thing."

The parentless parents version of Grandparents Day could never be confused with the Day of the Dead in Mexico. We don't honor our parents alongside the rest of the country, and entire neighborhoods don't pour into Tibbetts Brook Park to celebrate with us. But on a much smaller scale, Grandparents Day is a time when we don't have to carry the burden of grieving and remembering alone. As Hilari Graff explains, "You're sharing something with people who can understand your feelings in a way that even your closest friends may not."

Chapter 10

Loss Can Make Better Parents

"There is nothing I can do to bring them back so I try not to get upset about it. Sure, I would have loved for my daughter to know them but the best I can do is have her experience my parents through my actions."

"I love how my boys have bits of my parents in them. It brings me great joy to see it."

"Do I wish my children had grandparents? Absolutely! Do I wish I had a shoulder to cry on over the years? Definitely! But I have used the experience to show my children that we are all stronger than we think. While it's difficult to see the blessings in losing my parents so young, I am who I am today because I did."

—from the Parentless Parents Survey

T*his book ends where it* began—at my brother's house in Pennsylvania. It was December, and Mark and I went down with the kids to celebrate Chanukah. The trip took a little longer than usual, and soon after we arrived Mark offered to unpack and get Jake and

Lexi settled so I could go for a walk. Jay jumped at the chance to get some fresh air, too, and joined me.

My brother lives in the suburbs of Philadelphia, but if you were air-dropped there, you'd assume you'd landed somewhere in the English countryside. He doesn't live so much in a neighborhood as in a rolling landscape dotted with stone houses, some dating back to the 1700s. The paths near his house are a great place to talk, and when we were about twenty minutes into our walk, I don't know exactly why I did it, but I asked Jay a question that I'd been curious about for years but was always too self-conscious to ask. I was afraid he'd be dismissive, and that it would sound harsh and odd coming out of my mouth, which it did.

"Why do you always seem so happy?"

"What are you talking about, Ali?" Jay responded hesitantly.

"I mean, don't you ever miss Mom and Dad? You always seem so fine. Like nothing's ever wrong."

"Because everything is fine. What do I have to complain about?"

Are you joking?! Do we not have the same dead parents? Have you forgotten about Aunt Ronnie and Grandma Bertha, too? Nearly our entire family is gone!

We strolled on without saying another word for five minutes or so, until we could see his house growing bigger and bigger ahead of us. Our walk was clearly almost over, and if left to me the conversation would have ended, too, but at the last possible minute Jay stopped, turned to me, and said with the kind of compassion a teacher shows a struggling student, "Mom and Dad died, and that sucks. But I have a great wife and two great kids. I have a nice house. I like what I do for a living. I have a pretty terrific life. I really don't have much to be upset about." And he added in the most loving, big brotherly way he could, "You have a great life, too, Ali. You married a great man — a man you met when you were eighteen years old. Your kids are healthy and smart," and as a final point of punctuation he added imploringly, "Look forward, Allison."

Like most little sisters, I became instantly defensive. "I do look forward," I protested. "I know I have a lot to be thankful for."

Jay leaned over and wrapped his arms around me on nearly the exact spot where we'd had that uncomfortable embrace so many years before, right after Dad died. "I love you," he said softly into my ear, "but it seems to me like you look back more than you look ahead." He let go of me and turned to walk inside the house. Speechless, I stood in the driveway watching the back of his head until it disappeared behind the side door.

All at once I realized that the anger I had felt toward my brother — for not remembering the anniversaries of Mom's and Dad's deaths, for not needing to talk about them as much as I did — had been thoroughly without cause. What I had long considered indifference was actually Jay's conscious decision to look in a different direction. There was a reason why he had that huge smile on his face when we came to his house that first Thanksgiving after Dad died. He really *was* happy. Not pleased, of course, that Mom and Dad were gone, but happy that I was there. And that I had Mark. And, at that point, Jake. And that he had Randi, and Dexter, and Ria. And we both had Cheryl. He recognized then what I couldn't yet see. Jay was happy because we still had each other.

The Red Sea didn't part that day, and lightning didn't strike. The conversation did, however, lay the foundation for what would become a slow and evolving change in my thinking. Gradually, I've been able to embrace an attitude of gratitude and replace feelings of despair with an appreciation that at least I had parents worth missing.

That's what Sandy Taradash chooses to focus on, too. She told me, almost defiantly, that she's counted her blessings ever since the car accident that landed her in the hospital and killed both her parents. If you're skeptical, as I certainly was at first, here's how she explained her thinking to me:

"Let me tell you this one story that will help define where I come from. When they put me in the hospital, they put me in a room with a girl who had broken her neck in a car accident a few months before I got there. I don't know if you've ever seen a patient who has broken their neck — it's horrible. She was forced to lay flat on her back with two heavy sand bags attached to what looked like nails in her skull to keep her neck from moving. Her father never came to see her in the hospital. Never. She used to cry at night that her daddy didn't care about her.

"Well, lo and behold, a week or so after we were put together, her father called. She was crying, 'Why haven't you come to see me?' At some point when she was off the phone I said, 'At least you *have* a father. He's alive.' Well, she practically screamed at me. She yelled, 'But at least yours died loving you!'

"That one moment changed my entire life. I have never been bitter or angry that my parents were gone because of that moment. I was luckier than she was. My parents didn't want to leave me. They loved me more than anything in the world. What good would it have done me, my children, grandchildren, to be a victim and mope and cry all these years? I have one life to live and I'm not going to live it in a victim-ish mode. That would trickle down."

What we choose to do with our grief will affect our children. How they see us dealing with adversity can inform their developing attitudes about loss and their perceptions of the world and their place in it. In the best case, we can use our experiences of loss to teach our children lessons that other parents — the ones who still have their parents — may not be able to pass on nearly as well.

Lessons for Our Children

Empathy Is Important

Until a few years before she died, Jayne Jaudon Ferrer's mother had always been an involved grandmother. Jayne's sons had such a close relationship with her that when she was diagnosed with Alzheimer's, the writer, who is also a published poet, didn't think twice about asking her mother to move into their Greenville, South Carolina, home. For three years, Jayne, her husband, and their three boys took care of Jayne's mom. Jayne's youngest sons were in kindergarten and second grade at the time. Her oldest was in middle school.

The living arrangements worked out well until the disease progressed so much that Jayne's mother became violent. Mostly she was fine, but there was the morning she slapped one of Jayne's sons across the face and the afternoon she threw a glass at another. Jayne was urged by her mother's doctor to admit her to a specialized facility for Alzheimer's patients, but Jayne resisted. She felt she could handle it, and in the back of her mind she believed caring for their grandmother would be a good lesson for the boys.

Her mother's behavior, though, became increasingly erratic. When she pulled a kitchen knife on Jayne's youngest son, it was time for her to leave. Jayne's mom moved to a nearby nursing home, and Jayne and her sons visited regularly. Jayne says those visits were also important and powerful experiences. "All three developed relationships with the nurses, the aides, and some of the other residents," Jayne recalls proudly. And she says, "I think they learned a compassion that maybe they wouldn't have learned otherwise. There's a tenderness there."

That tenderness was in full view when Jayne's mother passed away at the age of ninety-one. "During Mother's funeral my sons were the ones that were actually there for me. They're now all over six feet tall, and even though they were grieving, too, they just physically gave me so much comfort. And now, especially during Christmas, when it's particularly hard for me, they go into that comfort mode."

Joanne Greene says her sons are also better off because she and Fred purposefully exposed them to her mother's illness. "Often boys don't get the message 'This is what we do.' It was hard for my younger son sometimes, but I would say, 'Buck up. If you were in the hospital, it would make Grandma plenty queasy, but she'd be there. You need to learn to live with that queasy because it's more important right now that you show her support and be there for her." The fifty-three-year-old mom is convinced that because she didn't shield her sons, they've grown into more understanding and kindhearted young men.

Sandy Taradash has found her own way to teach the same lessons. When it comes to the car accident story, she has purposefully told her family every last detail. "I believe children must know the world around them. I would rather my children and grandchildren live in a big world than a box. You live in a box, you become solitary and self-ish and your mind and heart will never open up. If they know my parents died, they will have more compassion. Not just for me, but for other people in the world. If they see an advertisement on TV for a poor child, one who doesn't have a mother or father, they will have just a little more appreciation and be better people because of it. Understanding how my parents died—and how I lived—that will make them better, kinder, and more loving people."

"Dead" Is Not a Four-Letter Word

I have made the intentional choice in this book not to discuss the "how-to's" of talking with your children about death. Libraries and bookstores are filled with books that can help you find the right words. If you'd like a list of some of the best literature on the subject, please see Appendix B. What I do want to address, however, is the importance of discussing the subject—no matter how you choose to do it.

The Barr-Harris Children's Grief Center in Chicago says parents who talk openly about death and dying do their children an invaluable service. Barbara Hozinsky, a therapist with Barr-Harris for eighteen years, says direct conversations serve a dual purpose. For children who knew their grandparents, candid dialogue can help them cope with their own grief. "To not include them is to not respect the fact that they are mourning. Children should go to funerals. They should participate in memorial services. They should be invited to express their feelings. This is sometimes intolerable for adults because we don't want to arouse pain in our children, but it's so important to how they will ultimately manage their losses." Secondly, Hozinsky says, "It teaches a child that no one is forgotten. It gives children a sense of history and the passage of generations. Not to acknowledge this to a child would be as if that person didn't matter."

Parentless parents are uniquely equipped to talk to their children about grief and may be more likely than other parents to expose them to life's more unpleasant moments. When Joanne Greene's mother was dying, she and Fred allowed their children to see everything. "I didn't want to paint a picture of the aging process that was different than it was," she told me. "We're not big shielders, I have to say. I think that would have been more unfair." You wouldn't accuse Lisa Petersen, the raspy-voiced ICU nurse in Michigan, of trying to sugarcoat life, either. "In our home," she told me, "I talk about dying more. My friends who have parents don't ever talk with their children about their own mortality."

As in all aspects of parenthood, if we can take advantage of our past experiences we can help our children better understand their present and future. And that includes preparing them for our own deaths. That's why it's not astonishing that virtually 60 percent of mothers and fathers who took the Parentless Parents Survey said they'd made it a priority to have their wills and other important family documents in order. By comparison, according to a survey conducted by the online legal information website Findlaw.com, just over 40 percent of Americans have a will. The contrast becomes even more striking when you compare the responses from the youngest respondents. In the Findlaw.com survey, about a quarter of the people polled between the ages of twenty-five and thirty-four have a will. In the Parentless Parents Survey, the number skyrockets to 71.2 percent for the same age group.

Life Is Short

A few years ago, Colleen Orme did something so unthinkable, so unimaginable, her friends in suburban Washington, D.C., thought she was nuts. She temporarily took all three of her boys out of team sports. "I'd be walking around school and people would be whispering, 'Colleen, I heard you took your kids out of sports.'" They couldn't believe it was true.

In this day of travel teams that begin when kids are in first grade, taking children out of organized sports may in fact be unheard of. But none of this mattered to Colleen. She didn't care if her boys pushed back, which they did. Colleen just wanted to give her children something else to see on the weekends besides the back of her head driving them to and from soccer games.

"People would say to me, 'I talk to my kids in the car on the way to practice.' But that's not the same as going away for the weekend and forging new experiences. I didn't mean this in an insulting way, but their priorities, in my opinion, were skewed. I see the world from a far different perspective because I've lost my parents and they have their parents. I realize there's a limited amount of time before they leave for college to instill the kind of family values I want them to have. I want them to know that in this harried, crazy, stupid lifestyle that this generation lives — where we drive an hour away for a seven-year-old's sports game — that we might be sacrificing relationships and real quality time together. My parents' deaths allowed me to have a stronger perspective of what's really important."

Colleen's outlook is one of the unforeseen benefits of loss, according to Dr. Kenneth Doka, who besides being past president of the Association for Death Education and Counseling is also senior consultant to the Hospice Foundation of America. "When your parents die, especially at a younger age, your experience of mortality is sharpened and it challenges your assumptive world," he says. "It creates this unique awareness that life isn't always what we'd like and that we should take the time to make it more meaningful." Deciding to act on that perspective is easier to do, however, if you've come to terms with the death of your parents.

According to Abigail Stewart, professor of psychology and women's studies at the University of Michigan, you can turn loss into an advantage if you're able to put pain in its proper place—in the past. In a bereavement study she conducted, Stewart found that subjects who made peace with their regrets and didn't dwell on the past recovered faster from their losses, had higher levels of self-awareness, and were generally happier. And if we successfully deal with loss, our children, always sponges, will see that, too. "You can increase your capacity to remain proportional and model that for your kids," Stewart told me in a telephone interview. "You can recast things as inconvenient, not a catastrophe. We can help place in its proper context what's a big deal and what's not."

Paralegal Anne Condon Habig believes it's because she had to deal with her parents' deaths that handling her teenage son isn't so hard. "If my son's rude to me, I don't really care because I know it's coming from something else. I mean, there are limits for sure, but I always think, *Pick your battles.* I think life is short and people make things important that aren't. And I've always wanted to be somebody he could really talk to about whatever's on his mind. He doesn't always, of course. He is a teenager. But I think he knows things with me are negotiable. I've learned from what I've been through that things change and we have to go with it." That's an approach Nancy Dickinson, the mom of two boys who lives in the Arizona outback, would agree with. "I'm not as driven with them as I used to be. Before my parents died, I was like, 'You must go to college. You will get a good job.' But since my parents died, I have taken the stance that life is more about following your bliss. 'Go to college, don't go to college.' All I ask is that they make enough money to support themselves and be happy doing whatever it is they choose to do. Our time is so limited on this planet, why should they be miserable?"

As with 48 percent of all survey respondents, the deaths of Fred Greene's parents also shaped the way he views work. Fred built his high-tech office, the one where he created that incredible Photo-shopped image of his father, son, and nephew, to support his growing home-based new media company. Working from home allowed him to have dinner with his children every night. "Knowing that it could be over at any moment, my career wasn't really as important. I mean, it was important to provide for my family, and I've done a pretty good job at that, but I wanted to work out of my house so that when my kids came home from school, even if I could only spend five to ten minutes before I had to go back to work, I could be there." What's more im-portant, he says, is how strong his relationship is with his sons as a result. "My closeness with our kids, my parenting, is all in relationship to the fact that I didn't have parents growing up. There's no question in my mind."

The corporate world wasn't for Lynn Burkholder either. The mom from Canada spent nearly a decade crisscrossing Ontario trying to find a career that excited her. Two years per job was about all she could handle before becoming antsy and uninspired. She worked for an insurance company, then landed a position in retail management, followed by a stint in the communications office of a major U.S. auto company. All along Lynn knew she didn't want to end up like her par-ents, who always said they'd have more fun when they retired, but died before they stopped working. "I knew I needed to be happy," she said.

Lynn's perfect job would allow her to leave the cubicle world behind and work for herself. She figured by owning her own business she could spend more time with her son, Michael, and have the freedom to do more yoga, which she also loved. Interestingly, after so many years spent unfulfilled, Lynn became a career coach helping others discover their true callings. "I am much happier now," she laughed into the phone when I asked about the transition. Then quickly added with more seriousness, "My hope is that Michael can see there are other ways to make money than by punching a clock, like I did. He can take control, because I took control. By making this choice I was being a good model for my son."

Lessons for Ourselves: Being a Parentless Parent Is Easier Than Just Being Parentless

In so many ways, having children — no matter how difficult raising them is without our parents — makes grief more manageable. What is it about being a parent that makes being parentless easier? I think there are a number of factors.

You Can See Your Parents in Your Children

When her mother died, Jayne Jaudon Ferrer says she'd just look at her sons and feel better. She'd get the same calming effect from spending time with her nephew. "My son, Jaron, has a dry wit that reminds me of my dad. My brother's son walks exactly like my daddy did, and has his ears. It's not the same as having a parent, but it's like a piece of him is here. Here's this configuration of DNA — it's not in the same form — but at least [there's] some tangible piece of that person there for you."

Tarah Epstein Baiman feels the same type of warmth when she

looks at her son, Jesse. "My husband and I are both dark. Jesse is fair-skinned with blue eyes, like my dad. When I look at Jesse, I see my dad and it's an incredible comfort to me," she says.

I've had to work hard at this kind of thinking. For much of their lives, when I looked at Jake and Lexi, I sometimes saw only what was missing from mine. Jake has my dad's redheaded complexion, and that resemblance made me sad. Slowly (and not altogether smoothly, I admit) I've been trying to change my way of thinking so that similarities that once brought me pain now bring me pleasure. For example, Jake is a social animal just like my mom. While some children drop their best friends from year to year, Jake keeps adding. The fact that Jake seems so much like my mom in this way makes me happy. And likewise, when Lexi paints, draws, or sculpts a house of clay, instead of thinking how sad it is that my dad's not here to see his architectural talents passed on to his granddaughter, I now try to focus on how great it is she even has some of his abilities at all.

You Can Share Stories with Your Children About Your Parents

Nearly 60 percent of all parentless parents say being able to share memories with their children makes them feel better about having lost their parents, including school secretary Cindi Hartmann in Michigan. "You know, your friends don't want to hear that," Cindi says. "Your neighbors and coworkers aren't going to want to hear that. Only through the eyes of a child can you laugh at those things again and relive them a little bit."

If your children knew your parents, as Cindi's did, you may also feel comforted when your children proactively share their memories of your parents with you. "When they start the conversation, it makes me feel really good. I might be standing there and one of the kids will come in and say, 'Hey, I was just remembering when we were at Nanny and Poppa's house.' Or 'Poppa would have been on the golf course today, it's such a beautiful day.' My girls are just two more people who knew my parents intimately. I couldn't imagine being parentless without them."

Even though they never met her parents, Sandy Taradash says her children and grandchildren also make life without her parents easier. "A couple months ago," Sandy told me enthusiastically over the phone, "I told my grandson a story, and one day, out of the blue, he looked at my daughter and completely repeated the story. I just wanted to laugh and cry all at the same time," she said. "Because those stories will just keep going and going."

You Can Experience the Holidays Through Your Children

Christine Haynes couldn't bring herself to put up a Christmas tree when her daughters Ramsey and Jour'dan were infants. She didn't spend much time decorating her house when they were toddlers either. The Maryland mother just couldn't get into the holiday spirit, and when friends would ask why she didn't put up a tree, she'd fire back that Santa Claus would come whether she bothered with a tree or not.

"Part of me just didn't want to commit," she explains. "I had a tree growing up and my mother would decorate it. It would be awesome and fabulous and it would take up the whole, entire apartment. I think part of me just didn't want to celebrate."

It wasn't until the girls were seven and two that a Christmas tree finally went up in the Haynes household. And that December, for the first time in a long time, Christine felt as happy as a little girl who'd been reunited with a lost doll. Just seeing her daughters marvel at the lights eased some of her pain. "It took me out of the stew that I usually sit in and helped me focus on how happy they were. They were like, 'Mama, it's so pretty!' I was actually so preoccupied with how excited they were I didn't pay attention to the loss."

And similarly for Judy Kalvin-Stiefel, the onetime bodybuilder turned public relations executive, there's no doubt in her mind that the holidays are easier because she can share them with her daughter. "I enjoy it because I enjoy her. I enjoy making her happy and making our own traditions. I enjoy it," she says finally, "for the sake of who we are now."

You Can Develop Unexpected Relationships — Even with Yourself

When Richard Rivera, the dad from the Bronx, turned forty, his wife threw him a surprise birthday party. At one point during the celebration he pulled his daughter, Indi, aside, and while looking around the reception hall packed with his closest friends, he said, "Take a look around. All of these people love you. They're all family."

Richard had a fantastic time that night and says he felt blessed to have so many friends in the same room and the same time. Richard's sense of peace, though, comes from how he's redefined the word "family." He believes you shouldn't limit your definition of family to people related to you by blood. "I've lost both my parents, but we've kind of substituted them in. I have all these really good friends." In fact, he's always encouraged his daughter to call his dearest friends "Tio" and "Tia" — the words for aunt and uncle in Spanish. But that night of his surprise party, overcome by all the love he felt around him, Richard couldn't resist telling her again.

Lynn Burkholder shares Richard's flexible definition of family. She, too, looks to friends to make up for some of what she and her son have lost. "I guess for me, I'd rather seek out people my son can have relationships with here and now. It's not that I don't want him to know where he came from. I want him to understand his lineage. But because my parents died so long before I had Michael, I would rather focus on what's available to him now." And Christine Haynes found a surrogate grandmother for her daughters. Christine met Osha in church, and she's now such a big part of her daughters' lives they call her Grammie Osha. "If her real grandchildren are invited to something, she invites my girls," Christine says. "She's awesome. She just loves them." It was Grammie Osha who pushed Christine the hardest to put up that Christmas tree.

And then there's what Jayne Jaudon Ferrer managed to pull off in South Carolina. Jayne comes from a very large family — her mother had seven sisters and a brother and her father had seven brothers and a sister. And after Jayne's mother died, she made it a point to get her sixty first and second cousins together. "We held reunions at her house for six or seven years. That was such a source of comfort because you could just feel her presence in the house. Most of the cousins have lost at least one parent, and when we're all together in one house we can see and feel our parents in each other." Jayne says these reunions would never have been meaningful to her if her parents were still alive. Of her cousins, aunts, and uncles she says, "They're my hidden blessing."

Surprisingly, my stepmother, Cheryl, has become my hidden blessing. She may live two hours away, but she babysits so often that she knows the location of Jake and Lexi's every school activity, what they like for dinner, and where I keep their class lists. And it was Cheryl who jumped at the chance to help with the kids when I went to Mexico.

Jake and Lexi are so close to Cheryl that they argue about whose turn it is to go to "Grandma Camp." Grandma Camp isn't really "camp" at all — it's just two or three days when Cheryl alternates bringing Jake and Lexi up to her house for some special one-on-one time. The highlight of Grandma Camp, by far, is the Hunt Club — a group Cheryl joined after Dad died. No hunting actually takes place — it's really just a kennel that houses dozens of professionally cared for beagles and foxhounds, and you can't help but smile when you visit. As soon as you enter, the dogs start yelping and bouncing up and down as if their hind legs are made of springs. On any given day, members take about thirty beagles out at a time for long, vigorous walks in the countryside. Most of the dogs aren't on leashes, and they learn to obey verbal commands and stay together as a pack. The most obedient compete in shows up and down the East Coast.

The fact that Jake and Lexi go to Grandma Camp, or call Cheryl "Grandma" at all, is still somewhat unbelievable to me. If you had asked me how I felt about Cheryl when my mother was still alive, especially when she married my father, I would have told you I hated her. In my juvenile view, she was the only person responsible for my parents' divorce and I vowed never to forgive her.

Cheryl also looks very different from my mom, and for years I despised her for that, too. My mom and I looked so much alike. We were the same curvy size, and I constantly raided her closet for clothes. Cheryl, on the other hand, is so long-legged and slim my father affectionately called her "Bones." Dad knew how much I disliked her and feared I'd cut her out of my life if he died first. But his death, and my mother's years before, had just the opposite effect.

At first, Cheryl and I started becoming close out of necessity. She liked having grandchildren and I liked having the extra help. Jake and Lexi were the buffer that made being close easier. We also reached out to each other because we are both living connections to my father. She sees my dad in us, and she is one of the closest links to my father I can offer my children. And over time, dare I say it, I actually began to like Cheryl—even after the kids went to bed. My parents' deaths freed me to like her. And now I love her.

Thanks to Cheryl, Jake and Lexi can hear stories about me when I was a child. She was there for most of it and remembers. And thanks to Cheryl, I have new words dancing around my brain, too. Instead of names for cancer drugs and surgical procedures, my vocabulary now includes the names of all those beagles. There's Wyatt, Whiskey, Wombat, Wiggy, Winter, and Willow. And Yogi,

Yukon, Yahtzee, Yingling, and Y'all. And, my favorite litter, the T's: Tulip, Tender, Truffle, Tornado, Truman, Tilson, and Teapot. One afternoon when the puppies were jumping all over us and licking our faces, I asked Cheryl, "Do you think Dad would have been into the beagles?"

"Are you serious?!" she laughed, pulling her mouth away from Wombat's face. "He would never have done this. He would have joined me once or twice, but he would have gotten bored. It wouldn't have been his scene at all."

The most surprising relationship I've developed since my parents died, however, is the one I've cultivated with myself. For the longest time, just like Colleen Orme in Virginia, I wanted to be rescued. I wanted my friends to care for me more than they did, and I expected Mark to anticipate my needs, even take my parents' place. But he can't. My friends aren't my mom and Mark isn't my dad and my parents are never going to fly back into my living room with their capes and magic rings and make everything better. What I've learned is that I can no longer go through life just being a mother, wife, writer, and home-maker. I need to take on one more additional role. I also need to be a parent to myself.

If Mark and I want to go out to dinner and see a movie, I stop feeling sorry for myself and call a babysitter. If I want to take the kids to an event my parents would have enjoyed but Mark has no interest in, I take Jake and Lexi and give Mark the afternoon off. And on Mother's Day, I give myself permission to spend the day the way I want to. All of this represents a sea change in my thinking. I used to wake up Mother's Day and hope Mark would surprise me with a gift certificate to get a massage or give me "permission" to skip Mother's Day with his mom so I could take a class at the gym. I'd invariably get disappointed if he failed to read my mind, and start missing my parents even more. *Surely they would have given Mark a friendly poke to treat his wife to a few hours of free time. Surely they would have coddled me the way I so desperately long to be coddled.* But the truth is I don't need to wait for anyone to treat me to anything. And I don't think my parents would have wanted their daughter to rely solely on somebody else to take care of her needs, either. My parents, after all, taught me to be self-sufficient.

By putting my oxygen mask on first, I am able to be a less bitter daughter-in-law and a more patient and tolerant mother. I am able to embrace Mark's parents and understand how lucky we *all* are to have them. It is a blessing, not a curse, to be surrounded by his family, and I am the only person to blame for the distance that once existed between us. I am the one who pitted my in-laws against the memory of my parents. I'm the one who made a contest of a situation that required no competition. Not feeling the need to keep score is freeing. Absence and presence can coexist.

This new outlook cuts down the friction between me and Mark and makes me a better wife. I can stay focused on the present, and my thoughts don't always leap to the past. And when Mark and I cuddle in bed at night, I can be there with him, fully, in both body and mind.

Over time, I've gained clarity in other areas as well. I had been so preoccupied with imagining what my parents would do and say at every turn that I all but forgot to have faith in myself. It wasn't until I came across the book *Raising America: Experts, Parents, and a Century of Advice About Children* that I truly came to accept that my mom and dad would never have been able to answer all my parenting questions. Author Ann Hulbert traces the history of parenting advice in the United States and shows how each generation gets caught up in a particular brand of expert opinion. In the late 1890s and 1920s babies were put on unyielding feeding schedules and mothers were warned not to play with, cuddle, or kiss their children lest they become too soft. Contrast that to the modern orthodoxy of "on demand" nursing and how often today parents are accused of being overly involved and indulgent.

Understanding that parenting advice always changes has been liberating. My parents are irreplaceable in myriad profoundly important ways, but they wouldn't have been omniscient. And because my mom wouldn't have been able to advise me about nursing (like most babies in the early 1970s, I was bottle fed), Mark and I probably would have hired Susan Esserman, the doula, anyway. Jake and Lexi only have one set of parents. Not my mom and dad. And not my in-laws.

Mark and I are it.

Dr. Carrie Barron, a psychiatrist and assistant clinical professor at Columbia University's Center for Psychoanalytic Training and Research, says this realization is significant because it means I am giving myself permission to be me—a grown woman separate from my parents. She calls this separation-individuation. "Losing your parents can launch you into a deep and strong sense of your independent self if you let it. It can be deeply liberating. By working through grief and facing the good and bad in our parents, we can take what worked and what we admired and reject what we found troubling. Think of the absence as a blank canvas upon which you get to parent the way you want to parent. You are not your parents, and you have to know that, and act on it, in order to be happy. If you know who you are, the possibilities for pleasure are endless."

This awareness has also allowed me to manage the pangs of jealousy I still feel sometimes when I see other children with their grandparents. And interestingly in this regard, I think parentless parents can learn a lot from Alcoholics Anonymous. Fully recovered alcoholics aren't bothered when people drink in front of them because their old cravings no longer cause them pain. Alcoholics Anonymous calls this being "in a position of neutrality." Certainly AA knows a thing or two when it comes to dealing with longings, jealousy, and resentment. There's a section of the Big Book, the basic text for Alcoholics Anonymous, first published in 1939, that I think is particularly germane to parentless parents who find themselves jealous of other people's parents:

"Assuming we are spiritually fit, we can do all sorts of things alcoholics are not supposed to do. People have said we must not go where liquor is served; we must not have it in our homes; we must shun friends who drink; we must avoid moving pictures which show drinking scenes; we must not go into bars; our friends must hide their bottles if we go to their houses; we mustn't think or be reminded about alcohol at all. Our experience shows that this is not necessarily so. We meet these conditions every day. An alcoholic who cannot meet them, still has an alcoholic mind; there is something the matter with his spiritual status." Likewise, parentless parents can't live in avoidance of other people's parents.

So how do we get to this place, this "position of neutrality"? Is there a way to wipe away the jealousy we feel when we see our friends with their parents and our in-laws with our children? The answer is tucked away in the very first sentence I quoted from the Big Book. "Assuming we are spiritually fit . . ." Happiness builds immunity.

I am the only one who can drive through the fog and embrace what's on the other side. My children. My husband. My in-laws.

My life.

One evening when Lexi was six, she made an unusual request before she went to bed. "Mom," she said as I was tucking her in, "can we read my birthday cards tonight?" While I was surprised by the request (we had been reading a lot of Shel Silverstein then), I knew exactly what she meant. Ever since Jake and Lexi's first birthday, I've saved a few of their birthday cards thinking they'd have fun one day reading some of the silly ones their relatives and friends had gotten for them when they were small.

"Sure, Lex," I said, and went over to her desk to get them. The cards were stored inside a Ziploc bag, and it was hard to find at first because it was buried under a pile of more important items — a glitter-covered notebook, stickers, and dozens of loose markers that rolled back and forth like the tide as I opened and shut the drawer. When I found the bag, I announced victoriously, "Here they are," and walked to the front of Lexi's room to dim the light.

I squeezed into her twin-sized bed next to her and carefully opened the clear plastic bag that was sitting on my chest. "Let's see what we have here," I said. "This one's from Uncle Richie. "It says, 'Hi Sweetheart. I hope you have a wonderful birthday. I love you!!!!!!"

The next few cards were from her friends at school. One had an illustration of a friendly green dinosaur eating the number four and another featured Winnie the Pooh and Piglet giggling. The last card had a picture of Sleeping Beauty on the cover, and inside it said, "Happy Birthday, Princess!"

"Who's it from?" Lexi asked, her voice getting sleepier.

I whispered, "It's from Grandma." And before I could say another word she asked, "Which one?"

Which one.

They were two simple words, but when strung together so innocently they taught me something I desperately needed to hear. My daughter just wanted to know if Grandma Marilyn, Sandy, or Cheryl had gotten her that birthday card, and all I could think of when I told her 'Grandma Marilyn' was how lucky we both were. Lexi has three grandmothers. Lexi has three grandmothers who are active and involved and had shaped her into the smart and feisty little girl who was then reclining half-awake beside me.

Yes, in my mind Lexi is missing the most important grandma. Yes, her life would be richer if my mom were alive. But it was all too clear to me at that moment that perhaps the void was much more mine than hers.

Smiling, I slipped the Ziploc bag onto the floor and leaned over to give her a kiss good night.

"Night, Lex. Love you."

"Love you, too."

With one final kiss, I got up to leave the room. But when I got to the door, I stopped, feeling an unshakable urge to come back inside. "What is it, Mom?" Lexi asked. I waited a half second before responding.

Turning around, I took a few steps back into her room and knelt down by the head of her bed. "Lex," I whispered, and smoothed her soft brown hair away from her eyes, "did I ever tell you the story about the card *Grandma Lynn* got me for my sixth birthday? It was *gigantic*."

"How big was it?"

And I told her all about it.

A Memory Journal
for Parentless Parents

T*he genesis of the Parentless* Parents Memory Journal came from the interview I did with Colleen Orme. About forty-five minutes into our conversation we started talking about those ever-present journals that encourage grandparents to write down their memories for their grandchildren. You've seen them. They have titles like *Memories for My Grandchild, A Grandparent's Legacy,* and *Grandparents Journal.* Colleen mused with frustration, "Those books are nice, but they're for living grandparents to fill out. What do we have?" Then she added hopefully, "I wish somebody could come up with some format, some really successful bridge, for people like us." The idea sat with me for a while, but I admit I did nothing with it until about a month later, when I met Fredda Wasserman at Our House.

Our House provides grief support to men, women, and children living in Southern California, and Fredda graciously allowed me to use their beautiful office space for the focus groups I conducted in Los Angeles. An hour before one of the sessions was scheduled to begin, I arrived to set up and meet Fredda for the first time. As we began chatting, she proudly showed me their newest tool to help adults and teens heal after loss. It's an 8.5-inch-by-5.5-inch navy blue spiral-bound notebook with the words "My Grief Journal" printed in white lettering across the front. When I first opened it, I just saw empty lined pages. But when I looked closer, I noticed a gentle prompt written in the upper left-hand corner of nearly every page. Incomplete sentences, like "The time of day that's hardest is . . ." and "What I will always love about you is . . ." That's when the lightbulb went on. On the plane home to New York, I opened my laptop and started typing what you'll see on the following pages. Thank you, Colleen and Fredda.

My hope is that the Parentless Parents Memory Journal makes sharing information about your parents easier. Perhaps it will inspire you, maybe even challenge you, to consider your children's relationship with their grandparents in a different way.

I've provided room to record your responses here, but you may prefer to write in your own journal or on the computer. You may also decide to use the prompts as conversation starters and not write anything down at all. Whatever you choose, my deepest wish is that the journal is a practical tool — enabling you to more effortlessly and concretely connect your children to their grandparents.

The Parentless Parents
Memory Journal

1. When I look at you, this is what reminds me of your grandparents:

_____

_____

_____

_____

_____

_____

_____

2. This is when you remind me most of your grandparents:

_____

_____

_____

_____

_____

_____

_____

3. I hope you'll always remember this about your grandparents:

_____

_____

_____

_____

_____

_____

_____

_____

_____

_____

_____

_____

4. If your grandparents were alive, this is the most important lesson they'd teach:

_____

_____

_____

_____

_____

_____

_____

_____

_____

_____

_____

_____

5. When I was little, this is how I celebrated the holidays with your grandparents:

_____
_____
_____
_____
_____
_____
_____
_____
_____
_____
_____

6. When I see you do this, I know your grandparents would be proud:

_____
_____
_____
_____
_____
_____
_____
_____
_____
_____
_____

7. This is what I loved most about your grandparents:

_____
_____
_____
_____
_____
_____
_____
_____
_____
_____
_____
_____
_____

8. This is what made me most upset about your grandparents:

_____
_____
_____
_____
_____
_____
_____
_____
_____
_____
_____
_____
_____

9. This is what your grandparents believed in most:

_____

_____

_____

_____

_____

_____

_____

_____

_____

_____

_____

_____

10. Your grandparents taught me the value of this:

_____

_____

_____

_____

_____

_____

_____

_____

_____

_____

_____

_____

11. Your grandparents used to say this all the time:

_____

_____

_____

_____

_____

_____

_____

_____

_____

_____

_____

_____

12. All of these items once belonged to your grandparents:

_____

_____

_____

_____

_____

_____

_____

_____

_____

_____

_____

_____

_____

13. This is what I remember about where your grandparents were born:

_____

_____

_____

_____

_____

_____

_____

_____

_____

_____

14. This is what I remember about the way your grandparents grew up:

_____

_____

_____

_____

_____

_____

_____

_____

_____

_____

15. This is what your grandparents did for a living:

_____

_____

_____

_____

_____

_____

_____

_____

_____

_____

_____

_____

16. These are the traditions that mattered most to your grandparents:

_____

_____

_____

_____

_____

_____

_____

_____

_____

_____

_____

_____

17. These are the foods that remind me most of your grandparents:

_____
_____
_____
_____
_____
_____
_____
_____
_____
_____
_____

18. This song, or type of music, reminds me of your grandparents:

_____
_____
_____
_____
_____
_____
_____
_____
_____
_____
_____

19. You get this from your grandparents:

_____

_____

_____

_____

_____

_____

_____

_____

_____

_____

_____

_____

20. If your grandparents were alive, this is what they'd say to you:

_____

_____

_____

_____

_____

_____

_____

_____

_____

_____

_____

_____

Appendix A

The Parentless Parents Survey

Every one-on-one interview I conducted for *Parentless Parents* was indispensable in the writing of these pages. To drive my research forward, however, I knew I needed quantitative data as well.

The Parentless Parents Survey was constructed with the help of Dr. Tracy E. Costigan, principal research scientist with the American Institutes for Research in Washington, D.C. It was built solely for online use and collected 1,298 eligible responses between November 30, 2008, and December 31, 2009. Participants represented forty-eight states and the following countries: Australia, Canada, France, Germany, Ireland, Italy, Japan, the Netherlands, New Zealand, Singapore, South Africa, and the United Kingdom.

One of the most important and ultimately moving aspects of the survey turned out to be the written responses that ended many of the sections. After each set of questions on a particular topic, respondents would find an empty space, without character limits, to add their thoughts and feelings. In this way, I got not only the aggregate data I needed, but also the real-time reflections these very difficult questions often provoked.

Thank you to all the men and women who took the time to take the Parentless Parents Survey. No survey like it had ever been done before, and I hope your participation will inspire experts — far more schooled than this journalist — to conduct the scientific research needed on the parentless parent population.

Parentless Parents Survey Summary

- Three-quarters (75%) of parentless parents lost both parents by the time their oldest child was twelve. Almost six in ten (59%) were parentless by the time their oldest child was six. 34% had lost both parents before becoming parents themselves.

Before first child was born	34.1%
By the time the first child was 6	59.0%
By the time the first child was 12	74.7%

- Of respondents who lost both parents before their first child was born, 60% report feeling overwhelmed a lot or most of the time during their baby's early years.

- In response to every question regarding pregnancy, childbirth, and emotions about children entering school and celebrating important milestones, respondents of every age report having felt more isolated than supported. Indeed, 57% of all parentless parents say they didn't have enough parenting support when their children were young.

- 69% say friends with living parents don't understand what it's like to be a parent without parents; less than half (42%) think their spouse understands; and fewer than 20% say their in-laws understand.

- Almost 70% of all respondents report feeling jealous when they see other children with their grandparents. This awareness is often heightened in social settings such as school events and playdates.

- Mother's Day and Father's Day are particularly challenging. 47% of the respondents say they grieve more on these holidays than celebrate.

- Nearly 58% of parentless parents fear that they'll die young and leave their children without a mother/father.

- There is a clear distinction between men and women during the early years of parenthood. In nearly every case parentless mothers report fewer positive emotions and more negative emotions than parentless men. The exception is when their children enter school — when parentless mothers report a slightly higher degree of satisfaction.

- Parentless parents tend to parent alongside spouses and partners who have one, if not both, living parents. In almost two-thirds (66%) of cases the spouse or partner has at least one living parent.

- Differing exposure to parent loss is hard on marriages. Parentless parents say they receive nearly double the amount of emotional support from friends who have also lost parents (82%) than they receive from their own husbands and wives (42%). In addition, more respondents indicate their spouses *don't* understand what they're going through (48%) than *do* (42%).

- Relationships with in-laws are delicate and conflicted. While nearly half (46%) of parentless parents get jealous when their in-laws are with their children, 68% say they're grateful their children have them as grandparents. Despite welcoming their presence, 29% resent their in-laws' influence over their children.

- When it comes to keeping the memory of their parents alive, almost two-thirds (61%) of the respondents say it's an activity they enjoy doing. Nearly 10%, however, find it a burden.

- Among the positive aspects reported by parentless parents, almost seven in ten say they appreciate their kids more than they would have if they weren't parentless, and more than half (55%) say they're more understanding with their children because they've lost their parents. Nearly 60% say sharing memories with their children about their deceased parents makes them feel better about having lost them.

- The majority, almost 60%, of the respondents have made it a priority to get important documents, such as a will, in order. For respondents between twenty-five and thirty-four, the rate rises to over 71% — nearly triple the rate for the general population in the same age group.

- A whopping 84% of parentless parents, among the largest affirmative responses in the survey, say they appreciate the family they still have. A similarly universal response is found in the comfort parentless parents derive from others in similar situations. More than 80% say their friends who have also lost both parents truly understand what it's like to be a parentless parent.

The Parentless Parents Survey

Part I: Let's get started. First, please tell us a little about yourself.

1. Gender

Male	14.5%
Female	85.5%

2. Age

25–34	7%
35–44	30%
45–54	39%
55 and above	24%

3. How many children do you have?

1 child	30%
2 children	47%
3 children	16%
4 children	5%
5 or more	2%

4. What is your marital status?

Married	79.3%
Separated or Divorced	12.8%
Living with Partner	3.3%
Never Married	2.0%
Widowed	1.7%
Other	0.9%

5. What is your highest level of education?

Some high school	0.4%
High school graduate	2.9%
Some college	11.9%
Associate's degree	6.9%
Bachelor's degree	34.1%
Graduate degree	43.7%

6. Race

Asian	2.8%
Black or African American	3.5%
White	93.0%
Other Race	1.5%

Categories add up to greater than 100% because
respondents could endorse more than one category.

7. Please tell us about your spouse/partner's parents:

Both parents alive	40%
Both parents deceased	24%
Father alive, mother deceased	7%
Father deceased, mother alive	19%
Not applicable	10%

Part II: Early Parenthood Without Your Parents

1. When you were pregnant (or the mother of your children was pregnant), did you feel _____ because/even though your parents were not alive?

	Never/Rarely	Sometimes	A lot of the time/ Most of the time
Overwhelmed	32.5%	37.8%	29.6%
Angry	45.4%	35.3%	19.3%
Sad	10.9%	43.1%	46.0%
Supported	34.2%	30.7%	35.0%
Happy	8.1%	36.9%	55.0%
Depressed	38.7%	42.9%	18.3%
Peaceful	33.3%	40.3%	26.5%
Isolated	25.9%	30.0%	44.2%
Confident	26.3%	39.6%	34.1%
Optimistic	11.1%	40.2%	48.8%

Other representative responses include: *deprived, bitter, cheated, totally alone, almost abandoned, jealous, grateful*

2. When your first child was born, did you feel _____ because/ even though your parents were not alive?

	Never/Rarely	Sometimes	A lot of the time/ Most of the time
Overwhelmed	18.6%	31.4%	50.0%
Angry	43.6%	35.6%	20.8%
Sad	13.2%	46.0%	40.7%
Supported	35.8%	33.4%	30.8%
Happy	8.4%	33.2%	58.4%
Depressed	36.0%	42.6%	21.4%
Peaceful	36.6%	38.0%	25.5%
Isolated	20.9%	31.8%	47.3%
Confident	28.4%	39.7%	31.9%
Optimistic	14.5%	40.0%	45.6%

Other representative responses include: *ripped off, unconnected, resentful, envious, blessed, joy*

3. When any of your subsequent children were born, did you feel _____ because/even though your parents were not alive?

	Never/Rarely	Sometimes	A lot of the time/ Most of the time
Overwhelmed	19.5%	37.2%	43.3%
Angry	37.2%	41.2%	21.6%
Sad	17.8%	47.7%	34.5%
Supported	40.3%	30.8%	28.9%
Happy	10.6%	37.3%	52.1%
Depressed	34.3%	41.5%	24.1%
Peaceful	35.4%	43.8%	20.9%
Isolated	23.5%	34.4%	42.1%
Confident	19.4%	42.7%	37.9%
Optimistic	16.1%	40.5%	43.3%

Other representative responses include: *emotionally tired, jealous, heartbroken, disappointed, worried, blissful*

4. When your children entered school, did you feel _____ because/even though your parents were not alive?

	Never/Rarely	Sometimes	A lot of the time/ Most of the time
Overwhelmed	38.2%	36.5%	25.3%
Angry	51.7%	34.2%	14.1%
Sad	18.7%	50.6%	30.7%
Supported	42.8%	31.5%	25.6%
Happy	8.3%	41.5%	50.2%
Depressed	37.8%	44.9%	17.3%
Peaceful	33.1%	42.8%	24.0%
Isolated	25.4%	34.5%	40.1%
Confident	19.3%	40.4%	40.4%
Optimistic	13.4%	37.3%	49.2%

Other representative responses include: *anxious, nostalgia, jealous, excited, relieved, proud*

5. When your children reach important milestones (e.g., birthdays, graduations, etc.), do you feel _____ because/even though your parents are not alive?

	Never/Rarely	Sometimes	A lot of the time/ Most of the time
Overwhelmed	48.3%	33.3%	18.5%
Angry	47.5%	30.2%	22.3%
Sad	7.3%	36.5%	56.3%
Supported	37.7%	34.9%	27.3%
Happy	8.5%	34.3%	57.2%
Depressed	35.7%	45.1%	19.2%
Peaceful	29.7%	42.2%	28.0%
Isolated	28.0%	34.5%	37.5%
Confident	15.4%	42.1%	42.4%
Optimistic	9.6%	41.1%	49.3%

Other representative responses include: *wistful, numb, empty, jealous, love, thankful*

6. How much do you agree with the following statements?

	Disagree	Neither Agree nor Disagree	Agree
I had a good sense of what to do with a newborn.	38.8%	12.0%	49.2%
I had enough parenting support during my children's early years (e.g., in-laws, babysitters, baby nurses, family, friends).	57.0%	9.5%	33.5%
My new parenthood experience was tarnished because I couldn't share it with my parents.	22.5%	23.3%	54.2%
My new parenthood experience was better than I expected because my parents weren't telling me what to do.	65.6%	25.9%	8.5%
I was worried something bad would happen to my unborn child, including the possibility of miscarriage.	33.8%	18.1%	48.1%

7. Please share your thoughts about being a new parent without your parents. Your reflections may span pregnancy through the first few years of your children's lives.

Sample Responses:

- I don't know anyone else who has given birth without parents by their side. It can make you feel alienated very quickly.

- My happiness is always tainted by sadness.

- What I miss is the validation that everything I go through is a stage.

- I think that not having someone who remembers when you were a baby is especially hard to take. You want to ask, was I like x, and there's no one who can tell you.

- I didn't want to ask anybody for help because I felt I would look foolish and inadequate.

- I'm sad when I'm at the playground and the other children's grandparents are there to watch them play. I wonder if the moms and dads realize how lucky they are to have their parents with them.

- It's very sad at school functions when everyone's grandparents attend and my kids don't have any.

- I felt lonely and really missed having someone who unconditionally loved me and could be proud of me.

- Remember when you were in school and you got a good grade on a report? The first thing you want to do is show your parents your accomplishment. Well, my kids are my greatest accomplishment and I feel as though no one is here to share that with. I have an amazing husband and I am very close with my in-laws, but it is not the same.

Part III: Beyond the Early Years

1. How much do you agree with the following statements?

	Disagree	Neither Agree nor Disagree	Agree
When I see other children with their grandparents, I get jealous.	15.7%	15.2%	69.1%
In social settings with my children (e.g., playdates, school functions) I am more conscious of my parents' absence.	22.3%	21.0%	56.7%
Parenting has always been harder for me than other parents because my parents are gone and theirs are alive.	29.5%	27.1%	43.4%
Parenting has always been easier for me than other parents because my parents can't interfere with or judge how I parent my children.	62.7%	27.6%	9.7%
If my parents were alive, I don't think my experience of parenthood would be that much different than it is now.	63.7%	14.3%	22.0%
If my parents were alive, I'd be the same kind of parent I am now.	24.5%	28.7%	46.8%

2. The following set of statements deals specifically with your children's birthdays, holidays, and other special celebrations. How much do you agree with each of the following statements?

	Disagree	Neither Agree nor Disagree	Agree
I force myself to enjoy the holidays for the sake of my children.	40.9%	20.1%	39.0%
I've been distracted and sad during my children's birthday parties because I wish my parents could be there.	53.9%	17.7%	28.4%
I've chosen not to attend, or have removed myself from, holiday celebrations with my children because I've been upset about my parents' absence.	85.3%	6.9%	7.8%
On Mother's/Father's Day, I find myself grieving my own mother/father more than I celebrate my life as a mother/father.	37.5%	15.0%	47.5%
Holidays are joyous occasions, even without my parents.	20.7%	16.0%	63.3%
I use holidays and other special occasions to talk about my parents.	25.4%	20.1%	54.4%
Holidays and other special celebrations are less painful than other times because I can talk about my parents without feeling self-conscious.	48.9%	35.2%	15.9%
On Mother's/Father's Day, I take time to remember my parents and talk about them with my children.	21.4%	19.4%	59.2%

3. What do you do specifically during the holidays and other celebrations to evoke your parents for your children?

Sample Responses:

- Tell stories of how we celebrated as a family when I was a child. Usually, I try to make the stories funny, as I think humor has more staying power than seriousness.

- I pass on the same traditions that I had as a child. By doing that it connects my children to my parents.

- It is too painful.

- I almost never talk about my parents.

- This thought never occurred to me!

- We give gifts to the kids and say to consider it from either grandparent because we know it's something they would have bought them.

- My son is just under three. I have actually not made a big deal out of the holidays because if anything ever happened I would not want him to feel the extra loss.

4. The following set of statements explores how the loss of your
parents informs the way you currently relate to your children
and the concerns you may have about the future.

	Disagree	Neither Agree nor Disagree	Agree
I've made it a priority to get my family's important documents in order (e.g., wills, life insurance).	21.3%	19.0%	59.6%
My children remind me of my parents and that makes me happy.	18.0%	28.0%	54.0%
My children remind me of my parents and that makes me sad.	61.3%	19.8%	18.9%
I've emotionally disengaged from my children at times because I've been preoccupied with my own sadness and loss.	59.1%	11.0%	29.9%
I've emotionally disengaged from my children because I don't want them to become too attached to me.	86.0%	7.5%	6.5%
I fear that I'll die young and leave my children without a mother/father.	25.2%	16.9%	57.9%
I expect to see my children get married and have children of their own.	11.3%	19.7%	69.0%
I expect to live beyond the age my parents died.	14.1%	25.8%	60.1%

Additional Comments:

- I sometimes find that I have more angry reactions to incidents
  with the kids because I may be in a funk related to missing
  my mother/father.

- I'm very organized with my kids' records and photo albums and scrapbooks.

- I feel incredibly lucky to have had the chance to become a parent and relive some of my own childhood fun. I feel closer to my mother, feel I understand her a bit better, since I've become a mother.

- I worry that I will not be able to see my children grow to get married and have children of their own.

- Parenting without my parents is like living in a home without a roof. There is the constant feeling of being exposed and feelings of grief and loss often cover my home like clouds — appearing without warning and dulling all else.

- I have only left my children twice in their entire lives for an overnight trip. Twice in five years. Both of those times they were left with my sister. The last overnight trip, I made a comment on Facebook about if anything happened to me, my sister was to be my children's guardian. Everyone thought I was being cute, but I just needed that additional assurance that everyone know my final wishes should anything happen to me.

- I'm always trying to give them advice on the big stuff — what kind of people I want them to be, to always look out for each other.

Part IV: Where Do You Turn for Support?

1. Please respond to the following statement: My _____ truly understand(s) what it's like for me to be a parentless parent.

	Disagree	Neither Agree nor Disagree	Agree
My sibling(s) truly understand(s) what it's like for me to be a parentless parent.	25.9%	13.1%	61.0%
My other relatives truly understand what it's like for me to be a parentless parent.	47.4%	27.8%	24.9%
Friends who have living parents truly understand what it's like for me to be a parentless parent.	68.7%	19.6%	11.7%
Friends who have deceased parents truly understand what it's like for me to be a parentless parent.	3.2%	15.3%	81.6%

2. If you are parentless and your spouse/partner is not, how has this affected your family relationships?

	Disagree	Neither Agree nor Disagree	Agree
My spouse/partner truly understands what it's like for me to be a parentless parent.	48.0%	10.0%	42.0%
My in-laws truly understand what it's like for me to be a parentless parent.	61.6%	20.3%	18.1%
My in-laws appreciate how hard it is for me to accept them as the only grandparents my children have.	52.2%	36.2%	11.6%
My spouse/partner has a much easier time being a parent than I do.	51.2%	27.4%	21.3%
I have a much easier time being a parent than my spouse/partner.	36.7%	35.7%	27.6%
I'm more controlling of my children because I know how quickly life can end.	45.9%	19.8%	34.3%
I'm more lenient with my children because I know how important it is for my children to be independent, in case I die young.	49.9%	23.6%	26.5%
I'm jealous of my spouse/partner's relationship with his/her parents.	47.6%	17.2%	35.2%
When I see my children with their living grandparents I get jealous.	38.8%	14.8%	46.4%
I've not always supported my children's relationship with their living grandparents.	61.8%	10.5%	27.7%
I resent the disproportionate influence my in-laws have over my children.	54.9%	16.3%	28.8%
I'm grateful for my in-laws. They are the only grandparents my children have.	15.5%	16.3%	68.3%

Additional Comments:

- I continuously think, "Why couldn't they be the parents that are gone." And worst of all, How do I express these things and to whom? It is socially unacceptable to do so. It makes me sound like a hateful person, which I am not. I have no outlet for all the stress and pressure within our marriage.

- I think part of the reason why my spouse and I are separated is I overcompensated for my parents not being alive. I am very involved with my kids so they never had to feel the need for grandparents.

- It is hard sometimes to see how close my children are to their living grandparents.

- I've gone out of my way to make sure my daughter has a relationship with my in-laws.

- I truly appreciated the support my in-laws gave us as young parents.

- I get so irritated with my in-laws. Would it kill you to admit he may actually look like me or someone in my family?! He is 50% of me too!

- I felt angry that every Mother's Day, etc., I was expected to be a visitor.

- I am divorced from my children's father. The influence of his parents had a huge impact on our marital demise.

3. Do you belong to any organizations, community groups, and/ or religious institutions that provide support to you as a parent?

Yes	23.2%
No	76.8%

Sample Responses of Helpful Organizations:

• Church

• Synagogue

• School

• Playgroups

• Online social networks

• Support groups, including Parentless Parents

4. Are you satisfied with how much support you are able to receive from these organizations as a parent without parents?

Yes	42.8%
No	57.2%

Sample Responses:

• Meeting people in the same situation is very comforting.

• It doesn't come close to offering the kind of emotional support that a grandparent would offer.

- There's no complete solution.

- A Motherless Daughters group only addresses half of my emptiness. I'm sad my mother died, but devastated I lost my father. I haven't found a place to support me in that grief.

- Our community of friends from our daughter's school is very supportive. In many ways it replaces extended family for us. We share parenting stories, concerns, and often exchange child care.

- I have support from my spouse and he has support from me. That seems to be enough.

Part V: Keeping the Memory of Your Parents Alive

1. How do you keep the memory of your parents alive for your children?

Show pictures	23%
Tell stories	23%
Display heirlooms	17%
Cook certain foods	16%
Play specific music	7%
Follow specific traditions	14%

Other Sample Responses:

- Sing specific songs.

- Visit places they enjoyed.

- Introduce my son to people who knew my
  parents.

- Point out similarities between them and their
  grandparents.

- I make sure to let my daughter know when Grandma and
  Grandpa are "paying" for something—a trip, special camp,
  college. I know they would be paying for these special
  experiences if they were still alive.

- I use the reasons for both of their deaths—lung cancer/
  cigarettes—to keep my kids from developing that habit and
  to keep them mindful of their health and the fragility of life.

- Bedtime stories. They aren't true but they are a way for me to
  reach out and keep the names alive.

2. How would you characterize the responsibility of keeping the
   memory of your parents alive?

Burdensome	7%
Something I must do	32%
Enjoyable	61%

Sample Responses:

- It's an honor.

- Sad, because I feel like I'm too young to be introducing my
  toddler to her grandparents with nothing more than stories,
  pictures, music, etc. I wish they were here for her to know in
  person.

- I love to talk about them.

- I don't think I do it well enough.

- I didn't have enough information about them.

- It's not a necessity to keep memories alive for my kids. I am the embodiment of my parents' upbringing.

- I don't make them more than they were. I spell out what they did right and where they failed so my kids can learn from their mistakes.

3. Please describe any creative ways you've developed for keeping the memory of your parents alive for your children.

Sample Responses:

- I sometimes relate different historical events to how it affected my parents.

- We have visited their hometowns and houses.

- I brought home some of my mother's ridiculous old clothes and hats and my kids use it for dress-up.

- My son knows all the funny things my parents used to do. We talk about the jokes, the laughs. That way, my son thinks of them in a good way. It also makes it easier for me to talk about them without getting upset.

- Over the years we put in a lot of effort keeping up connections with relatives.

- I made him a shield (he is into knights) with his paternal family crest on it. He likes to brandish it in play saying, "This is the crest of my father and his father!" That makes me feel good.

· My children hear me talking about them as frequently as if they were alive.

Part VI: The Overall Impact of Being a Parentless Parent

1. If there is anything positive that has come from being a parentless parent, it is:

	Disagree	Neither Agree nor Disagree	Agree
I appreciate my children more.	6.0%	24.0%	69.9%
I'm more understanding with my children because I have lost my parents.	11.5%	34.0%	54.5%
I can parent my children any way I want to.	26.2%	35.0%	38.8%
I appreciate the family I still have.	3.5%	12.2%	84.2%
I've moved and now live in a location that's best for my children.	23.0%	50.0%	27.0%
I've switched jobs or made different career choices in order to spend more time with my children.	21.2%	30.6%	48.2%
I can share memories of my parents with my children and that makes me feel better about having lost them.	15.9%	25.7%	58.5%

2. This is when I am most impacted by being a parentless parent:

Sample Responses:

- When I cannot tell my son what I was like as a child.

- Mother's Day, Father's Day, Grandparents Day, Special Occasions, Holidays.

- I feel like a perpetual outsider even though my in-laws are kind to me. No matter how accepted I am, it is always as my husband's wife, not a daughter.

- When the important milestones come — my son's science team winning a state championship. I would love to brag to someone about the scholarship, but no one will be happy for me without a twinge of jealousy, too.

- It catches me totally by surprise.

3. Overall, I think the most important issue facing me as a parentless parent is:

Sample Responses:

- Trying to make my parents real to my kids.

- Fear of my own death.

- Feeling untethered.

- Lack of support.

- Resenting others who still have their parents.

- Trying to fill the void in my children's lives from not having grandparents. I've spent most of my time trying to figure out what I can give them to replace it.

- Missing out on sharing the joy and pride I feel for my children and their accomplishments.

- The additional responsibility of caring for my grandparents.

- I need to be better at nurturing myself.

- Patting my own back.

- To find the carefree joy I used to carry.

- The lack of unconditional love is devastating and makes every aspect of parenting more difficult.

- The tension/jealousy I sometimes feel toward my spouse and in-laws.

- Keeping family traditions and passing them on.

- Not idealizing my parents.

- To appreciate the family I still have.

- Accepting what I cannot change.

Appendix B

Recommended Reading

If you ran a bereavement center for children in the United States, it's very likely you'd turn to the National Alliance for Grieving Children for help. The NAGC acts as an umbrella organization—linking otherwise independent organizations so they can more easily share resources and ideas.

Because the Alliance has such a unique and unparalleled bird's-eye view of everything happening in the field of children and grief, when I decided to compile a list of books for parentless parents and their children, I called the president of NAGC, Paul Golding, for recommendations. But I didn't want just a list of any books dealing with grief and loss. I wanted a list specifically geared to children coping with the loss of grandparents.

To help with my request, Golding consulted with the NAGC's board of directors and received their input and guidance. And while the recommendations below are by no means exhaustive, the list and descriptions Paul provided represents their collective thinking about some of the best books available for children who have lost their grandparents.

MY GRANDSON, LEW (Charlotte Zolotow) (Grades Pre – 2)
Young Lewis misses his grandfather, even though he died when Lewis was only two. Lewis and his mother learn that remembering Grandpa together is less lonely than each remembering him alone.

MY LETTER FROM GRANDMA (Ruth V. Cullen)
(Grades Pre – 2)
A girl reads a letter that her grandmother left for her when she died. This letter brings healing and love with its words.

SOPHIE (Mem Fox) (Grades Pre – 2)
Sophie loves her grandpa and he loves her. Then one day he dies suddenly. Winner of Parents' Choice Award.

THE TWO OF THEM (Aliki) (Grades Pre – 2)
A story that describes the relationship between a girl and her grandfather from her birth to his death.

REMEMBER THE BUTTERFLIES (Anna Grossnickle Hines)
(Grades Pre – 3)
One summer, two children bring a dead butterfly to their grandfather and he explains the life cycle of the butterfly to them. After their grandpa dies, they talk about all the things he shared with them and how they are a part of a life cycle.

ANNIE AND THE OLD ONE (Miska Miles) (Grades K – 3)
When Annie's Navajo grandmother says that she will die when Annie's mother's rug is completely woven, Annie tries to hold back time by

unweaving the rug in secret. This book gently explains the reality and inevitability of death.

COME BACK GRANDMA (Sue Limb) (Grades K–3)
When Bessie's grandma dies, she misses her and can't forget her. The story moves ahead to when Bessie grows up, marries, and has a daughter of her own who reminds her of her grandma.

GRANDMA'S SHOES (Libby Hathorn) (Grades K–3)
A young girl misses her grandmother terribly after she dies. She slips her feet into her grandma's shoes and is transported on a journey filled with images reminding her of her grandma.

THE WALL (Eve Bunting) (Grades K–3)
A young boy and his father travel to Washington to find his grandfather's name on the Vietnam Veterans Memorial wall.

ANIMAL CRACKERS: A TENDER BOOK ABOUT DEATH AND FUNERALS AND LOVE (Bridget Marshall)
(Grades K–4)
This book explores aging, memory loss, and a special kind of love when a young child's nanny must go to a nursing home and later dies.

THE BUTTERFLY BUSH: A STORY
ABOUT LOVE (Dawn Michelle Evarts) (Grades 3–5)
Lindsay's grandmother gives her a butterfly bush that becomes very special to her after her grandmother dies.

BLACKBERRIES IN THE DARK (Mavis Jukes) (Grades 3–6)
After the death of his grandfather, Austin and his grandmother create new memories while holding on to old ones.

A RING OF ENDLESS LIGHT (Madeleine L'Engle)
(Grades 6 – 8)
The cycle of life and death becomes a difficult burden for sixteen-year-old
Vicky Austin as she watches her grandfather who is dying from cancer.

THE CREATIVE JOURNAL FOR TEENS (Lucia Capacchione)
(Teens)
Offers easy techniques for journal writing that enable expression of
feelings and self-understanding.

THE GRIEVING TEEN: A GUIDE FOR TEENAGERS AND
THEIR FRIENDS (Helen Fitzgerald) (Teens)
In brief sections, teens learn what others have faced during the death
of someone they cared for, whether the cause was old age, violence,
suicide, or through accident or illness.

HELPING TEENS COPE WITH DEATH
(The Dougy Center for Grieving Children) (Teens)
An immensely useful book that explains common grief reactions of
teenagers and offers advice for parents on supporting teens in grief—
with helpful hints on handling the holidays and anniversaries.

I WILL REMEMBER YOU: WHAT TO DO WHEN SOMEONE
YOU LOVE DIES—A GUIDEBOOK THROUGH GRIEF FOR
TEENS (Laura Dower) (Teens)
This book helps teens explore their choices about grief. It encourages
the understanding that there are no rules to follow and that grieving
is what you make it. Includes sections entitled "50 Ways to Remember" and "Why It's Different for Teens."

Appendix C

Resources

In Chapter 5, I offer a wealth of ideas for keeping the memory of your parents alive. If you're interested in reading more fun and creative suggestions, please go to www.allisongilbert.com, where I've launched the "Keeping Their Memory Alive" blog. Here, I present even more tips and resources.

I also welcome you to share your best ideas with me. Please email me your suggestions, the ones that have been most meaningful to you and your family, at allison@allisongilbert.com. I promise to feature many of them on the blog so we can all learn from each other.

There are other ways to connect as well. Parentless Parents is on Facebook. Join our growing community by searching "Parentless Parents" like you would any friend on the site.

You can also meet other parentless parents in person. By visiting www.allisongilbert.com, you can locate a Parentless Parents chapter near you. If none exists where you live, feel free to start your own group. If you need help, don't hesitate to reach out; I'd be very happy to lend a hand.

And finally, for readers who simply want to connect with the artists and companies I wrote about, below is their contact information in the order I presented them in the chapter:

Kim Screen
Good Stock
www.good-stock.com
info@good-stock.com

Marita Gootee
www.maritagootee.com
marita@maritagootee.com

The Gazebo
www.thegazebo.com
robert@thegazebo.com

Robert Dancik
www.robertdancik.com
playcik@yahoo.com

Acknowledgments

In March 1996, just a few weeks after my mother died, I walked through the familiar red doors of Gilda's Club New York City to attend my weekly support group. I had been making the trip downtown for nearly a year to talk about my mother and her diagnosis with ovarian cancer. If you were there, you would have seen men and women of various ages and backgrounds coming together in a room decorated like a finely appointed living room — couches in warm colors and floral prints, coffee tables made of wicker and wood, and small lamps that shed the kind of light perfect for laughing and crying. Each of us was coping with the pending death or loss of a parent, and every seven days that room on the second floor was my refuge.

The leader of our meetings was a gentle man and I remember him being so good at facilitating our discussions that he made all of us feel like we had equal time to vent, scream, or sob. One day I guess I was in unusually bad shape and he invited me to stay and talk with him a little longer after the session ended. Back in his office, he handed me a book that he said was relatively new.

The book was Hope Edelman's *Motherless Daughters*. How could this book exist?! I thought to myself. *Yes, that's who I am. I am a motherless daughter.* Hope put into words what I was unable to articulate myself. Yes, I was a daughter without a mother and that's why I hurt so much.

No other book had ever been written like Hope's. It gave voice to countless women, including me, who had previously suffered without the right vocabulary. Hope and I didn't meet until I began writing my previous book, *Always Too Soon: Voices of Support for Those Who Have Lost Both Parents,* and soon after our first conversation she became a treasured friend and mentor. When I first had the idea for *Parentless Parents*, Hope was the only person I told, besides my husband, Mark. I wanted her support, and in deference to her inspirational work, her blessing. I thank her for both and so much more.

This book would not be in your hands today if it weren't for my agent, Richard Morris, at Janklow & Nesbit. He believed what I wanted to say needed to be written and held my hand until it was. We are truly a great team. And for introducing me to Richard, my deepest gratitude goes to Natalie Robins and Christopher Lehmann-Haupt, and their daughter, my friend, Rachel Lehmann-Haupt. I am truly lucky to have three such amazing champions in my life. Thank you for believing in me.

My sincerest thanks also to Sarah Landis, my editor at Hyperion. Sarah's guidance made every page in this book better. To truly understand her enormous impact, one would only have to read the earlier versions of this book. And to the rest of the Hyperion team, I could ask for no better. Any author would be lucky to work with Ellen Archer, Marie Coolman, Christine Ragasa, Leslie Wells, Colin Fox, Bryan Christian, and Katherine Tasheff. Thank you so much, and for everything.

At CNN, I remain awestruck by the massive support I received from Rick Davis, Carolyn Disbrow, and Barbara Levin. Thank you for supporting my passions outside of work.

There are also several individuals I'd like to thank specifically for their logistical support and generosity. Fredda Wasserman, of Our

House, who graciously provided me the space to conduct focus groups while I was in Los Angeles. Heidi Lurensky, Heather Brown, Patty Diaz, and Susie Kessler at the JCC in Manhattan for doing the same for my groups in New York. My gratitude also extends to Heather Cabot and Irene Rubaum-Keller for offering the kind of guidance that was truly invaluable during my time in LA.

My trip to Hunuku, Mexico, would never have been possible without my expert guide, Lalo Hernández. Thank you, Lalo, for introducing me to the Tuz family. And at Xcaret, I want to thank Martha Matu for making sure I saw everything I wanted to see and more. Thanks also to Kate Moeller, formerly of Club Med, and to the Ritz-Carlton's Paulina Feltrin for making many important and necessary introductions before and during my stay.

My sincerest gratitude also extends to Kathleen McQuade Eye for making my visit with her mother, Marian McQuade, possible. One of the most rewarding aspects of writing this book was meeting Marian McQuade, and it was with profound sadness that I learned of her passing a few months after our time together. Thanks also to retired West Virginia state senator Shirley Love for helping me comprehend her enormous undertaking.

Heartfelt thanks also to Jonathan Tisch and Dan Johnson of the Loews Corporation; John Mara, president of the New York Football Giants; and Janet Tweed, president of Gilbert Tweed Associates. Each of you should know what a difference you have made to the lives of my children. I also owe a great deal of thanks to their assistants Vicki Alfonzetti, Nicole Kelly, and Senada Fici. The "Grandma and Grandpa Tour" simply would not have happened without you.

I also want to say a very special thank you to Dave Eiland, formerly with the New York Yankees, for generously agreeing to speak with me during the regular season. And to Jason Latimer, my earnest gratitude, for making that important conversation happen. Without Jason, I never would have been able to connect with Dave Eiland in the first place.

Unparalleled thanks to Kenneth Land at Duke University and Steven Mintz at Columbia University. Your expertise and willingness to double-check my work gave me the confidence I needed to write about the sweeping changes happening within the American family.

There are many others who provided the necessary information I needed to write this book. To those I quoted, my sincerest thanks. To those unnamed in these pages, my thanks extends equally to, among others: Susan Martin, Erin Wallace, Jamie Poslosky, and Jay Berkelhamer at the American Academy of Pediatrics; Sarah Hutcheon at the Society for Research in Child Development; Audrey Hamilton at the American Psychological Association; Robert Bock at the National Institute of Child Health and Human Development; Lee Herring at the American Sociological Association; Barbara Cire at the National Institute on Aging; Krystal Gatling and Megan Cox at the National Center for Health Statistics; Robert Bernstein at the U.S. Census Bureau; Nancy Thompson and Amy Goyer at AARP; Kelly Sakai at the Families and Work Institute; Lynne Van Buskirk, formerly at the American Bar Association; Samantha Chernak at the Financial Planning Association; Carl W. Brown, Jr., at the Roper Center for Public Opinion Research; Glen Elder at the University of North Carolina at Chapel Hill; Laura Pittman at Northern Illinois University; Laura Scaramella at the University of New Orleans; Melissa Barnett at the University of Arizona; Arin Connell at Case Western Reserve University; and Maria Trozzi at Boston University School of Medicine and Boston Medical Center. I thank you all for your patience and for never turning me away when I had follow-up questions, which were many.

Particular thanks to Karen Brown, director of Cancer Genetic Counseling at Mount Sinai Hospital in New York City, who helped me untangle the data surrounding the BRCA gene. And for Anne Bush Feeley, oncology nurse at Mount Sinai, for reviewing my mother's medical records and showing me in black-and-white detail all that my mom had been through.

Thanks also to Adjoa Boateng, Rachel DeLevie-Orey, and Ginger Wilmot, for their superb research, fact-checking, and transcription assistance. And my friend, photographer Robert Tardio, for taking the picture of me that appears on the back flap of this book.

For building the Parentless Parents Survey and interpreting the results, my profound thanks to Dr. Tracy E. Costigan, principal research scientist at the American Institutes for Research. It is exciting to know that the Parentless Parents Survey will serve as the foundation for additional research in the future. Under your guidance, we are bound to learn even more about this previously underexplored population.

For giving the Parentless Parents Survey and the subject of parentless parenting unequaled prominence, enormous thanks to Alana B. Elias Kornfeld at the Huffington Post.

To my dear friends Betsy Cadel, Janet Rossbach, and editor extraordinaire Christina Baker Kline, thank you for looking over the earliest versions of this manuscript and for making important suggestions. Who better than your girlfriends to be so brutally honest? And to Beth Blass, Kristin Brandt, Tanya Hunt, and Janice Shepps, the kind of amazing friends I could always count on for a spontaneous cup of coffee or glass of wine when the going got tough or there was reason to celebrate.

To all the parentless parents who told me their stories in person, over the phone, via email, through the Parentless Parents Survey, and in focus groups, it's because of you that I knew this book needed to be written and it's because of you that I kept pressing forward when I doubted my own abilities. My deepest hope is that this book lives up to your expectations.

And to my family, thank you for understanding that I needed to write this book, especially when deadlines prevented me from attending family functions both close to home and far away. Thank you, too, for allowing me to publish such intimate details of our lives. This book represents my entire truth, not just the parts that were bland enough to share comfortably, and for that I am the most grateful. In that regard, I am particularly grateful to my in-laws, Jimmy, Sandy, and Marilyn; my brother, Jay; my stepmother, Cheryl; and my uncle Richie, for not only gladly reading this book and offering observations, but for never asking me to alter or remove passages they could have easily and understandably found objectionable.

For that—and more—I want to thank my husband, Mark. You are my best friend and love of my life. You are also an exceptional bedside therapist, Help Desk technician, editor, and proofreader. I was lucky to be your girlfriend when we were teenagers and feel luckier now to be your wife. Thank you for never letting go and always holding my hand in the dark.

And finally, to our two beautiful children, Jake and Lexi. You fill my days with joy and gratitude. When I look at you, I see the future.

All my love, Mom.

Notes

INTRODUCTION

6   *the age at which*: U.S. Census Bureau, "Families and Living Arrangements," Table MS-2, Estimated Median Age at First Marriage, by Sex:
1890 to the Present.

6   *average age for a woman*: National Center for Health Statistics, 2010. "National Vital Statistics Reports," Births: Final Data for 2007; vol. 58, no. 24,
p. 12.

7   *Between 1970 and 2007*: National Center for Health Statistics, 2002. "National Vital Statistics Reports," Table 1. Mean Age of Mother and Absolute Change by Live Birth Order: United States, 1970–2000; vol. 51, no. 1,
p. 6; National Center for Health Statistics, 2010. "National Vital Statistics
Reports," Births: Final Data for 2007, vol. 58, no. 24, p. 12.

7   *first child rose 3.6 years*: National Center for Health Statistics, 2009. "Delayed
Childbearing: More Women Are Having Their First Child Later in Life,"
NCHS data brief, no. 21, 2009, p. 1.

7   *for a sixty-five-year-old*: National Center for Health Statistics. 2009. "Health,
United States, 2009," Table 24, Life expectancy at birth, at 65 years of age,
and at 75 years of age, by race and sex: United States, selected years
1900–2006, p. 187; National Center for Health Statistics, 2010. "National
Vital Statistics Reports Web Release," Table 7. Deaths: Final Data for 2007,
vol. 58, no. 19, p. 26.

7   *having fewer babies*: National Center for Health Statistics, 2010. "National
Vital Statistics Reports." Births: Preliminary data for 2008. Births and birth
rates. vol. 58, no. 16, pp. 2–3.

7   *approximately 180,000*: National Center for Health Statistics, 1976. "Vital Statistics of the United States," Table 1–52. Live Births by Age of Mother, Live-Birth Order, Sex of Child, and Race: United States, 1972. Volume I— Natality, p. I–55.

7   *By 2008, that number*: National Center for Health Statistics, 2010. "National Vital Statistics Reports," Table 3. Live Births by Age of Mother, Live-Birth Order and Race and Hispanic Origin of Mother: United States, preliminary 2008, vol. 58, no. 16, p. 9; Pew Research Center, 2010. *The New Demography of American Motherhood*, p. 6.

8   *Fifty-seven percent*: Parentless Parents Survey, 2011, p. 239.

8   *approximately 69 percent*: ibid., p. 246.

8   *Nearly 70 percent*: ibid., p. 241.

8   *nearly double the amount*: ibid., pp. 246, 247.

8   *indicated their spouses*: ibid., p. 247.

8   *the majority of respondents*: ibid., p. 233.

9   *Nearly 30 percent of*: ibid., p. 247.

Chapter 1: EARLY PARENTHOOD

15   *This could explain*: Parentless Parents Survey, 2011. Statistic obtained by analyzing only those responses of individuals who indicated having lost both parents before first child was born.

18   *women reported significantly*: ibid. All gender-specific data obtained by analyzing survey responses according to sex of respondent.

18   *"mothers still spend"*: Families and Work Institute, 2008 National Study of the Changing Workforce, "Times are Changing: Gender and Generation at Work and at Home," p. 14.

18   *Women report taking*: ibid., pp. 17–18.

Chapter 2: THE "I" FACTOR

28   *Indeed, nearly 60 percent*: Parentless Parents Survey, 2011, p. 239.

28   *grandparents are caregivers*: U.S. Census Bureau, "Who's Minding the Kids? Child Care Arrangements: Spring 2005/Summer 2006," Current Population Reports, Table 2, "Preschoolers in Types of Child Care Arrangements by Employment Status and Selected Characteristics of Mother: Spring 2005," p. 3.

28   *Her data also show*: ibid., Table 3, "Primary Child Care Arrangements of Preschoolers with Employed Mothers: Selected Years, 1985–2005," p. 8.

28   *82 percent of respondents*: Gretchen Straw, Debbie Gann, Laura O'Connor, "AARP Grandparenting Survey," November 1999, p. 21.

28   *while 68 percent indicated*: Curt Davies, Dameka Williams, AARP, "The Grandparent Study 2002 Report," May 2002, p. 10.

28   *In 2000, approximately*: "AARP Public Policy Institute Analysis of the Census Bureau's Current Population Survey," March 2010.

29   *in response to every question*: Parentless Parents Survey, 2011, pp. 234–238.

29   *A staggering 79 percent*: ibid., p. 235. This statistic is the sum of the number of parents who reported feeling isolated "Sometimes" and "A lot of the time/Most of the time" after their first child was born.

Chapter 3: LATER PARENTHOOD

44   *nearly 60 percent of*: Parentless Parents Survey, 2011, p. 241.

44   *70 percent admit being*: ibid.

51   *opened an adaptation*: Hiawyn Oram, *The Lion, the Witch and the Wardrobe, Based on the Original Book by C. S. Lewis* (HarperCollins, 2004).

Chapter 4: THE GRANDPARENT GAP

55   *gathered in Budapest*: Peter K. Smith, *The Psychology of Grandparenthood: An International Perspective*, ed. Peter K. Smith (London and New York: Routledge, 1991), p. xiii.

56   *enormous impact on grandchildren*: Peter K. Smith, "Introduction: the Study of Grandparenthood," in *The Psychology of Grandparenthood*, pp. 9–10.

56   *In their study*: Piergiorgio Battistelli and Alessandra Farnetti, "Grandchildren's Images of Their Grandparents: a Psychodynamic Perspective," in *The Psychology of Grandparenthood*, pp. 143–156.

56   *focused on older children*: Maria Tyszkowa, "The Role of Grandparents in the Development of Grandchildren as Perceived by Adolescents and Young Adults in Poland," in *The Psychology of Grandparenthood*, pp. 50–67.

59   *children have better*: Shalhevet Attar-Schwartz, Ann Buchanan, Jo-Pei Tan, Eirini Flouri, Julia Griggs, "Grandparenting and Adolescent Adjustment in Two-Parent Biological, Lone-Parent, and Step-Families," *Journal of Family Psychology*, vol. 23, no. 1 (2009): 67–75.

60   *"They can reduce"*: American Psychological Association Press Release, "Children in Single-Parent Households and Stepfamilies Benefit Most Socially from Time with Grandparents," February 23, 2009.

61   *"It was his influence"*: Dr. Frank I. Luntz, *What Americans Really Want . . . Really: The Truth About Our Hopes, Dreams, and Fears* (New York: Hyperion, 2009), p. viii.

61   *she rails against*: Dana Bedford Hilmer, *Blindsided by a Diaper: Over 30 Men and Women Reveal How Parenthood Changes a Relationship* (New York: Three Rivers Press, 2007), p. 221.

Chapter 5: KEEPING YOUR PARENTS' MEMORY ALIVE

66   *Most often, according*: Parentless Parents Survey, 2011, p. 250.

67   *While 61 percent of*: ibid., p. 251.

74   *successful people thrive*: Malcolm Gladwell, *Outliers: The Story of Success* (New York: Little, Brown and Company, 2008).

77   *a teenager's bedroom*: "Problem Two: Redecorating," *Real Simple*, December 2008, p. TV6.

78   *started in 1918*: Jessica Helfand, *Scrapbooks: An American History* (New Haven and London: Yale University Press, 2008), p. 48.

79   *are "visual biographies"*: ibid., p. ix.

81   *was once featured*: "Memory Keepers," *Real Simple*, December 2008, p. 201.

82   *"Objects such as"*: Robert Dancik, *Amulets and Talismans: Simple Techniques for Creating Meaningful Jewelry* (Cincinnati, Ohio: North Light Books, 2009).

84   *"This is a soup"*: Tessa Kiros, *Falling Cloudberries: A World of Family Recipes* (Kansas City, Missouri: Andrews McMeel, 2004), p. 231.

84   *"reminds him of "*: ibid., p. 206.

88   *"Whenever you think"*: Tim Russert, *Big Russ and Me: Father and Son: Lessons of Life* (New York: Hyperion, 2004), p. 333.

96   *close to 10 percent*: Parentless Parents Survey, 2011, p. 251.

Chapter 6: FEAR OF DYING YOUNG

101   *Seven years after*: Throughout this chapter, I write about the difficult choice I made to have preventative cancer surgery. If you would like to learn more about the operation and the decisions I faced leading up to it, please see the pieces I wrote for The Huffington Post, portions of which were used in this book. Many of the posts can be found under the series entitled "My Journey to Prevent Ovarian Cancer."

102   *as high as 60 percent*: Karen L. Brown, Diana M. Moglia, and Sherry Grumet, "Genetic Counseling for Breast Cancer Risk: General Concepts, Challenging Themes and Future Directions," *Breast Disease*, 27 (2006–2007): 72.

102   *lifetime risk of 1.5 percent*: ibid.

105   *an 85 percent risk*: ibid.

105   *have a 13 percent chance*: ibid.

105   *which decreases up to*: Karen Brown, director of Cancer Genetic Counseling, Mount Sinai Hospital in New York City, multiple phone interviews with author, March 2010.

109   *"Death is as available"*: Robin Romm, *The Mercy Papers: A Memoir of Three Weeks* (New York: Scribner, 2009), p. 114.

110   *almost 58 percent fear*: Parentless Parents Survey, 2011, p. 244.

115   *addresses anxieties about*: Michael Schwartzman, *The Anxious Parent: How to Overcome Your Fears About: Discipline, Toilet Training, Feeding & Sleep-*

ing Difficulties, Separation, Sibling Rivalry and Other Childhood Problems (New York: Fireside, 1990).

Chapter 7: WHEN ONLY ONE SPOUSE IS PARENTLESS

130   *nearly 50 percent of*: Parentless Parents Survey, 2011, p. 247.

130   *and 29 percent railed*: ibid.

131   *Grandparents prefer to*: Peter K. Smith, ed., *The Psychology of Grandparenthood: An International Perspective* (London and New York: Routledge, 1991), p. 7.

131   *"Women are almost"*: Hope Edelman, *Motherless Mothers: How Mother Loss Shapes the Parents We Become* (New York: HarperCollins, 2006), p. 169.

131   *A team of*: Richard L. Michalski and Todd K. Shackelford, "Grandparent Investment as a Function of Relational Uncertainty and Emotional Closeness with Parents," *Human Nature*, vol. 16, no. 3 (Fall 2005): 293–305.

135   *"Without her ovaries"*: Masha Gessen, *Blood Matters: From Inherited Illness to Designer Babies, How the World and I Found Ourselves in the Future of the Gene* (Orlando Florida: Harcourt, 2008), p. 93.

135   *"Women who undergo"*: ibid., p. 101.

149   *nearly 50 percent of*: Parentless Parents Survey, 2011, p. 247.

149   *much more likely*: ibid., pp. 246, 247.

Chapter 8: A WORLD OF SUPPORT

153   *Obon takes place*: Katherine Ashenburg, *The Mourner's Dance: What We Do When People Die* (New York: North Point Press, 2002), p. 264.

153   *"To welcome them"*: ibid., pp. 264–265.

154   *"holding memorial services"*: ibid., p. 264.

154   *In North America*: ibid., p. 263.

164   *United States has*: Edward J. Madara, director of the American Self-Help Group Clearinghouse, multiple emails and phone conversations with author, September 2009–March 2010.

165   *hundreds of groups*: Barbara J. White and Edward J. Madara, eds., *The Self-Help Group Sourcebook: Your Guide to Community and Online Support Groups*, 7th Edition (Denville, NJ: American Self-Help Group Clearinghouse, Saint Clare's Health Services, 2002).

166   *close to 70 percent*: Parentless Parents Survey, 2011, p. 246.

166   *a massive 82 percent*: ibid., p. 246.

Chapter 9: A DAY TO CALL YOUR OWN

180   *In 2002, Dr. Keith*: Elaina M. Kyrouz et al., "A Review of Research on the Effectiveness of Self-Help Mutual Aid Groups," in *The Self-Help Group*

Sourcebook: Your Guide to Community and Online Support Groups, ed. Barbara J. White and Edward J. Madara, 7th Edition (Denville, NJ: American Self-Help Group Clearinghouse, Saint Clare's Health Services, 2002), pp. 71–85.

180   *We are a nation*: Barbara Ehrenreich, *Bright-Sided* (New York: Metropolitan Books, 2009).

180   *Remarkably, nearly 50 percent*: Parentless Parents Survey, 2011, p. 242.

181   *Americans purchase more*: Hallmark, "Holidays & Occasions," http://news room.hallmark.com/Holiday.

Chapter 10: LOSS CAN MAKE BETTER PARENTS

197   *virtually 60 percent of*: Parentless Parents Survey, 2011, p. 244.

198   *just over 40 percent*: FindLaw.com, "Most Americans Don't Have a Will," http://company.findlaw.com/pr/2008/063008.estate.html.

198   *about a quarter*: ibid.

198   *the number skyrockets*: Parentless Parents Survey, 2011. This tabulation stems from analyzing only those responses to the same statement of men and women between the ages of 25 and 34.

199   *In a bereavement study*: Cynthia M. Torges, et al., "Regret Resolution, Aging, and Adapting to Loss," *Psychology and Aging*, vol. 23, no. 1 (2008): 169–180.

200   *As with 48 percent*: Parentless Parents Survey, 2011, p. 253.

202   *Nearly 60 percent of*: ibid.

208   *traces the history*: Ann Hulbert, *Raising America: Experts, Parents, and a Century of Advice About Children* (New York: Alfred A. Knopf, 2003).

209   *in the early 1970s*: Jacqueline H. Wolf, PhD, "Low Breastfeeding Rates and Public Health in the United States," *American Journal of Public Health*, vol. 93, no. 12 (2003).

209   *"position of neutrality"*: Alcoholics Anonymous (New York: Alcoholics Anonymous World Services, Inc., 2001), 4th Edition, p. 85.

210   *"Assuming we are"*: ibid, pp. 100–101.

Index

101353